ASCENT®

CENTER FOR TECHNICAL KNOWLEDGE

CATIA V5-6R2017: Functional Tolerancing & Annotation

Learning Guide
1st Edition

ASCENT - Center for Technical Knowledge®
CATIA V5-6R2017: Functional Tolerancing & Annotation
1st Edition

Prepared and produced by:

ASCENT Center for Technical Knowledge
630 Peter Jefferson Parkway, Suite 175
Charlottesville, VA 22911

866-527-2368
www.ASCENTed.com

Lead Contributor: Scott Hendren

ASCENT - Center for Technical Knowledge is a division of Rand Worldwide, Inc., providing custom developed knowledge products and services for leading engineering software applications. ASCENT is focused on specializing in the creation of education programs that incorporate the best of classroom learning and technology-based training offerings.

We welcome any comments you may have regarding this learning guide, or any of our products. To contact us please email: feedback@ASCENTed.com.

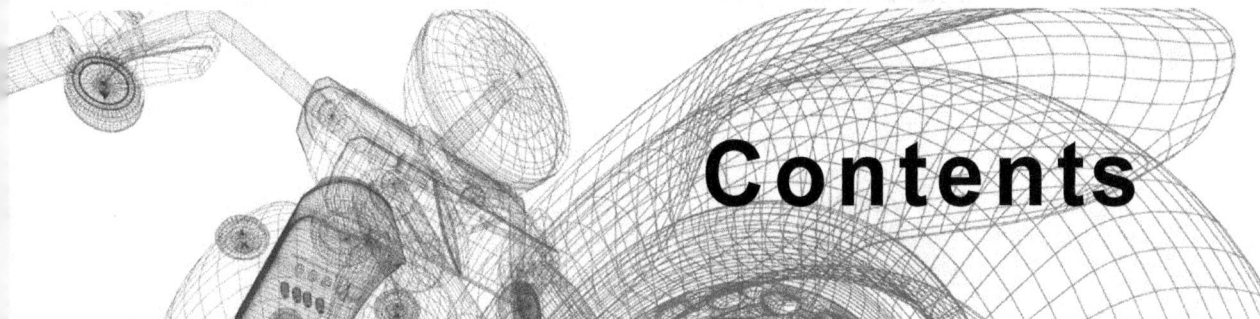

Contents

Preface

The *CATIA V5-6R2017: Functional Tolerancing & Annotation* learning guide is extensive hands-on course with numerous practices that helps you acquire the skills to create and display engineering, manufacturing, and assembly information directly on the 3D part, assembly, or process model. Students attending this course will receive a thorough understanding of geometric tolerances, dimensions, notes, and other annotations critical to the accurate and cost-effective creation of mechanical parts and assemblies. The 3D Functional Tolerancing and Annotation course complies with the industry and government initiated American Society of Mechanical Engineers' (ASME) Y14.41 3D standards for the creation and submission of model only, paperless design applications.

Topics Covered

- Introduction to Functional Tolerancing & Annotation

- Workbench overview

- Annotation process

- Extracting 2D view from the 3D model

- Annotation planes and extraction views

- Construction geometry

- Semantic and non-semantic annotations

- Datum Reference Frames

- Tolerance Advisor

- Basic Dimensions

- Annotations: Text, Flag Notes, Datum Elements, Datum Targets, Roughness, Dimensions

- Restricted Areas

- Threads

- Annotation Visualization Tools: Query, Grouping, Leader Symbols, Annotation Mirror and Transfer, Filters

- Cameras and Captures

- Geometry Connection Management

- FT&A analysis and reporting

- Product Functional Tolerance and Annotation workbench

Note on Software Setup

This learning guide assumes a standard installation of the software using the default preferences during installation. Lectures and practices use the standard software templates and default options for the Content Libraries.

This course was developed against CATIA V5-6R2017, Service Pack 1.

Lead Contributor: Scott Hendren

Scott Hendren has been a trainer and curriculum developer in the PLM industry for over 20 years, with experience on multiple CAD systems, including Pro/ENGINEER, Creo Parametric, and CATIA. Trained in Instructional Design, Scott uses his skills to develop instructor-led and web-based training products.

Scott has held training and development positions with several high profile PLM companies, and has been with the Ascent team since 2013.

Scott holds a Bachelor of Mechanical Engineering Degree as well as a Bachelor of Science in Mathematics from Dalhousie University, Nova Scotia, Canada.

Scott Hendren has been the Lead Contributor for *CATIA: Functional Tolerancing & Annotation* since 2013.

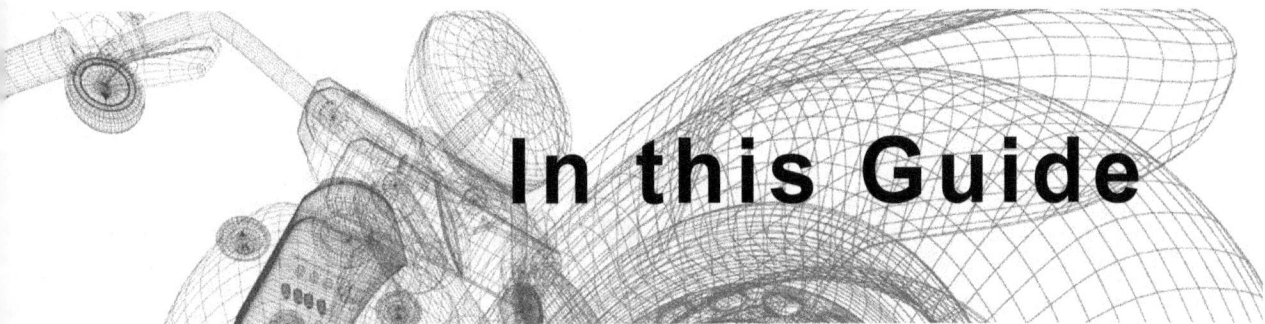

In this Guide

The following images highlight some of the features that can be found in this guide.

Practice Files

The Practice Files page tells you how to download and install the practice files that are provided with this guide.

FTP link for practice files

Chapters

Each chapter begins with a brief introduction and a list of the chapter's Learning Objectives.

Learning Objectives for the chapter

The page shows a reproduction of sample textbook pages alongside explanatory callouts.

Getting Started

1.3 Working with Commands

Starting Commands

The main way to access commands in the AutoCAD software is to use the Ribbon. Several of the file commands are available in the Quick Access Toolbar or in the Application Menu. Some commands are available in the Status Bar or through shortcut menus. There are additional access methods, such as Tool Palettes. The names of all of the commands can also be typed in the Command Line. A table is included to help you to identify the various methods of accessing the commands.

When typing the name of a command in either the Command Line or Dynamic Input, the **AutoComplete** option automatically completes the entry when you pause as you type. It also supports mid-string search by displaying all of the commands that contain the word that you typed, as shown in Figure 1–12. You can then scroll through the list and select a command.

Figure 1–12

You can also click **(Customize)** *to display the Input Settings for the AutoComplete feature.*

To set specific options for the **AutoComplete** feature, right-click on the Command Line, expand Input Settings, and select from the various options, such as the ability to search for system variables or to set the delay response time, as shown in Figure 1–13.

Figure 1–13

If you need to stop a command, press <Esc> to cancel. You might need to press <Esc> more than once.

As you work in the AutoCAD software, the software prompts you for the information that is required to complete each command. These prompts are displayed in the drawing window near the cursor and in the Command Line. It is crucial that you read the command prompts as you work, as shown in Figure 1–14.

© 2015, ASCENT - Center for Technical Knowledge®   1–9

Sample page 2 content:

Getting Started

Practice 1c   **Saving a Drawing File**

Practice Objectives

- Open and save a drawing.
- Modify the **Automatic Saves** option.

Estimated time for completion: under 5 minutes

In this practice you will open a drawing, save it, and modify the **Automatic saves** option, as shown in Figure 1–51.

Figure 1–51

1. Open **Building Valley-M.dwg** from your class files folder.
2. In the Quick Access Toolbar, click (Save). In the Command Line, _QSAVE displays indicating that the AutoCAD software has performed a quick save.
3. In the Application Menu, click Options to open the Options dialog box.
4. In the Open and Save tab, change the time for Automatic save to **15 minutes**.

Callouts:

Side notes

Side notes are hints or additional information for the current topic.

Instructional Content

Each chapter is split into a series of sections of instructional content on specific topics. These lectures include the descriptions, step-by-step procedures, figures, hints, and information you need to achieve the chapter's Learning Objectives.

Practice Objectives

Practices

Practices enable you to use the software to perform a hands-on review of a topic.

Some practices require you to use prepared practice files, which can be downloaded from the link found on the Practice Files page.

Practice Files

To download the practice files for this guide, use the following steps:

1. Type the URL shown below into the address bar of your Internet browser. The URL must be typed **exactly as shown**. If you are using an ASCENT ebook, you can click on the link to download the file.

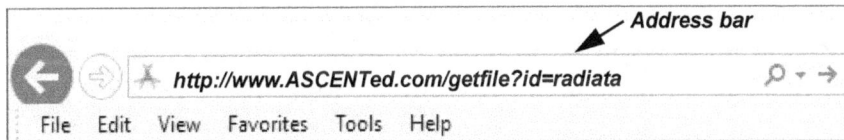

Address bar

http://www.ASCENTed.com/getfile?id=radiata

File   Edit   View   Favorites   Tools   Help

2. Press <Enter> to download the .ZIP file that contains the Practice Files.

3. Once the download is complete, unzip the file to a local folder. The unzipped file contains an .EXE file.

4. Double-click on the .EXE file and follow the instructions to automatically install the Practice Files on the C:\ drive of your computer.

   Do not change the location in which the Practice Files folder is installed. Doing so can cause errors when completing the practices.

http://www.ASCENTed.com/getfile?id=radiata

Stay Informed!

Interested in receiving information about upcoming promotional offers, educational events, invitations to complimentary webcasts, and discounts? If so, please visit:

www.ASCENTed.com/updates/

Help us improve our product by completing the following survey:

www.ASCENTed.com/feedback

You can also contact us at: *feedback@ASCENTed.com*

Introduction to FT&A

The goal is to teach you how to create tolerances and annotations to detail a model using the CATIA: Functional Tolerancing & Annotations workbench. You should already have a foundation level understanding of the rules, standards, and types of geometrical tolerances, dimensions, and annotations.

Learning Objectives in this Chapter

- Understand the usage of tolerancing and annotations.
- Understand the use of the FT&A Workbench.
- Recognize the FT&A interface and tools.
- Understand the annotation process.
- Create drawings from an annotated model.
- Learn how to access annotations and set annotation references.

1.1 Tolerancing and Annotations

Tolerances and annotations provide the details required to manufacture and fabricate a model designed in CATIA. Tolerances and annotations guide a Manufacturing group in the following ways:

- Details the acceptable standards.

- Provides the window for geometric variances and imperfections in parts and assemblies.

- Facilitates the production process and manufacturing standards.

Traditionally, these annotations are placed in the 2D drawing. Using the Functional Tolerancing & Annotation workbench, all annotations are stored directly in the 3D model. This eliminates the need to develop a drawing, and supports a paperless design and manufacturing environment. An example of an annotated part model is shown in Figure 1–1.

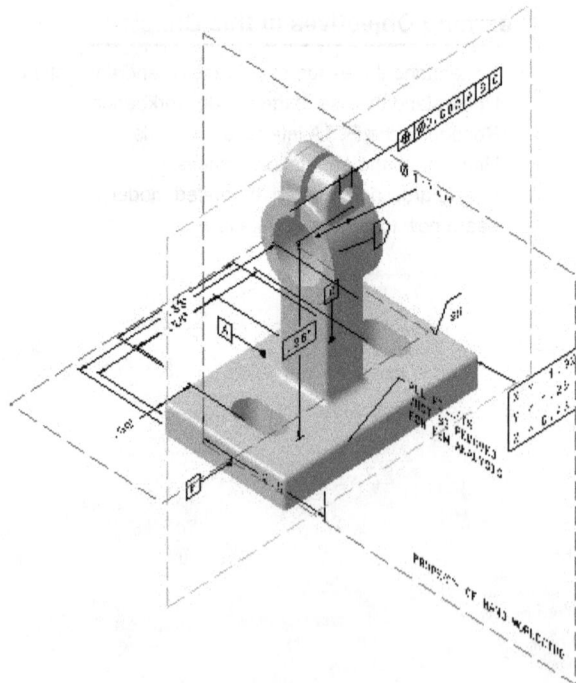

Figure 1–1

Placing the tolerances and annotations directly into the 3D design enables the manufacturing process to be considered throughout the design cycle, specifically in the initial stages. This helps avoid conflicts between design and manufacturing as early in the product life cycle as possible.

Annotations can be created in the following CATIA model types:

Model Type	File Extension	Workbench
Part	*.CATPart	Functional Tolerancing & Annotation
Assembly	*.CATProduct	Product Functional Tolerancing & Annotation
Process	*.CATProcess	Process Tolerancing & Annotation

Although all annotations can be added to parts or products after their designs are completed, certain annotations can be created during the design process.

All annotations are organized in specific branches of an Annotation Set in the specification tree. An example is shown in Figure 1–2.

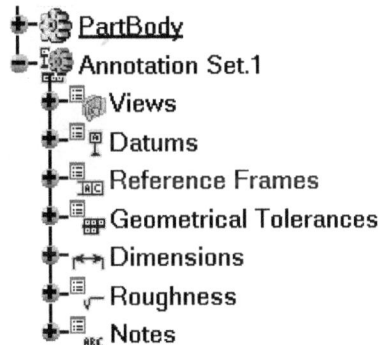

Figure 1–2

Annotation Standards

Similar to the drawing standards that are used to create 2D drawings, standards apply to the creation of annotations in a 3D model. For example, some annotations are created to match the ASME standard.

Since it is possible to break a rule of the applied standard, two annotation categories can be created:

- Semantic

- Non-Semantic

Semantic

This type of annotation always matches the rules, specifications, and designations assigned by the active standard. Semantic annotations are created using the Tolerance Advisor or Framed (Basic) Dimensions icons. The Tolerance Advisor dialog box is shown in Figure 1–3.

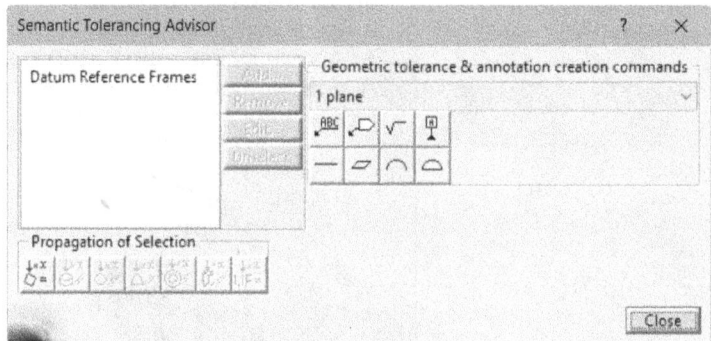

Figure 1–3

Non-Semantic

Non-semantic annotations might not necessarily match the active standard. Create this type of annotation when the active standard does not adequately represent the design intent of the model or the standards adopted by the designing company. Care should be taken when creating a non-semantic annotation to ensure that the end user of the annotation understands the designer's intent. Non-semantic annotations are created using the icons shown in Figure 1–4.

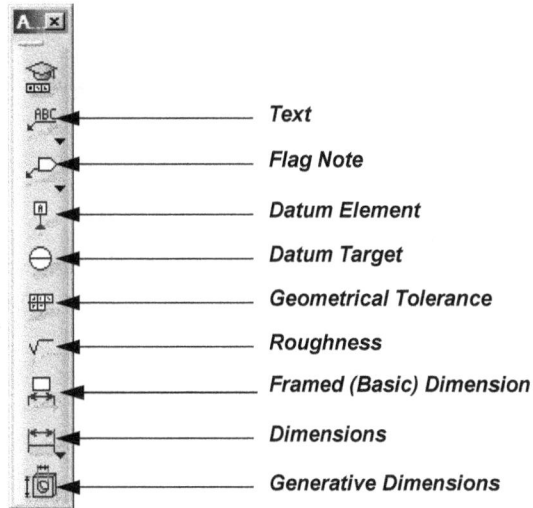

Text

Flag Note

Datum Element

Datum Target

Geometrical Tolerance

Roughness

Framed (Basic) Dimension

Dimensions

Generative Dimensions

Figure 1–4

1.2 FT&A Workbenches

You can create 3D annotation on CATIA models in three modes:

- Part

- Assembly

- Process

Part

The majority of this learning material focuses on the creation of annotations and tolerances for part models in the Functional Tolerancing & Annotation workbench. To access this workbench, select **Start>Mechanical Design>Functional Tolerancing & Annotation**. The workbench symbol changes to .

Assembly

To access the Product Functional Tolerancing & Annotation workbench, select **Start>Mechanical Design>Product Functional Tolerancing & Annotation**.

Process

To access the Process Tolerancing & Annotation workbench, select **Start>Digital Process for Manufacturing>Process Tolerancing & Annotation**.

1.3 FT&A Interface

The Functional Tolerancing & Annotation workbench interface displays, as shown in Figure 1–5.

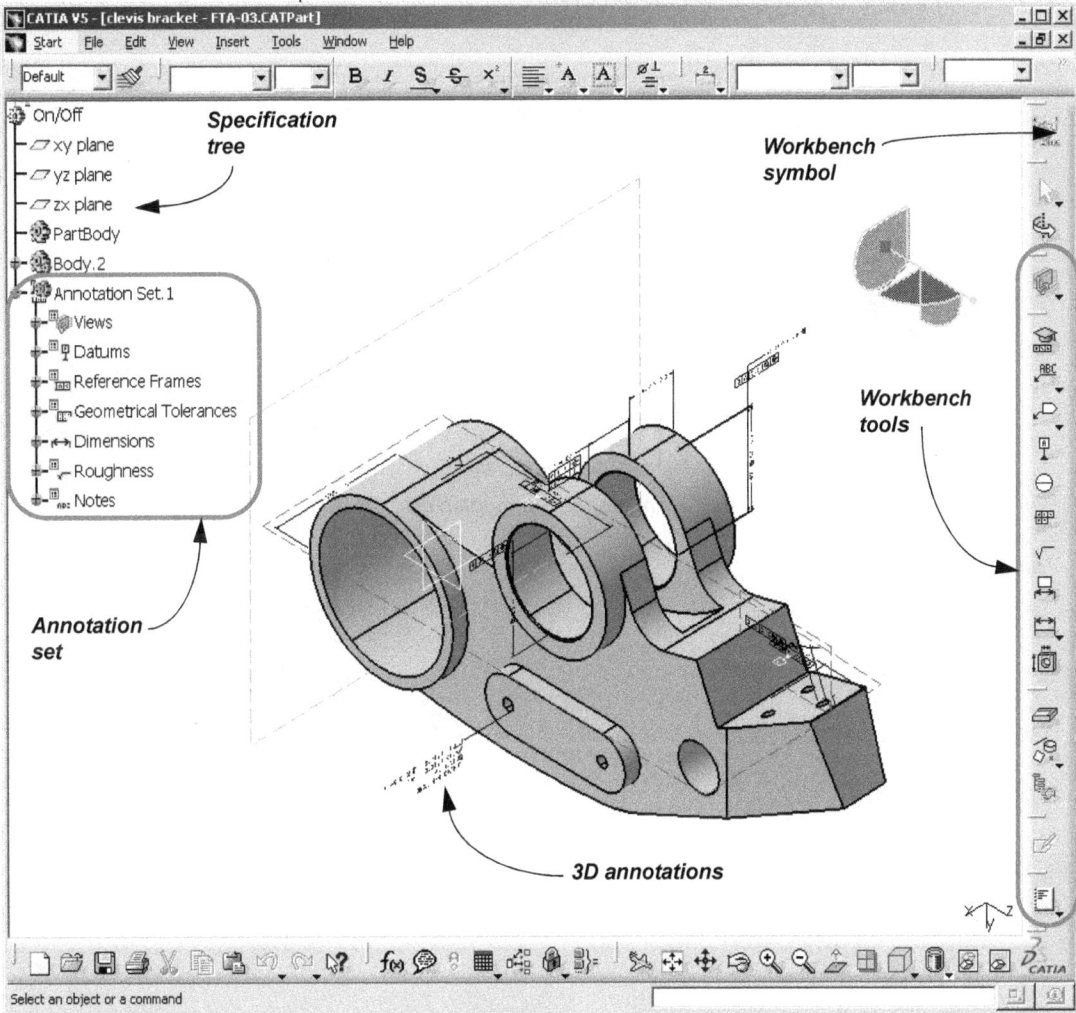

Figure 1–5

Annotation Switch On/Off

Since 3D annotations add visual complexity to the model, they can be toggled on and off to simplify the display. If you receive a model that has no annotations displayed, you must toggle on the annotation set. To toggle the annotations on and off, right-click on the annotation set and select **Annotation Set Switch On/Switch Off**. This is useful when viewing an annotated model in an assembly.

When an annotation set has been toggled off, the name of the annotation set displays in the specification tree, as shown in Figure 1–6. However, the branch cannot be expanded and no annotations display on the model.

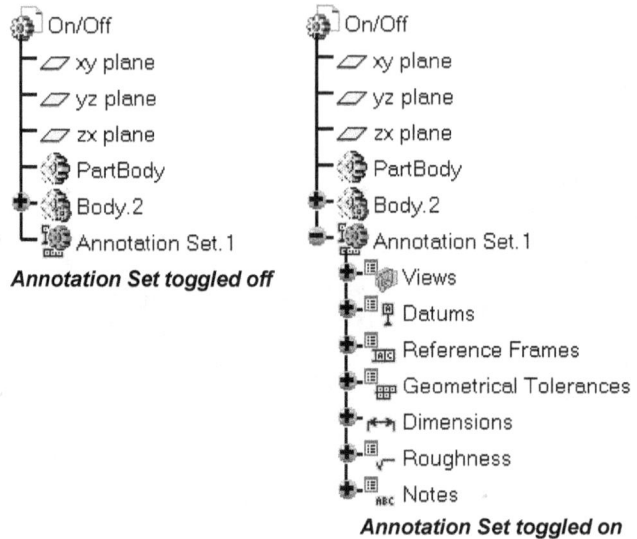

On/Off
- xy plane
- yz plane
- zx plane
- PartBody
- Body.2
- Annotation Set.1

Annotation Set toggled off

On/Off
- xy plane
- yz plane
- zx plane
- PartBody
- Body.2
- Annotation Set.1
  - Views
  - Datums
  - Reference Frames
  - Geometrical Tolerances
  - Dimensions
  - Roughness
  - Notes

Annotation Set toggled on

Figure 1–6

The display status of an annotation set can also be controlled by clicking ⬚ (List Annotation Set Switch On/Switch Off) in the Visualization toolbar. The Annotation Set Switch On/Switch Off dialog box opens, as shown in Figure 1–7.

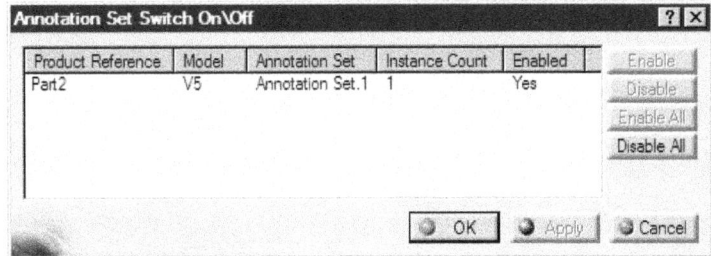

Product Reference	Model	Annotation Set	Instance Count	Enabled	
Part2	V5	Annotation Set.1	1	Yes	Enable
					Disable
					Enable All
					Disable All

Annotation Set Switch On\Off

OK   Apply   Cancel

Figure 1–7

To control the display of an annotation set, select it in the list and use the buttons on the right side of the dialog box. This tool is very useful when working in the Product Functional Tolerancing & Annotation workbench. It enables you to control the display of multiple part-level annotation sets in a single operation.

1.4 FT&A Tools

This section provides an overview of the different tools available in the Functional Tolerancing & Annotation workbench. The workbench consists of the following seven toolbars:

- Annotations

- Geometry for 3D Annotations

- Views/Annotation Planes

- Reporting

- Visualization

- Capture

- Grouping

Annotations

The Annotations toolbar contains all of the tools required to fully annotate and tolerance the part. The Annotations toolbar icons are as follows.

Option	Icon	Description
Tolerance Advisor		Creates semantic annotations based on the selected geometry.
Text flyout		
Text with Leader		Creates text with a leader to geometry in the annotation plane.
Text		Creates text in the annotation plane.
Text Parallel To Screen		Creates text referencing geometry or an annotation plane that is always parallel to the screen.
Flag Note flyout		
Flag Note with Leader		Creates a flag note with a leader to geometry in the annotation plane.
Flag Note		Creates a flag note in the annotation plane.

Datum Element		Creates a datum element from selected geometry.
Datum Target		Creates a datum target from selected geometry.
Geometrical Tolerance		Creates a geometrical tolerance for the selected geometry.
Roughness		Specifies the surface roughness.
Framed (Basic) Dimensions		Creates a basic dimension for the selected geometry.

Dimensions flyout

Dimensions		Creates dimensions for the selected geometry.
Cumulated Dimensions		Creates cumulated dimensions for the selected geometry.
Stacked Dimensions		Creates stacked dimensions for the selected geometry.
Coordinate Dimensions		Creates coordinate dimensions for the selected geometry.
Curvilinear Dimensions		Creates curvilinear dimensions for the selected geometry.
Generative Dimension		Creates selected model feature dimensions automatically.

Geometry for 3D Annotations

The Geometry for 3D Annotations toolbar is used to create and manage constructed geometry, which is used to correctly reference and annotate the part. The Geometry for 3D Annotations toolbar icons are as follows.

Option	Icon	Description
Restricted Area		Creates a restricted area from the selected geometry.
Geometry for 3D Annotations flyout		
Constructed Geometry Creation		Creates construction geometry based on selected element(s).
Constructed Geometry Management		Shows details of constructed geometry references.
Thread Representation Creation		Creates thread representation construction geometry.
Geometry Connection Management		Shows details of constructed geometry connections.

Views/ Annotation Planes

The Views/Annotation Planes toolbar contains the various view creation tools. These views are used to hold all annotations for the part, and can be extracted with their annotations to a 2D representation. The following describes the Views/Annotation Planes toolbar icons (flyout menu).

Option	Icon	Description
Principal Views		Creates the principal views (Front, Left, Right and so on).
View from Reference		Creates a view from the selected plane/planar surface.
Offset Section View/Section Cut		Creates an offset section view from the selected sketch.
Aligned Section View/Section Cut		Creates an aligned section view from the selected sketch.

Reporting

The Reporting toolbar is used to evaluate your annotations against specific checks developed from tolerancing standards. Annotations that do not meet the check criteria can be identified for resolution. The following describes the Reporting toolbar icons (flyout menu).

Option	Icon	Description
Report		Generates a report based on annotations.
Report Customization		Customizes report generation options.

Visualization

The Visualization toolbar tools can be used to investigate part/annotation relationships, filter and adjust the display of annotations, and better display the part and its details. The following describes the Visualization toolbar icons.

Option	Icon	Description
List Annotation Set Switch On/Switch Off		Enables annotation sets to be switched on and off.
3D-Annotation-Query Switch On/Switch Off		When active, selecting an element also highlights all associated geometry and annotations.
Filter		Enables annotations to be filtered and displayed.
Mirror annotations		Mirrors direction of text in the annotation plane.
Clipping Plane		Cuts part by selected annotation plane.
Analysis Display Mode		When enabled, it will color code dimensions that are invalid, linked to deleted geometry, or linked to unloaded files.
Analysis Blanking		Displays annotations with a blank background

Capture

The Capture tool is used to create snapshots of your model. Capture enables you to orient and display the part in a specific way, and to hide and show required annotations to clearly display the required information. The following describes the **Insert> Capture>Capture** tool.

Option	Icon	Description
Capture		Creates a capture in the Tolerancing Capture workbench.

Grouping

The Grouping tools can be used to clean up and organize the display. You can manually or automatically group annotations. The following describes the Grouping toolbar icons.

Option	Icon	Description
Automatic Grouping		Automatically groups selected annotations together.
Manual Grouping		Manually groups selected annotations together.

1.5 Annotation Process

General Steps

Use the following general steps to add annotations and tolerances to a model:

1. Define the tolerancing standard.
2. Define the annotation planes.
3. Create dimensions and tolerances.
4. Create datum reference frames.
5. Create geometrical tolerances.
6. Create basic dimensions.
7. Create additional annotations.
8. (Optional) Extract 2D drawing views.

Step 1 - Define the tolerancing standard.

The tolerancing standard defines the properties to which the annotations must conform. To define the standard, select **Tools>Options>Mechanical Design>Functional Tolerancing & Annotation** and select the Tolerancing tab. Select an option in the **Default standard at creation** drop-down list, as shown in Figure 1–8.

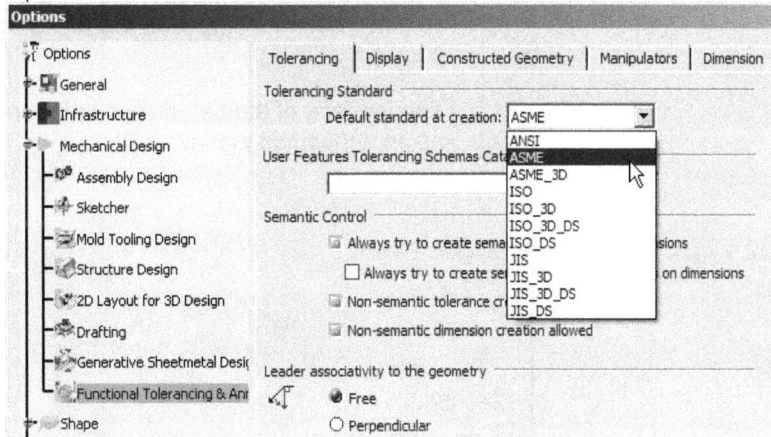

Figure 1–8

New models are created using the default standard. To change the standard for existing annotation sets, right-click on the Annotation Set.1 branch of the specification tree and select **Properties**. Use the drop-down list in the *Standards* tab of the Properties dialog box to change the standard for a model, as shown in Figure 1–9.

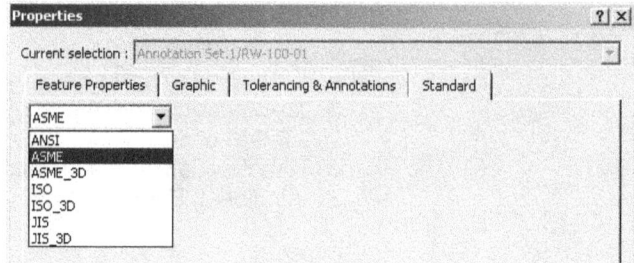

Figure 1–9

Step 2 - Define the annotation planes.

Before creating any annotations, define an annotation or view plane by referencing any planar face or reference plane in the model. The view plane provides an orientation reference for the annotation. When creating new annotations, they are associated with the active view plane. This enables annotations to be selected based on the view plane that was active during their creation.

The top face of the part shown in Figure 1–10 has been defined as an annotation plane.

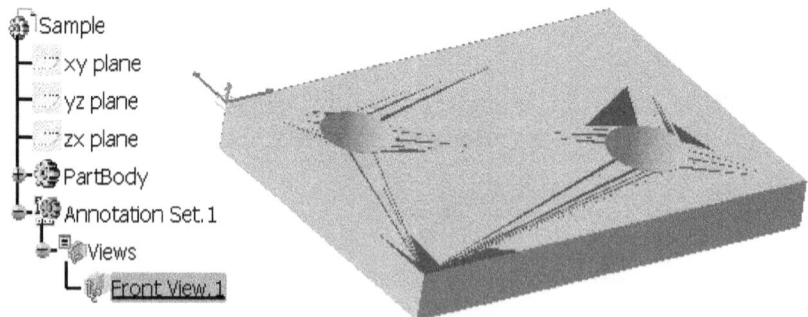

Figure 1–10

Active View

The active view plane is identified by a red border on the model. In the specification tree, the active view displays with a red plane and it is underlined, as shown in Figure 1–11. If no view planes exist, one is created that accommodates the annotation being defined.

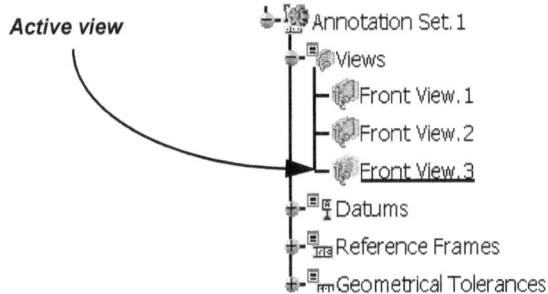

Figure 1–11

To activate a view plane, right-click on the view in the specification tree and select **Activate View**. You can also activate the view by double-clicking the view frame on the model.

Step 3 - Create dimensions and tolerances.

Dimensions and tolerances should be added as early as possible to support the datum reference frames and geometrical tolerances that are added to the model.

Dimensions can be toleranced using one of the following methods:

- General Tolerance (e.g., 90)

- Numerical Values (e.g., 90 ± 0.1)

- Tabulated Values (e.g., 90 H7)

- Single Limit (e.g., 90 MIN)

Some dimensions and tolerances have been added to the part, as shown in Figure 1–12.

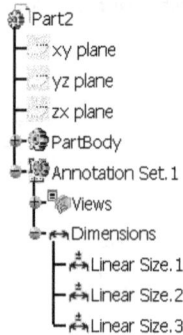

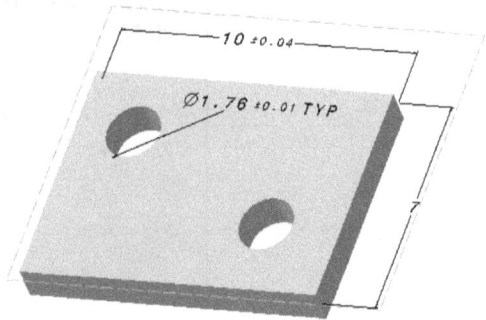

Figure 1–12

Step 4 - Create datum reference frames.

The next step is to define the semantic datums for the model. They can be defined on planar faces or reference planes in the model. If a non-planar surface is selected, datum target points must be defined to establish the datum.

In CATIA, Datum reference frames are also called Datum systems. The terms are used interchangeably.

Datum reference frames (DRF) provide the basis for all geometrical tolerancing in the model. The DRF's are developed from a selection of semantic datums. Once created, DRF's are added to the specification tree and the Semantic Tolerancing Advisor dialog box.

Three semantic datums (A, B, and C) and a datum reference frame (A|B|C) have been defined for the part model, as shown in Figure 1–13.

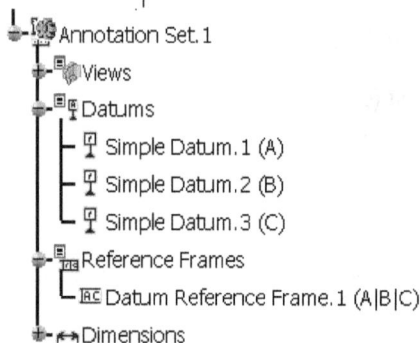

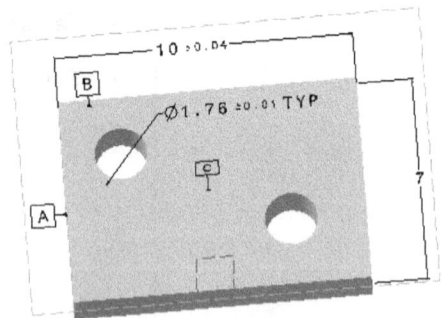

Figure 1–13

Step 5 - Create geometrical tolerances.

Since the geometrical tolerance must be constructed from one of the existing datum reference frames, they can only be added once the DRF's have been defined. A variety of geometrical tolerance types and conditions can be created in both semantic and non-semantic formats. A position tolerance has been added to the diameter dimension, as shown in Figure 1–14.

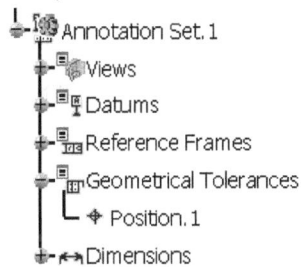

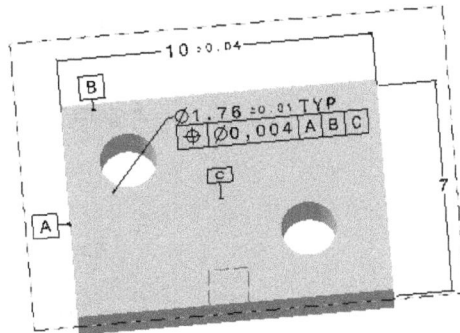

Figure 1–14

Step 6 - Create basic dimensions.

Basic dimensions are indicated by a frame or box around the dimension value. Since a basic dimension specifies a theoretically exact value, it must be associated with a datum reference frame to be created. A basic dimension has been added to the model, as shown in Figure 1–15.

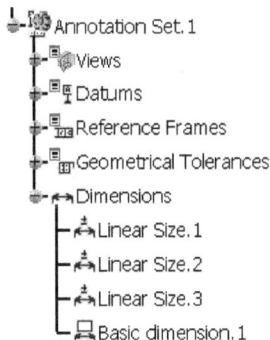

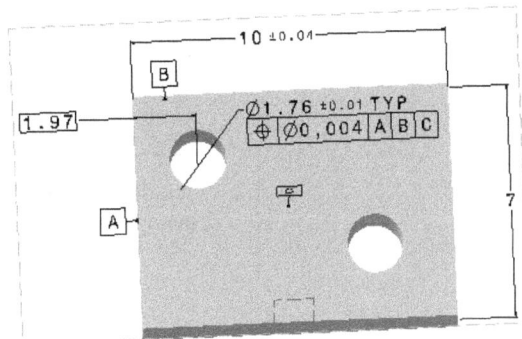

Figure 1–15

Step 7 - Create additional annotations.

The last step of the process is to complete the annotation of the model. The following list indicates some of the different types of additional annotations that can be defined:

- Text, including notes with leaders and title block information

- Flag notes

- Roughness symbols

A completely annotated model displays, as shown in Figure 1–16.

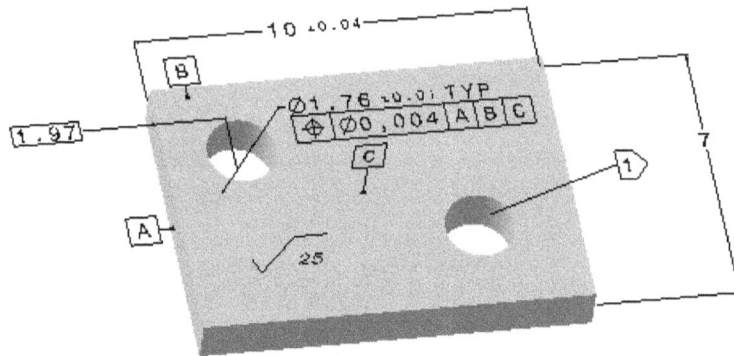

Figure 1–16

Step 8 - (Optional) Extract 2D drawing views.

Once the model has been fully annotated, you can extract drawing views directly from the annotation views.

1.6 Drawing Creation

Using the FT&A workbench simplifies the creation of drawing views. In the same way that drawing views can be extracted directly from the model, annotated views can also be taken directly from the model into the 2D drawing. This ability ensures that all engineering information is stored and extracted directly from the 3D model. It also enables the design and manufacturing process to minimize its reliance on the drawing for output.

General Steps

Use the following general steps to create a drawing using an annotated model.

1. Create a new drawing.
2. Extract a view from the 3D model.
3. Align the drawing views.

Step 1 - Create a new drawing.

With the annotated model open, create a new drawing. The tolerance standard and drawing standard must be the same to display an annotated view from a model.

Step 2 - Extract a view from the 3D model.

Before creating any drawing views, tile the windows (recommended) so that selections between the model and drawing can be facilitated. Select **Window>Tile Horizontally**.

In the Projections toolbar of the Drafting workbench, click

(View from 3D). Expand the specification tree for the annotated model and select an annotation plane in the Views branch. The system previews the annotated view in the drawing window. Position and orient the view using the drawing compass and then select anywhere in the drawing background to generate the view.

A drawing with multiple annotated views displays, as shown in Figure 1–17.

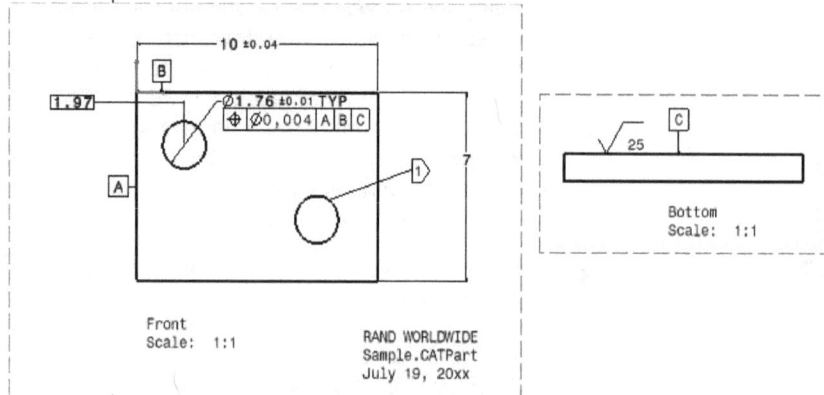

Figure 1–17

Step 3 - Align the drawing views.

By default, drawing views added from the model are not aligned correctly.

How To: Use the following steps to align the views:

1. Right-click on the border of the drawing view that moves into an aligned position and select **View Positioning>Align Views Using Elements**.
2. Select an element from each view to be aligned. For example, two edges are selected from the drawing views, as shown in Figure 1–18.

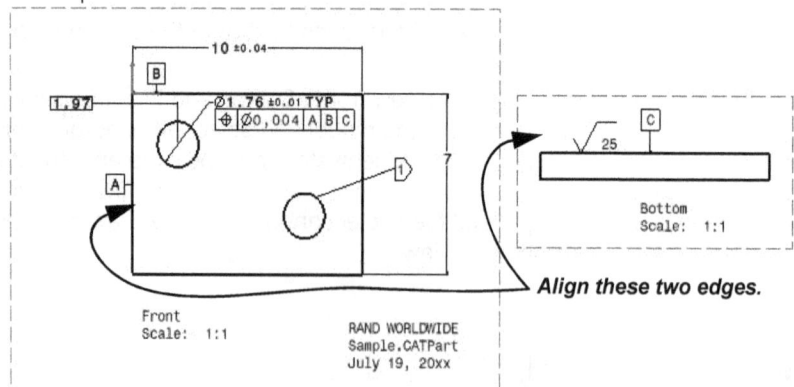

Align these two edges.

Figure 1–18

The aligned views display, as shown in Figure 1–19.

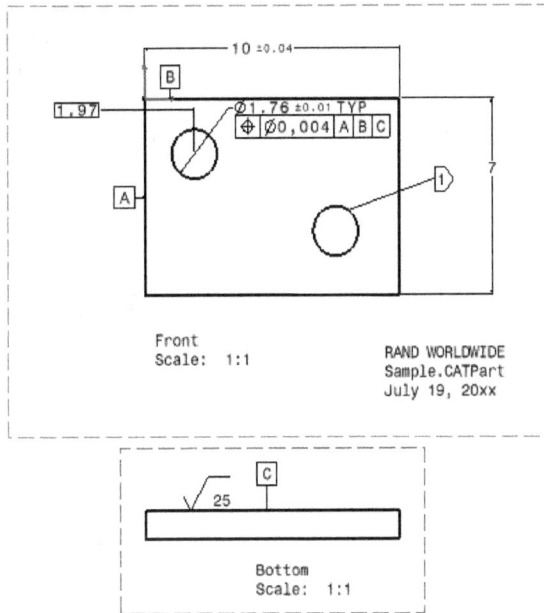

Figure 1–19

1.7 Accessing Annotations

The annotation set that is created to store all elements created in the Functional Tolerancing & Annotation workbench is viewable outside this workbench. Therefore, only the designers that are applying annotations require a license for FT&A. Anyone that is reviewing annotations and tolerances can do so using a Digital Mock-Up (DMU) license or can access them through another workbench that enables you to view CATPart and CATProduct files.

If you are using DMU to review part level annotations, you have to add the part to an empty CATProduct file. CATPart files cannot be directly opened in DMU. An example of an annotated model that has been inserted into a product in the DMU Navigator workbench displays in Figure 1–20.

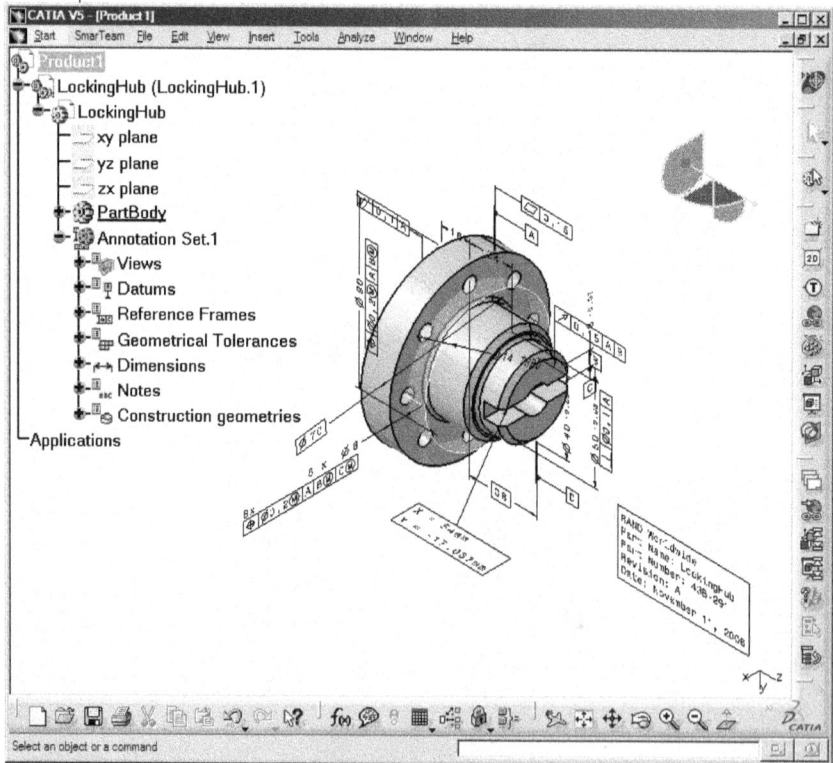

Figure 1–20

Remember that you might have to toggle on the annotation set before it can be viewed in the model. This is done by right-clicking on the annotation set and selecting **Annotation Set Switch On/Switch Off**.

1.8 Annotation References

You must select references when creating annotations. For example, the hole feature is selected to create the dimension and geometrical tolerance annotation shown in Figure 1–21. A parent-child relationship now exists between the hole and the annotation so that the annotation would fail if the hole were deleted.

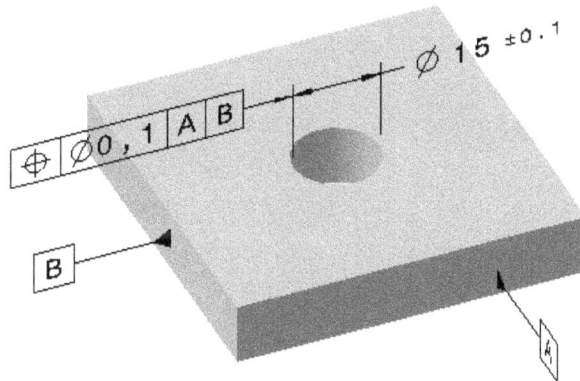

Figure 1–21

3D Annotation Query

The 3D Annotation Query tool (⬚) is used to identify the connection between a selected annotation and the rest of the model by highlighting elements on the model and in the specification tree when enabled. For example, the system highlights the hole feature if the toleranced dimension is selected, as shown in Figure 1–22.

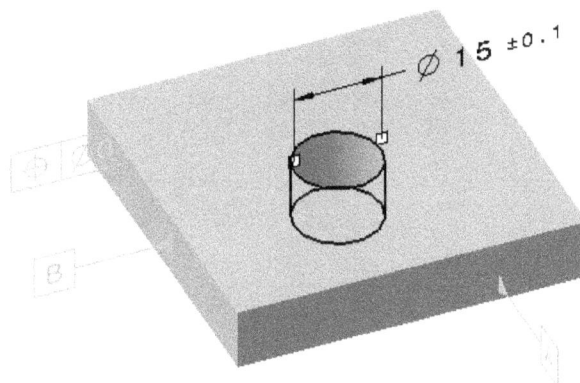

Figure 1–22

The 3D Annotation Query also considers the relationships between annotations. For example, if the geometrical tolerance is selected, the system highlights the hole feature and the Datum A and B annotations that are referenced by the geometrical tolerance.

By default, the **3D Annotation Query** tool is active. The icon is toggled on and off by selecting it in the Visualization toolbar, as shown in Figure 1–23.

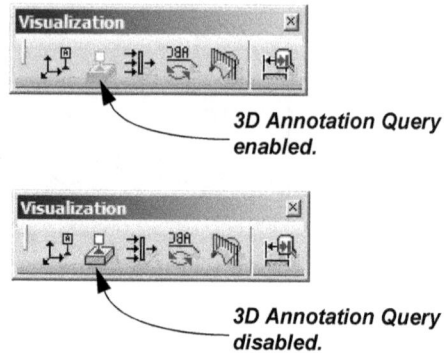

3D Annotation Query enabled.

3D Annotation Query disabled.

Figure 1–23

Practice 1a | FT&A Overview

Practice Objectives

- Review an annotated model.
- Activate a view.
- Create a note.
- Create annotated drawing views from a 3D model.

In this practice, you will review a model that contains a variety of tolerances and annotations. The intent of this practice is to become familiar with the FT&A workbench and the different types of annotations that can be created.

After reviewing the model, you create a new drawing file and extract annotated views from the 3D geometry. The intent is to reinforce the concept that all engineering information must be stored and extracted directly from the 3D model. This enables the design and manufacturing process to minimize its reliance on the drawing for output.

The model and completed drawing displays, as shown in Figure 1–24.

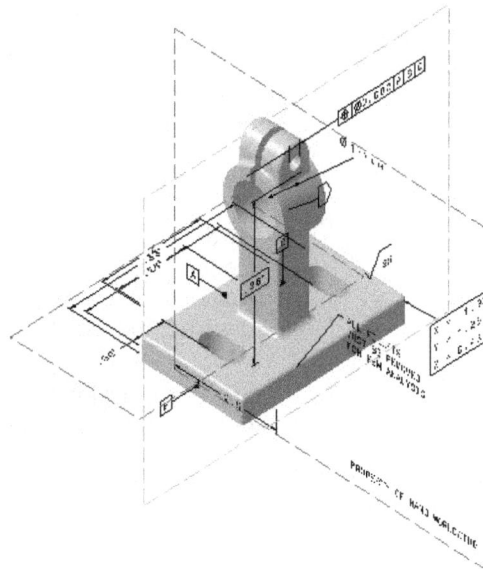

Figure 1–24

Task 1 - Open a part file.

1. Open **FlangeLock.CATPart**.

2. Verify that you are in the Functional Tolerancing & Annotation

   workbench. The workbench icon should be [icon]. To access
   the workbench, select **Start>Mechanical Design>
   Functional Tolerancing & Annotation**.

3. Select **Tools>Options>General>Parameters and Measure**
   and select the *Units* tab.

4. Select **Inch (in)** from the Length drop-down list, as shown in
   Figure 1–25.

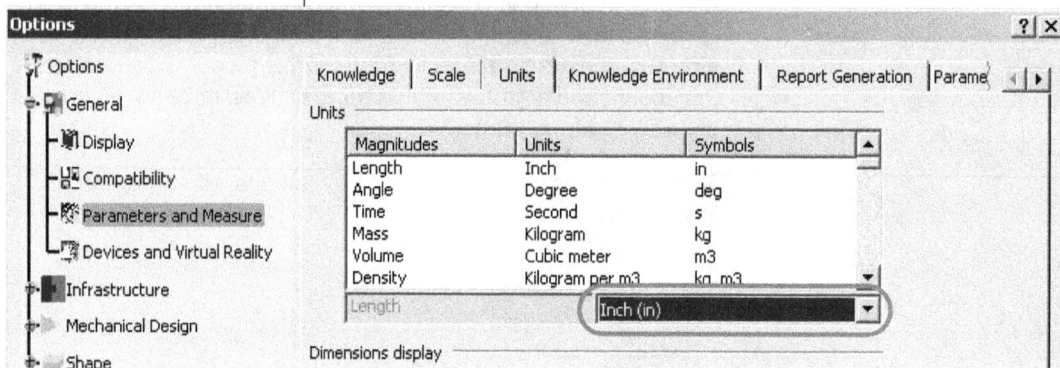

Options

Options
General
 Display
 Compatibility
 Parameters and Measure
 Devices and Virtual Reality
Infrastructure
Mechanical Design
Shape

Knowledge | Scale | Units | Knowledge Environment | Report Generation | Parame

Units

Magnitudes	Units	Symbols
Length	Inch	in
Angle	Degree	deg
Time	Second	s
Mass	Kilogram	kg
Volume	Cubic meter	m3
Density	Kilogram per m3	kg_m3

Length | Inch (in)

Dimensions display

Figure 1–25

5. Click **OK**.

6. By default, the 3D-Annotation-Query Switch On/Switch Off
   icon is enabled. This icon highlights geometry and reference
   frames that are associated to the selected annotation. If
   enabled, the icon highlights in orange. For now, disable this

   option by clicking [icon] (3D-Annotation-Query Switch
   On/Switch Off) in the Visualization toolbar.

Task 2 - Review the annotations.

The presence of FT&A annotations in the model can be detected by the Annotation Set branch in the specification tree. You can toggle the display of annotations on and off to simplify the display of the model. Currently, the display of annotations is toggled off.

1. Right-click on **Annotation Set.1** in the specification tree and select **Annotation Set Switch On/Switch Off**. Annotations display on the model, as shown in Figure 1–26.

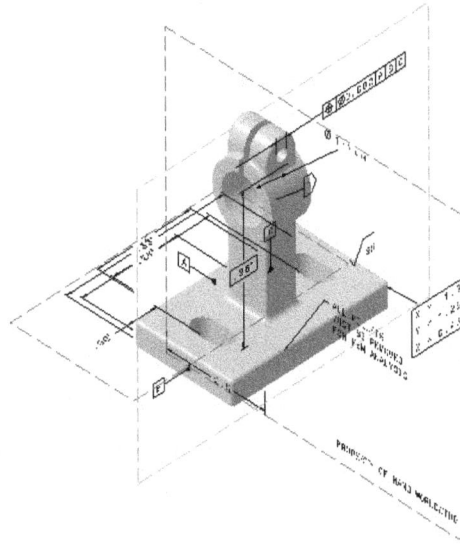

Figure 1–26

2. Expand the **Annotations** branch. A variety of annotations have been created in the model. Each annotation is organized in the tree by type, as shown in Figure 1–27.

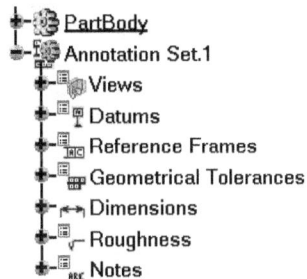

Figure 1–27

3. Expand the different branches of the specification tree and select a variety of annotations to become familiar with the different types. As tolerances are selected in the tree, they highlight on the model.

4. Click ⬛ (3D-Annotation-Query Switch On/Switch Off) so that it is enabled.

5. Select the **Position.1** tolerance, as shown in Figure 1–28. It also highlights the geometry associated to the tolerance (Datum Reference Frame A|B|C and Hole.2).

The other annotations are hidden in Figure 1–28 to simplify the display of the model.

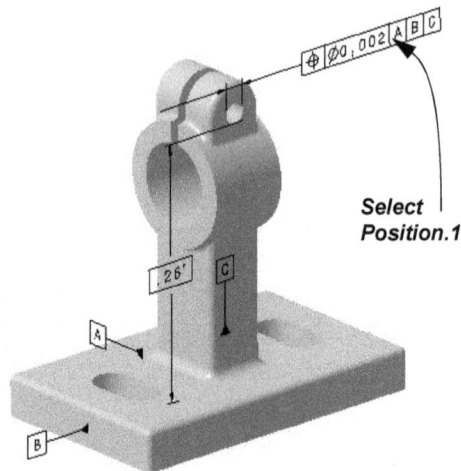

Figure 1–28

Task 3 - Modify the model.

The dimensional annotations are associative to the geometry on which they are based. In this task, you modify the Multipad base feature and then update the model to view changes to the associated annotations.

1. In the specification tree, expand **PartBody** and then **Multipad.1**. Double-click on **Sketch.1**. The sketch for the multipad feature displays.

2. Double-click on the **2.5** dimension, as shown in Figure 1–29.

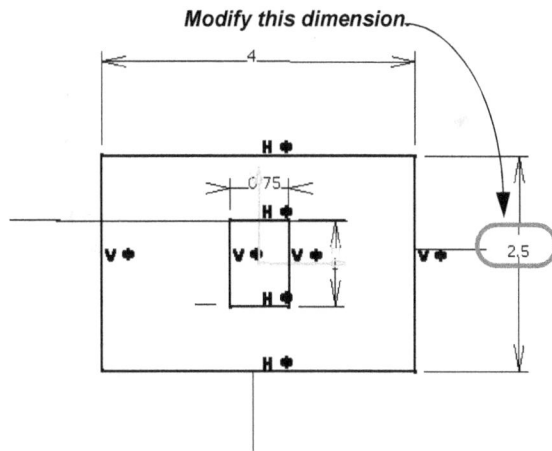

Modify this dimension

Figure 1–29

3. Enter a new value of **2.6** and click **OK**.

4. Click ⬆ (Exit workbench) to exit Sketcher. The system updates all geometry and annotations based on the design change, as shown in Figure 1–30.

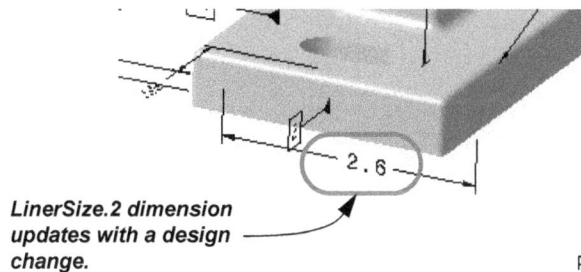

LinerSize.2 dimension updates with a design change.

Figure 1–30

Task 4 - Activate a view and add a note.

The frame of the currently selected view highlights in orange on the model and in the specification tree. Any annotations created are automatically associated with the activated view.

In this task, you add a text annotation to the model to demonstrate the properties of the active view.

1. Expand the **Annotation Set.1>Views** branch of the specification tree. The active view, **Front View.2**, is indicated by a orange plane in the specification tree and on the model.

2. Double-click on **Front View.1** in the specification tree to activate the view.

3. Click 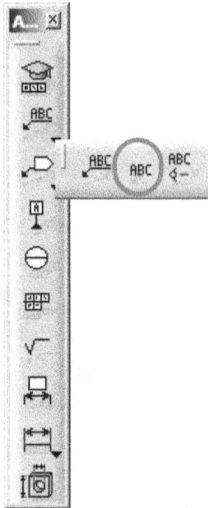 (Text) and select a location close to the one shown in Figure 1–31. The Text Editor dialog box opens.

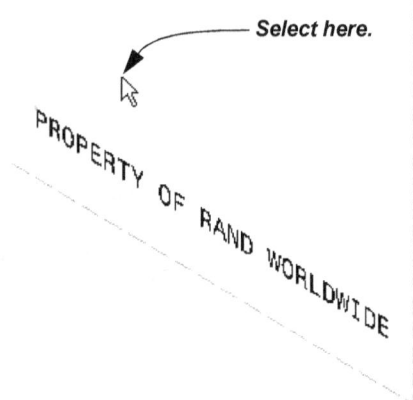

Figure 1–31

4. Enter the text **Material: Aluminum** and click **OK**. The annotation is added as **Text.3** to the Notes branch of the specification tree.

5. To orient the model using the view plane, click (Normal View) and then select **Front View.1** on the model or in the specification tree.

6. Position the text annotation, as shown in Figure 1–32.

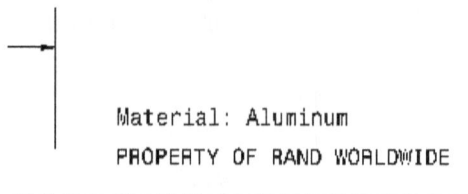

Figure 1–32

Task 5 - Create a drawing.

1. Select **Start>Mechanical Design>Drafting**. The New Drawing Creation dialog box opens, as shown in Figure 1–33.

2. Create the drawing using the following parameters:

   - *Automatic Layout:* **Empty sheet**
   - *Standard:* **ASME**
   - *Sheet Style:* **C ANSI**

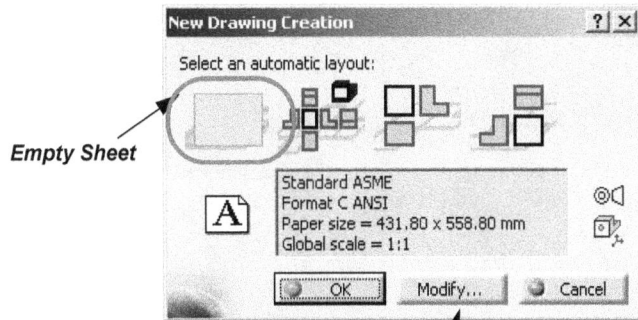

Empty Sheet

Click Modify to change the drawing standard and the sheet style.

Figure 1–33

3. Click **OK** to create the new drawing.

4. Select **Window>Tile Horizontally** to see the model and drawing simultaneously.

5. In the Projections flyout of the Views toolbar, click ⬚ (View from 3D).

6. Select **Front View.1** in the specification tree in the FlangeLock.CATPart window. The system displays this view and all annotations that are associated with it, as shown in Figure 1–34.

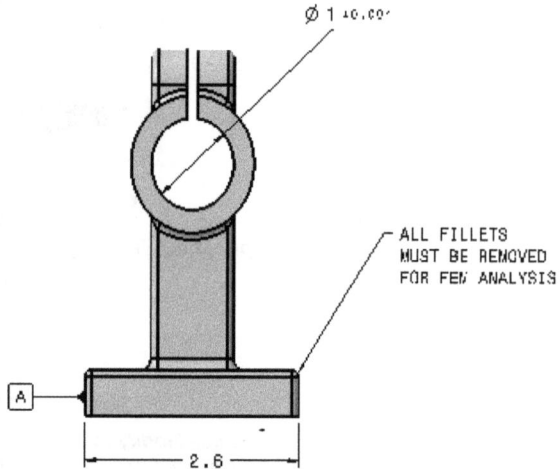

Ø 1 ±0.00′

ALL FILLETS
MUST BE REMOVED
FOR FEM ANALYSIS

A

2.6

Material: Aluminum

PROPERTY OF RAND WORLDWIDE

Figure 1–34

7. Click anywhere in the background of the drawing window to complete the view creation.

8. Create two more views using ⬚ (View from 3D), selecting **Front View.2** and **Front View.3**. Position the drawing views as shown in Figure 1–35.

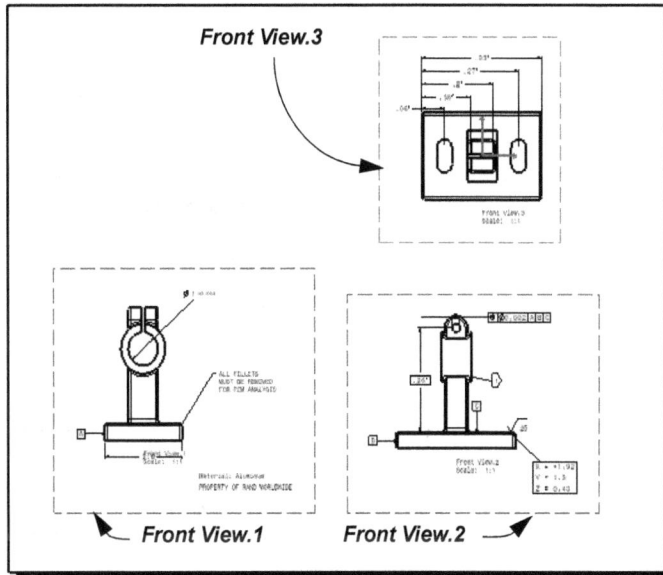

Figure 1–35

You can also correct this issue by recreating the dimensions in the 3D model using geometry that displays in the drawing view.

Two of the dimensions in Front View.3 have red x's over them. This is because their leaders are linked to geometry that is hidden in the current view. To correct this issue, you display hidden lines in the drawing view.

9. Right-click on the border of **Front View.3** and select **Properties**.

10. In the Properties dialog box, in the *View* tab, select **Hidden Lines**, as shown in Figure 1–36.

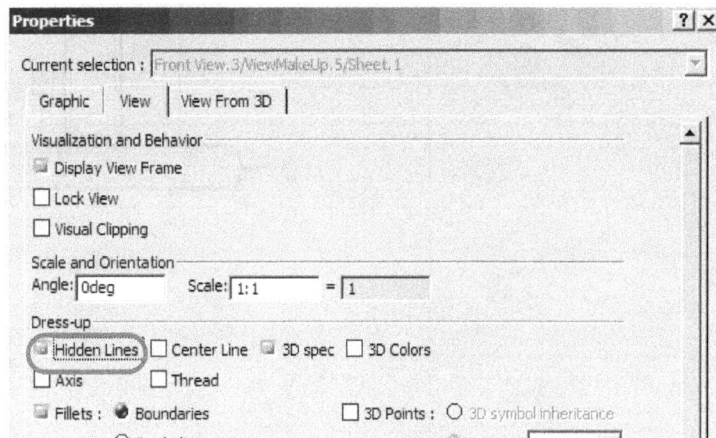

Figure 1–36

11. Click **OK** to close the Properties dialog box. The view is updated and the x's are now hidden.

Task 6 - Align the drawing views.

1. Right-click on the border of **Front View.3** and select **View Positioning>Align Views Using Elements**.

2. Select the entities from **Front View.2** and **Front View.3**, as shown in Figure 1–37.

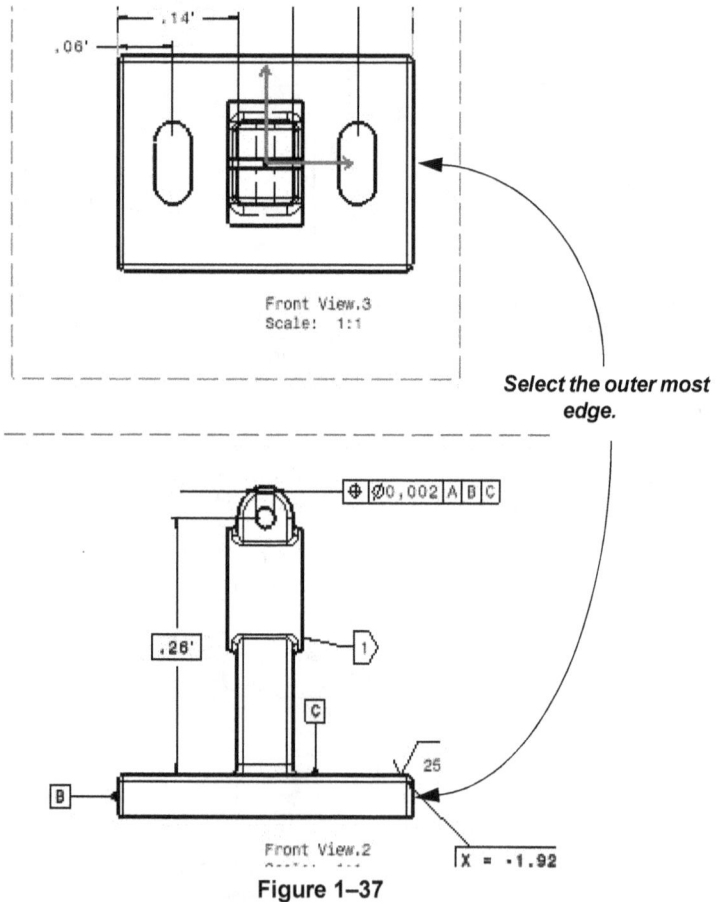

Select the outer most edge.

Figure 1–37

3. Repeat this operation to align **Front View.1** and **Front View.2**. The drawing displays, as shown in Figure 1–38.

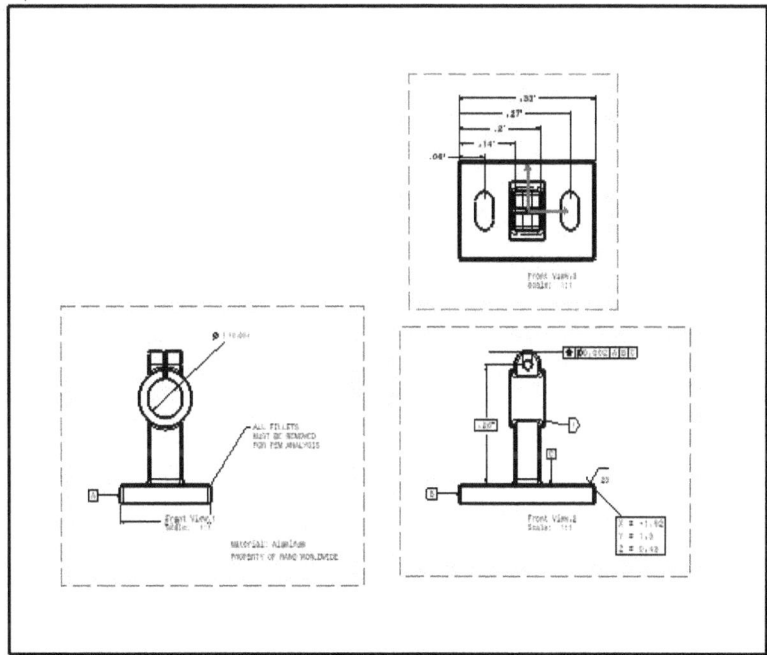

Figure 1–38

Task 7 - Transfer an annotation to another view.

1. Activate the FlangeLock.CATPart window and maximize the window.

2. Right-click on the **2.6in** dimension and select **Transfer To View/Annotation Plane**, as shown in Figure 1–39.

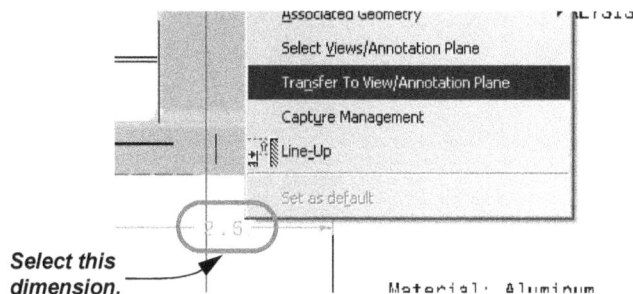

Select this
dimension.

Figure 1–39

3. Select **Front View.3** in the specification tree. The system transfers the 2.6in dimension to this view plane.

4. Drag the dimension to an appropriate location.

5. Select **Window>Drawing1**.

6. Update the drawing to reflect the modification made to the 2.6in dimension. The Front View.3 drawing view displays, as shown in Figure 1–40.

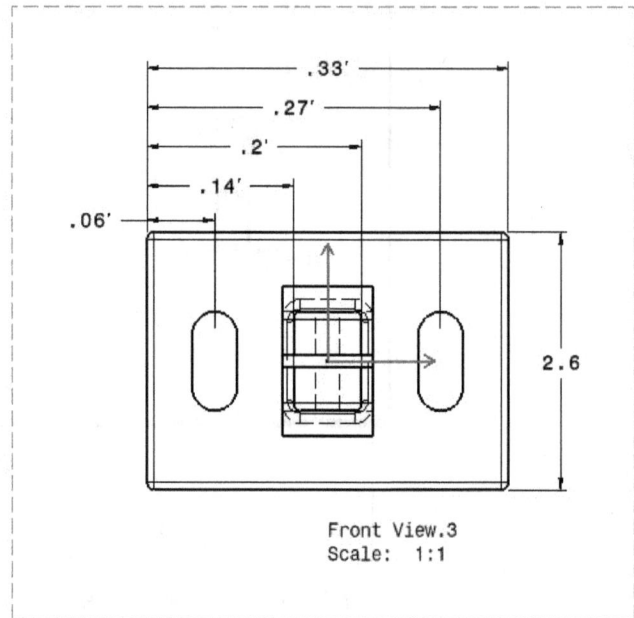

Figure 1–40

7. Save the model and drawing and close all windows.

Chapter

2

Preparing the Model

This chapter introduces how to create annotation planes and construction geometry. These features serve as the foundation of the annotations of a model.

Learning Objectives in this Chapter

- Create views, including Planar and Sketched views.
- Learn how to use a clipping plane.
- Understand the impact of view associativity.
- Understand the use of construction geometry.
- Create Principal views.
- Create Axonometric views.

2.1 Views

Views are used to locate and control the orientation of 3D annotations that are created on the model. Each annotation is associated with the view that was active during its creation. If a view has not been created, one is automatically added when the first annotation is created.

You can use views to orient the model. To do this, in the View toolbar, click ▱ (Normal View) and then select the view in the model or specification tree.

The Views toolbar and the different types of views that can be created are shown in Figure 2–1.

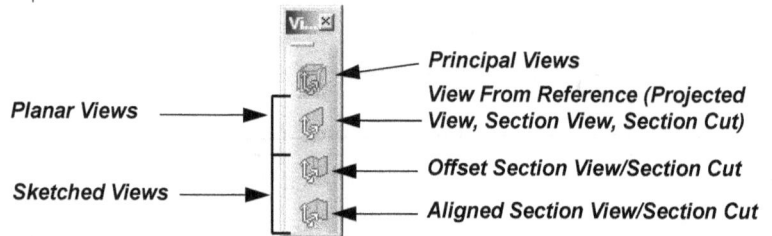

Figure 2–1

This toolbar can be divided into two types of views: planar and sketched. Planar views are created from a planar reference, while the sketched views are created from a sketch.

2.2 Planar Views

General Steps

Use the following general steps to create a planar view:

1. Select the view reference and planar view type.
2. Modify View Parameters.

> ## Step 1 - Select the view reference and planar view type.

Click ![icon] (View From Reference) to create a planar view. Select the reference and geometric element in the View Creation dialog box, enter a view name if required in the *Name* field. In the Type drop-down list, select **Projection View**, **Section View** or **Section Cut**, as shown in Figure 2–2.

Figure 2–2

Projected View

This view type creates an annotation plane by selecting a planar face, surface, or reference plane on the model. When used to add a drawing view, the projected view orients the model so that the annotation plane is parallel to the screen. A projected view is identified by a blue reference axis. An example is shown in Figure 2–3.

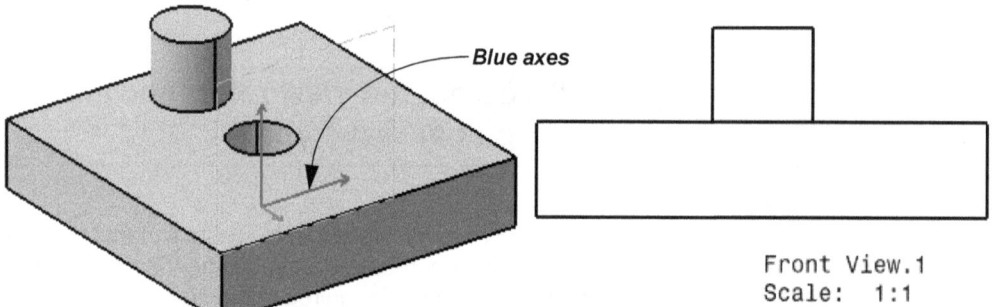

Front View.1
Scale: 1:1

Figure 2–3

Section View

A section view annotation plane defines both a viewing orientation and a cutting plane. When the view is extracted to the Drafting workbench, a section view is automatically generated. A section view is identified by a green reference axis. An example is shown in Figure 2–4.

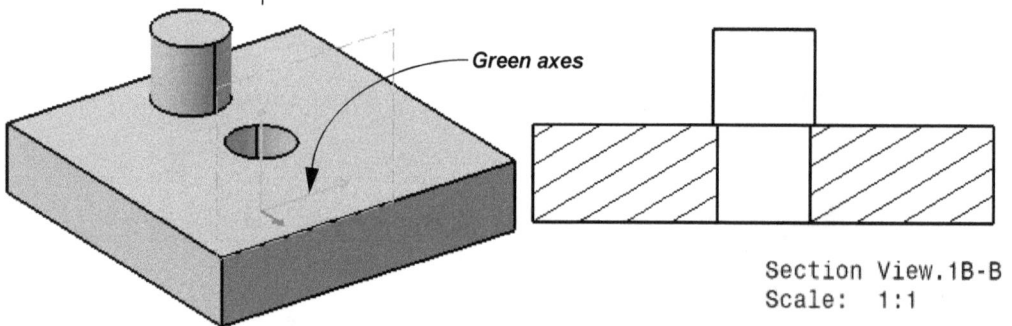

Section View.1B-B
Scale: 1:1

Figure 2–4

Section Cut

A section cut view annotation plane defines both a viewing orientation and a cutting plane. When the view is extracted to the Drafting workbench, a section cut view is automatically generated. The section cut only displays the geometry that lies on the cutting plane. All background geometry is not displayed. A section cut is identified by a yellow reference axis. An example is shown in Figure 2–5.

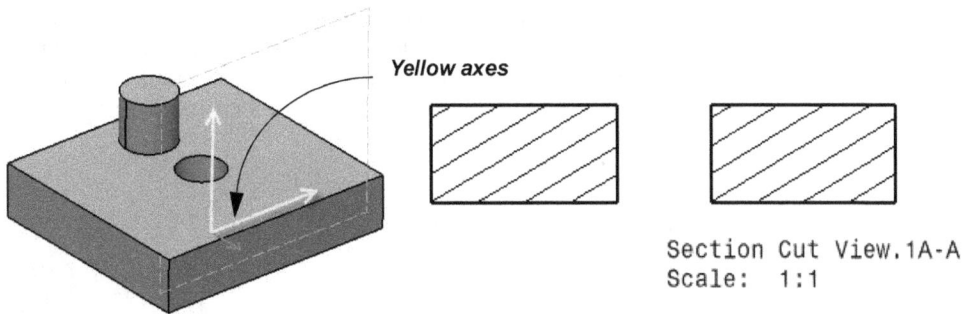

Yellow axes

Section Cut View.1A-A
Scale: 1:1

Figure 2–5

Step 2 - Modify View Parameters.

Optionally, modify the view parameters, such as **Ratio**, **Orientation**, and **View Normal**. Note that the reference element can also be replaced at this point, by clicking in the *Reference* field and selecting a new reference. Click **OK** to complete the view creation. The system adds the view to the model and specification tree and activates it. The active view is indicated by an orange border.

View Normal

When a view is being created, a reference axis is placed on the view to indicate the orientation of the view, as shown in Figure 2–6. If required, to invert the normal axis, select **Invert normal** in the View Creation dialog box. The axis that is normal to the view plane initially displays red when no annotations have been associated with the view.

Select the view from the specification tree or directly on the model to view the reference axis.

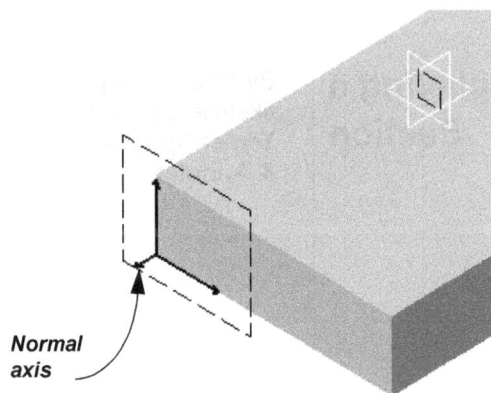

Normal axis

Figure 2–6

This normal axis determines the orientation of annotations that are placed on the view. An example is shown in Figure 2–7, where two parallel views have been created with normal axes in opposite directions. The annotation for Datum B has been inverted due to the orientation of the normal axis for Front View.2.

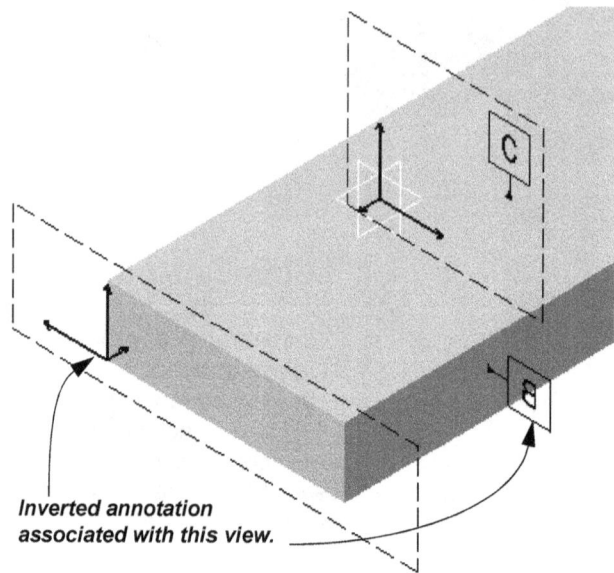

Inverted annotation associated with this view.

Figure 2–7

The view normal can only be inverted before annotations have been created on the view. If you want to invert the normal after annotations have been created, you can temporarily transfer the annotations off the view, invert the normal, and then transfer the annotations back. This enables you to invert the normal without deleting and recreating the annotations.

Displaying a Section

By default, the geometry of the section view (either planar or sketched) does not display on the 3D model. To display it, select **Tools>Options>Mechanical Design>Functional Tolerancing & Annotation** and select the *View/Annotation Plane* tab.

Next, enable the **Visualization of the profile in the current view** option in the *View/Annotation Plane Display* area, as shown in Figure 2–8.

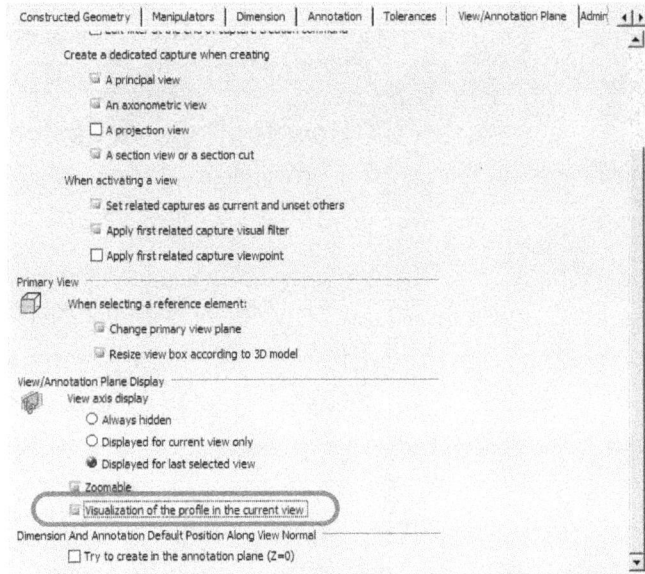

Figure 2–8

The model now displays the boundary generated by the section whenever the view is active, as shown in Figure 2–9.

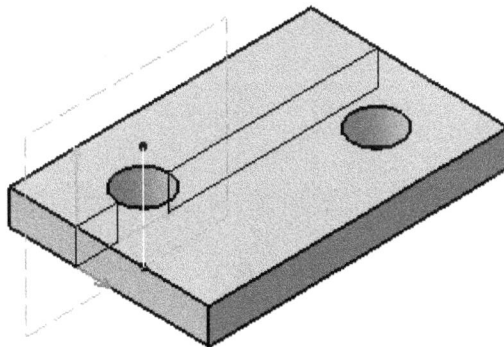

Figure 2–9

2.3 Sketched Views

This section provides the steps required to create Offset Section View/Section Cut and Aligned Section View/Section Cut views. These types of views are specifically targeted at preparing views for 2D extraction.

How To: Define a Sketched View

1. Define the type of section view to create by clicking one of the following two icons:

    - (Offset Section View/Section Cut) - The Offset View Creation dialog box opens, as shown in Figure 2–10.

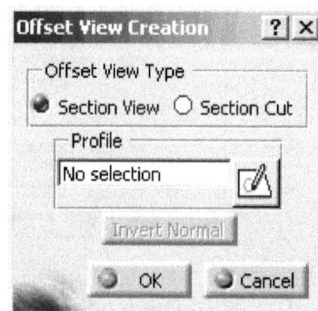

Figure 2–10

    - (Aligned Section View/Section Cut) - The Aligned View Creation dialog box opens, as shown in Figure 2–11.

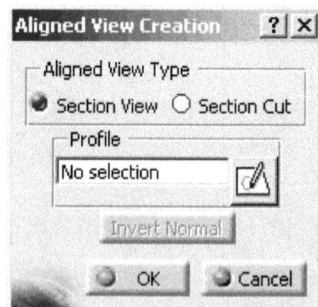

Figure 2–11

2. Select the type of view to be created by selecting the **Section View** or **Section Cut** option. The **Section View** option only impacts the drawing where a section view displays all geometry behind the cutting plane, while a section cut only displays the geometry on the cutting plane. An example is shown in Figure 2–12.

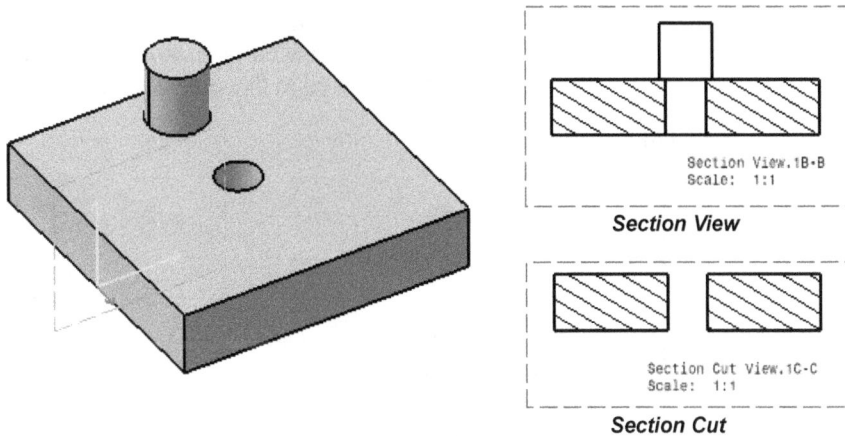

Section View.1B-B
Scale: 1:1

Section View

Section Cut View.1C-C
Scale: 1:1

Section Cut

Figure 2–12

3. Click (Sketch) and select a planar face, surface, or reference plane to sketch a profile for the extraction view. You can also select a predefined sketch feature. For an offset view, all of the lines in the sketch must be perpendicular or parallel to one another to be valid. An example sketch for an offset view is shown in Figure 2–13.

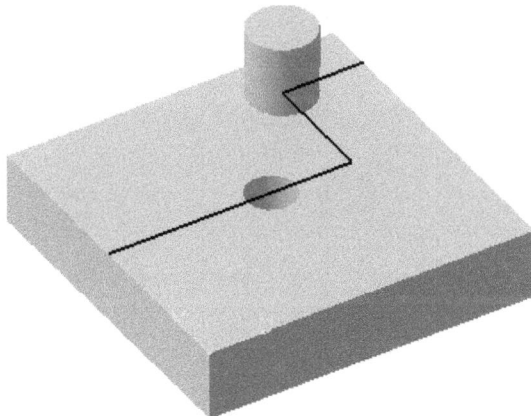

Figure 2–13

*You can invert the normal for a sketched view and at any time up until an annotation has been created. Activate the view, right-click, and select **Invert Normal**.*

4. If required, use **Invert Normal** to change the direction of the view normal. The arrow points opposite to the viewing direction.

5. Click **OK** to complete the view creation. The system adds the view to the model and specification tree, as shown in Figure 2–14. The **Offset Section View.1** cannot be activated and is only available for drawing view creation purposes. Beneath the offset section view are several section views. Each section view behaves like a standard section view that can be activated to place annotations.

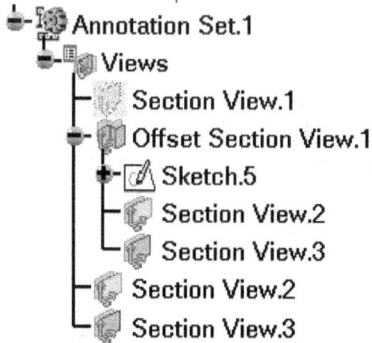

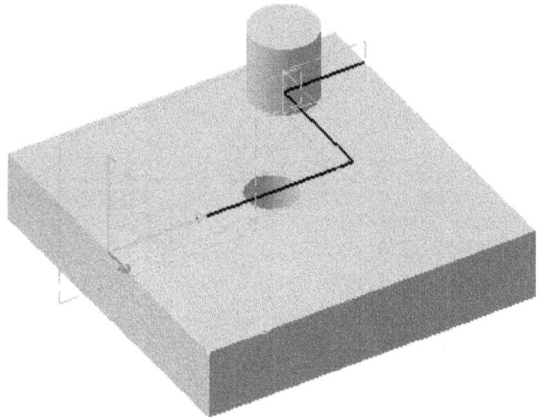

Figure 2–14

2.4 Clipping Plane

A clipping plane enables you to clip the geometry of the part using an existing view/annotation plane. A clipping plane is for visualization purposes only, as the view plane or part geometry are not permanently altered and no feature is created or added to the specification tree. An example is shown in Figure 2–15.

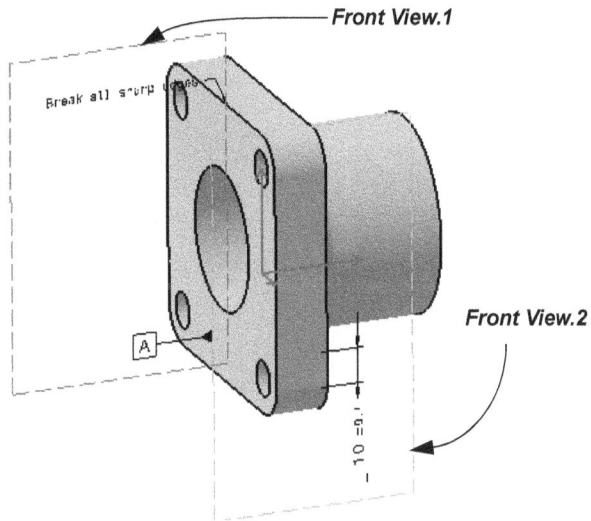

Figure 2–15

How To: Use the following steps to view a clipping plane:

1. In the Visualization toolbar, shown in Figure 2–16, click

    (Clipping Plane).

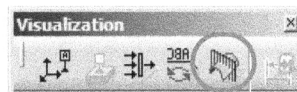

Figure 2–16

2. The application clips all of the geometry of the part at the active view/annotation plane.

Figure 2–17 shows the clipping plane using the **Front View.1** annotation plane.

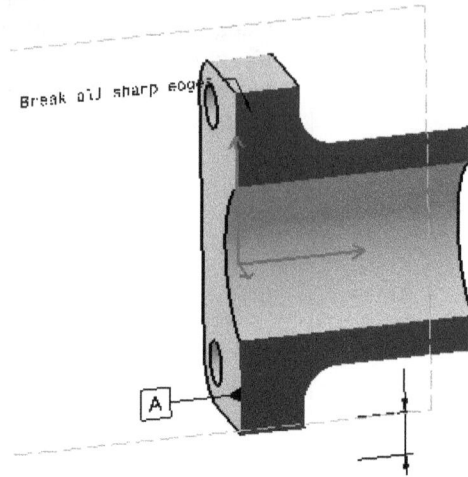

Figure 2–17

Figure 2–18 shows the clipping plane using the **Front View.2** annotation plane.

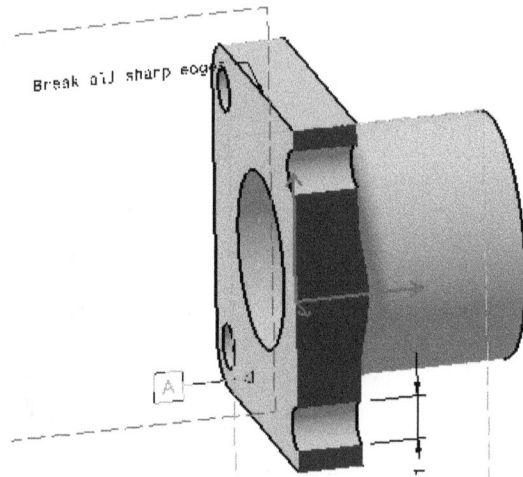

Figure 2–18

The clipping plane display is not saved with the model, however, they can be saved with the capture functionality.

3D Preview

When a view is selected, it is automatically displayed with the clipping plane regardless of whether or not ![icon] is active. If the view selected is a section view, the profile of the section displays as an orange line. You can disable this functionality by clearing ![icon] (3D Annotation Query Switch On/Switch off).

Display Settings

The clipping plane can be customized to display hatching, coloring, or dotting. This is very useful in assemblies to help distinguish the various components. Cross-hatching properties defined in the part also display in the drawing.

To display hatching, coloring, or dotting in the clipping plane, select **Tools>Options>Mechanical Design>Functional Tolerancing & Annotation**. Select the *Display* tab. In the *Hatching, coloring, or dotting for the clipping plane section*, enable the **Display** option.

If no material has been defined for the model, the color of the model is applied to the clipping plane.

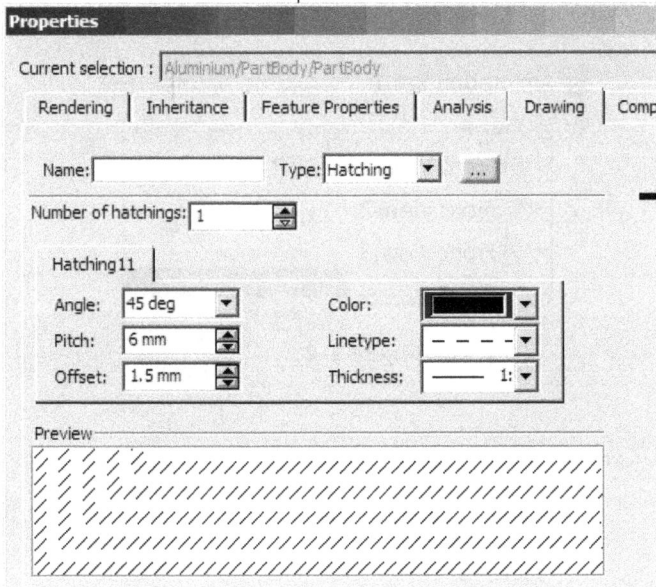

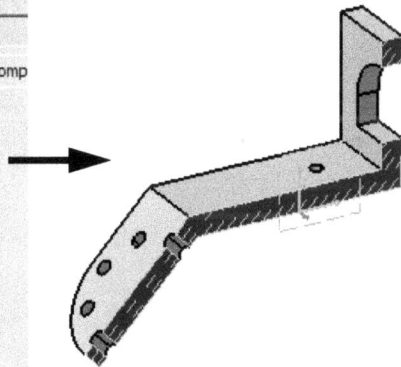

To display hatching, coloring, or dotting in the clipping plane, apply a material to the model. Right-click on the material in the specification tree and select **Properties**. In the *Drawing* tab define the type of display, as shown in Figure 2–19.

Figure 2–19

2.5 View Associativity

When a view is created, a link is generated to the selected geometry reference(s). For example, if an offset reference plane is selected to define a front view, the view is dependent on the position of the plane. If the plane is moved, the view updates. This is driven by a CATIA option that controls the associativity of an annotation plane to its referenced geometry.

To access this option, select **Tools>Options>Mechanical Design>Functional Tolerancing & Annotation**. Then select the *View/Annotation Plane* tab to access the **Create views associative to geometry** option, as shown in Figure 2–20.

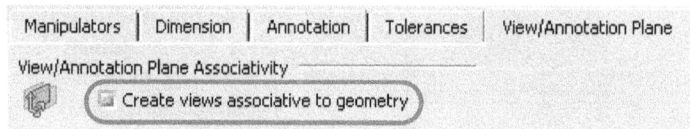

Figure 2–20

By default, this option is enabled. If it is disabled, the views do not update when modifications are made.

You can also disable or enable this option for specific annotation views. Right-click on the view and select **Change View Support**, as shown in Figure 2–21.

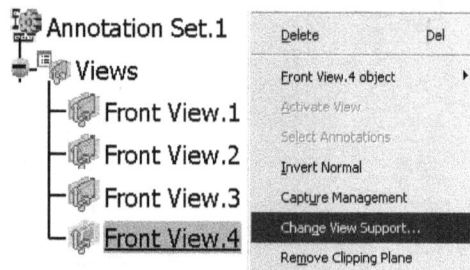

Figure 2–21

The Change View Support dialog box opens, as shown in Figure 2–22.

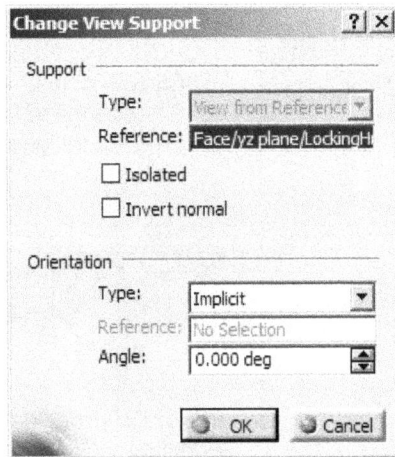

Figure 2–22

This dialog box is useful in the following situations:

- You require associativity, but views were created with **Create views associative to geometry** (in the Options dialog box) disabled. Toggle off the **Isolated** option and select reference element(s) for any views that you want to update with model changes.

- You require a view to reference a different geometric entity. In this case, you can click in the *Reference* field and then select a new planar reference.

2.6 Principal Views

General Steps

Use the following general steps to create a principal view:

1. Click Principal Views in the Views/Annotation Planes toolbar.
2. Select a plane to define the Front view plane orientation.
3. Select additional views to be created in the Principal View dialog box and click **OK**.

Step 1 - Click Principal Views in the Views/Annotation Planes toolbar.

Click ![icon] (Principal Views) to create a principal view. The Principal Views dialog box opens, as shown in Figure 2–23.

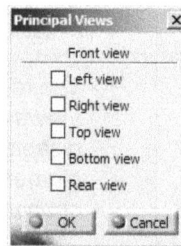

Figure 2–23

The primary view is **Front view**. To change the primary view, click the control arrows, as shown in Figure 2-24.

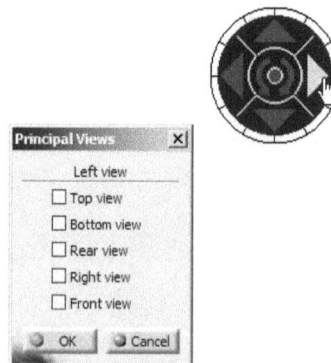

Figure 2–24

Depending on which arrow you clicked, the following combinations are applied:

Right arrow: FRONT > LEFT > REAR > RIGHT > FRONT.

Left arrow: FRONT > RIGHT > REAR > LEFT > FRONT.

Up arrow: FRONT > BOTTOM > REAR > TOP > FRONT.

Down arrow: FRONT > TOP > REAR > BOTTOM > FRONT.

The view bounding box displays as shown in Figure 2–25.

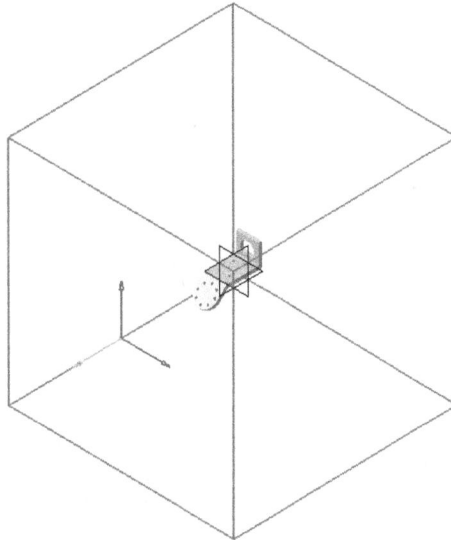

Figure 2–25

Step 2 - Select a plane to define the Front view plane orientation.

Select a plane to define the Front view plane orientation. The view box is resized according to the model size, as shown in Figure 2–26.

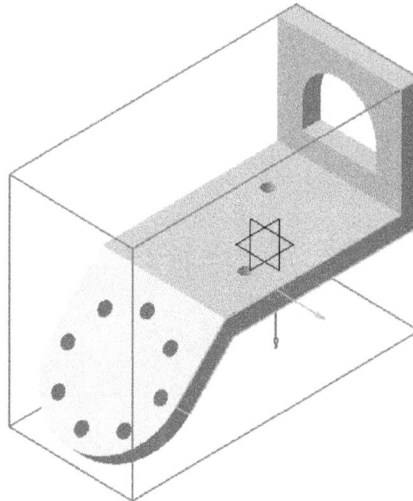

Figure 2–26

You can orient the view bounding box using the control and can modify the view bounding box angle using the green knob, as shown in Figure 2–27.

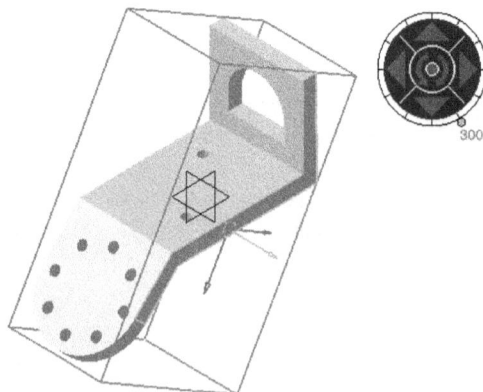

Figure 2–27

Step 3 - Select additional views to be created in the Principal View dialog box and click OK.

Select additional views to be created in the Principal View dialog box and click **OK**. Additional views display in the specification tree.

Created view/annotation planes are created as Projection View/Annotation and their reference planes are the faces of the bounding box.

Captures are automatically created and associated with the related views, and the names match, by default. However, if view names are edited, they will not automatically reflect in the capture names.

It is possible to have multiple views with the same name. If you want to ensure that all views have a unique name, click **Tools> Options>Infrastructure>Part Infrastructure>Display** and ensure that either **Under the same tree node** or **In the main object** are selected in the *Checking Operation when Renaming* area. A check is performed to ensure that two views do not bear the same name in a given annotation set.

2.7 Axonometric Views

An axonometric view enables you to manage 3D annotations in the same manner as for a Projection View/Annotation Plane, but uses the screen view orientation.

General Steps

Use the following general steps to create an axonometric view:

1. Click the View From Reference icon in the Views/Annotation Planes toolbar.
2. Select the Axonometric View icon from the Tools Palette.
3. Select a 3D point or vertex, or indicate a point on a surface or a curve.
4. Click **OK** in the View Creation dialog box.

Step 1 - Click the View From Reference icon in the Views/Annotation Planes toolbar.

Click (View From Reference) in the Views/Annotation Planes toolbar. The Tools Palette toolbar opens as shown in Figure 2–28.

Figure 2–28

Step 2 - Select the Axonometric View icon from the Tools Palette.

Select (Axonometric View) from the Tools Palette. Blue borders display at the four corners of the screen enabling you to define the view point.

You can set a 3D viewpoint and/or select a point to define the axonometric view.

Step 3 - Select a 3D point or vertex, or indicate a point on a surface or a curve.

Select a 3D point or vertex, or indicate a point on a surface or a curve, in the 3D window to define the origin of the view. The View Creation dialog box displays as shown in Figure 2–29.

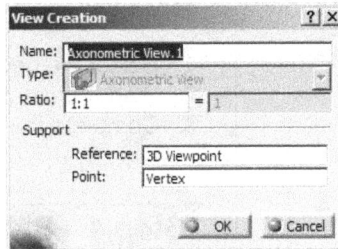

Figure 2–29

Step 4 - Click OK in the View Creation dialog box.

Click **OK** in the View Creation dialog box or click anywhere on the screen. The axonometric view is created as shown in Figure 2–30. Axonometric views are identified as Axonometric View in the specification tree.

Note that View Axis Display is toggled on in this image.

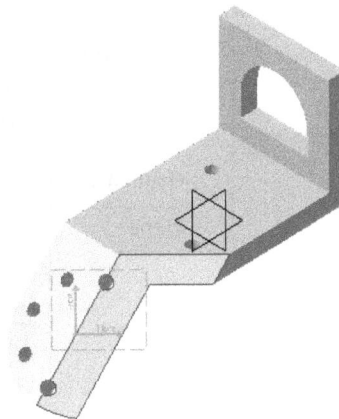

Figure 2–30

2.8 Construction Geometry

Construction geometry enables you to generate references to geometry that is not present in the design model. This provides a consistent and complete referencing scheme for annotations in the model.

General Steps

Use the following general steps to create a construction geometry:

1. Select the geometrical element(s).
2. Start the creation of the construction geometry.
3. Complete the creation of the construction geometry.

Step 1 - Select the geometrical element(s).

The construction geometry is created solely by referencing existing geometry. The type of construction geometry created depends on the reference(s) used. For example, you must preselect a hole to create an axis for it.

Step 2 - Start the creation of the construction geometry.

In the Geometry for 3D Annotations toolbar, click

(Constructed Geometry Creation). The Constructed Geometry Creation dialog box opens. Select the appropriate geometry to create from the available options, listed as follows:

Geometry	Image	Inputs and Outputs
Plane		Select two surfaces to create a plane that is equidistant between them, or that bisects the angle created between them.

Plane		To create a plane on which all entities lie select one of the following: • two coplanar edges, • an edge and a point, • three points, • two cylinders, • a cylinder and an edge, or • a cylinder and a point.
Plane		Select a surface and non-intersecting edge, or a surface and a cylinder to create a plane through the axis at an angle to the surface.
Plane		Select a cone to create a plane at either a specific cross-section diameter, offset from one plane, or equidistant between two planes. Selecting **Circle** creates a circle of the cone's cross-section.
Point		Select a surface and an edge, axis, or cylinder to create a point where the two intersect.
Point		Select a circle to create a point at its center.
Point		Select a cone to create a point at its apex.
Axis		Select two intersecting surfaces to create an axis along their intersection.
Axis		Select a cylinder or circular pattern to create an axis through its center.

Axis		Select a cone to create an axis through its center.
Cylinder		Select a cylinder and another cylinder, axis, or point to create a cylinder with its center as the first entity and a radius passing through the second entity.
Cylinder		Select a circular pattern to create a cylinder through the entities.

Step 3 - Complete the creation of the construction geometry.

Click **OK** to complete the feature. The model and specification tree update to display the construction geometry, as shown in Figure 2–31.

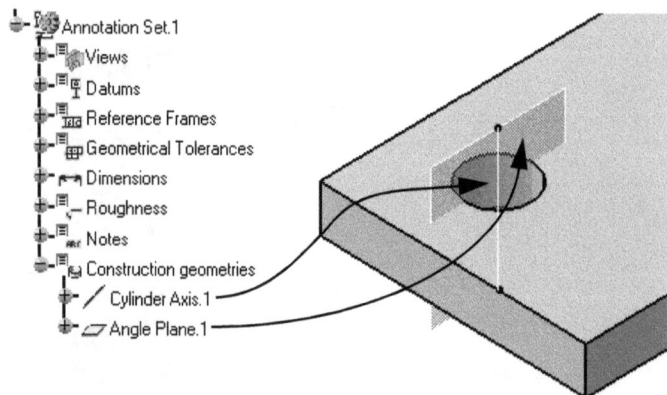

Figure 2–31

Practice 2a | Preparing the Model

Practice Objectives

- Define an annotation plane.
- Define a section plane.
- Create construction geometry.
- Invert the normal of an annotation plane.

In this practice, you will create section planes and construction geometry to prepare a model for annotation creation in the FT&A workbench. The completed model displays, as shown in Figure 2–32.

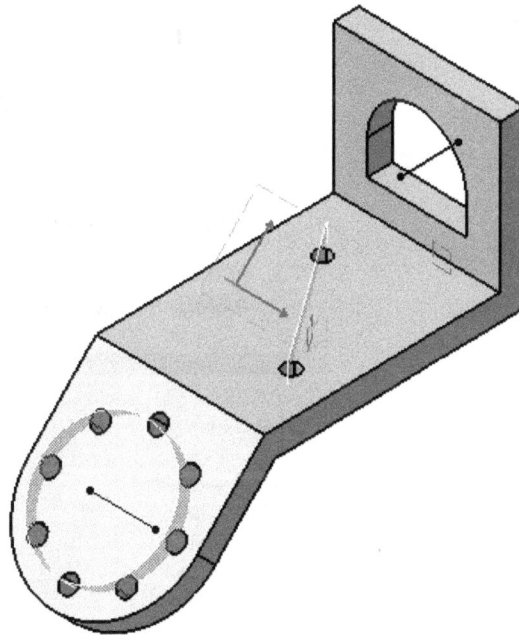

Figure 2–32

Once you finish preparing the model for annotations, you create a drawing for the model and add drawing views to show the properties of annotation planes and construction geometry.

Task 1 - Open a part file.

1. Open **Sample.CATPart**. The model displays, as shown in Figure 2–33.

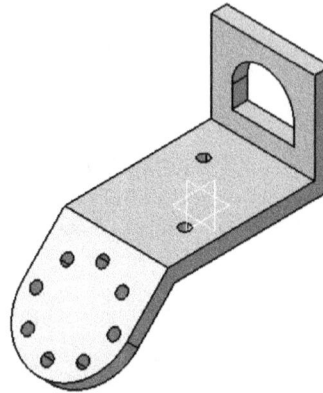

Figure 2–33

2. Select **Tools>Options>Mechanical Design>Functional Tolerancing & Annotation** and select the *Tolerancing* tab.

3. In the Default standard at creation drop-down list, select **ASME**, as shown in Figure 2–34.

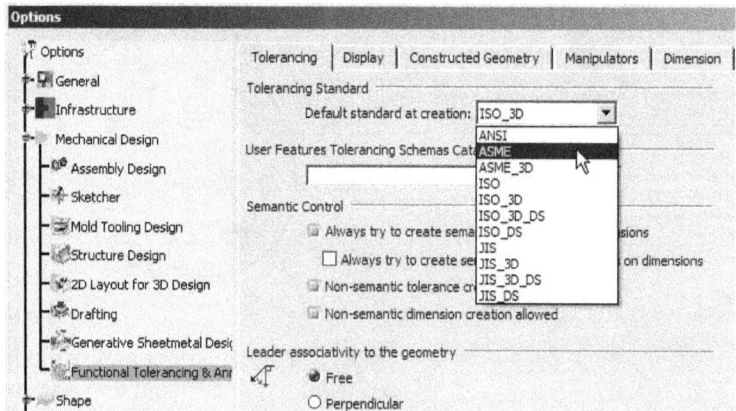

Figure 2–34

You may need to scroll down in the list to find the View/Annotation Plane Display area.

4. Select the *View/Annotation Plane* tab.

5. In the *View/Annotation Plane Display* area, enable the **Displayed for last selected view**

6. Select **General>Parameters and Measure** and select the *Units* tab.

7. In the Length drop-down list, select **Millimeter (mm)**, as shown in Figure 2–35.

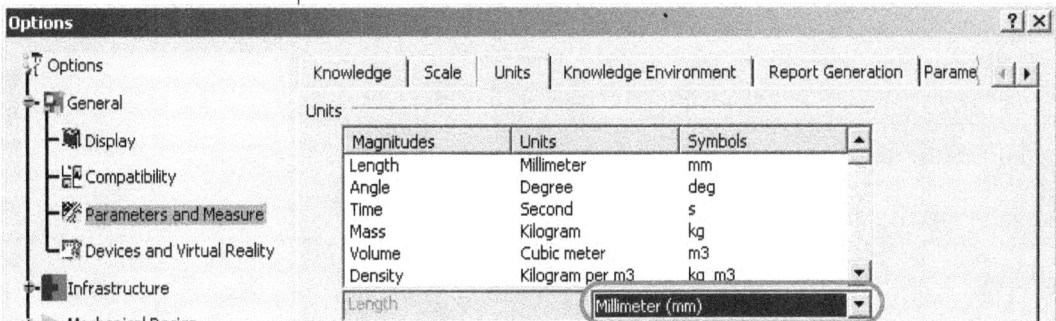

Figure 2–35

8. Click **OK**.

Task 2 - Define a projection view.

---

1. In the Views/Annotation Planes toolbar, expand the Views flyout and drag it to a floating location, as shown in Figure 2–36.

Figure 2–36

2. Click [icon] (View From Reference).

3. Select the face of the model, as shown in Figure 2–37. Once selected, the View Creation dialog box opens. The face selected is listed in the *Reference* field.

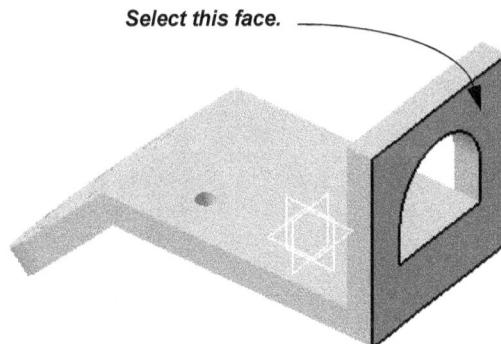

Select this face.

Figure 2–37

4. Accept all defaults and click **OK**. The system adds a view frame to the model and a **Front View.1** entry is added to the Views branch of the specification tree, as shown in Figure 2–38.

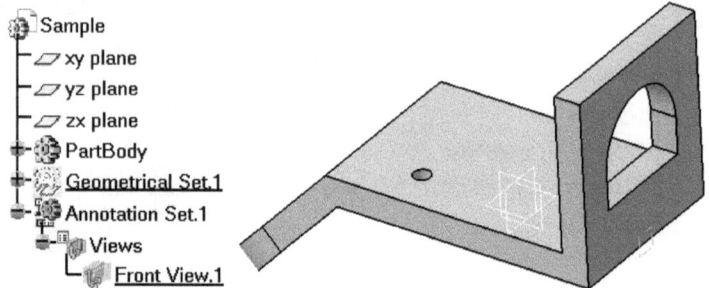

Figure 2–38

Task 3 - Define a section view.

In this task, you create a section view. A section view does not display a section profile on the 3D model by default. You can enable its display using the Options dialog box. A cross-section view is automatically created when this view is used to create a drawing view. You will display this view in a drawing at the end of the practice.

1. Click (View From Reference).

2. Select the ZX plane.

3. In the Type drop-down list, select **Section View**.

4. Accept all other defaults and click **OK**. The system displays the section view frame on the model and adds it to the Views branch of the specification tree, as shown in Figure 2–39.

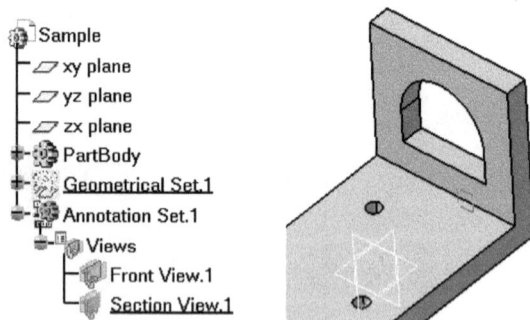

Figure 2–39

5. In the Visualization toolbar, click ⬚ (Clipping plane). The model displays as shown in Figure 2–40.

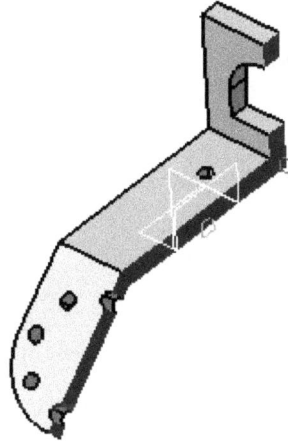

Figure 2–40

Design Considerations

*The clipping plane can also be toggled off by right-clicking on the view and selecting **Remove Clipping Plane**.*

Although the clipping plane can be used to cut the part in any view, the tool is especially useful when trying to visualize how a section cut will display on the 3D model.

6. Click ⬚ (Clipping plane) again to clear it.

7. Expand the Views branch of the specification tree and select **Section View.1**. Selecting a view applies a clipping plane. The section profile also highlights in orange because this is a section view.

8. Click on the screen to clear the section view.

9. Select **Tools>Options>Mechanical Design>Functional Tolerancing & Annotation** and select the *View/Annotation Plane* tab.

You may need to scroll
down in the list to find
the visualization option.

10. In the *View/Annotation Plane Display* area, enable the
Visualization of the profile in the current view option, as
shown in Figure 2–41.

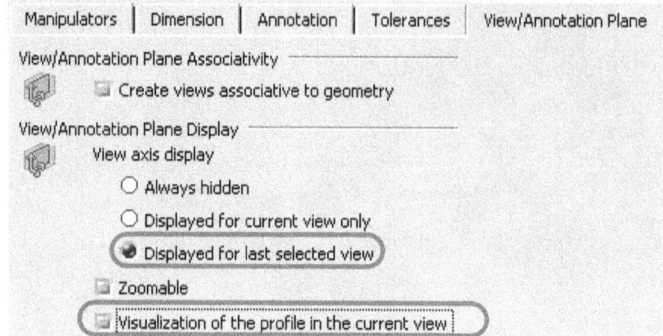

Manipulators	Dimension	Annotation	Tolerances	View/Annotation Plane

View/Annotation Plane Associativity

☐ Create views associative to geometry

View/Annotation Plane Display

View axis display

○ Always hidden

○ Displayed for current view only

● Displayed for last selected view

☐ Zoomable

☐ Visualization of the profile in the current view

Figure 2–41

11. Click **OK**. The model updates to display the section profile, as
shown in Figure 2–42.

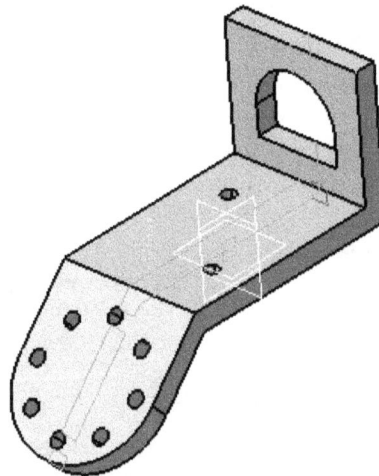

Figure 2–42

12. Clear the **Visualization of the profile in the current view**
option.

13. Hide the three default reference planes to simplify the display
of the model.

Task 4 - Create a construction plane.

In this task, you create a construction plane that passes through the axes of the two holes on the top face of the part. This plane is then used to develop an annotation plane.

1. In the Geometry for 3D Annotations toolbar, click

     (Constructed Geometry Creation), as shown in Figure 2–43.

Figure 2–43

2. Select the cylindrical surface of the hole shown in Figure 2–44. Ensure that you select the hole from the model and not from the specification tree. Based on the selection, the Constructed Geometry dialog box opens with the option to create an axis.

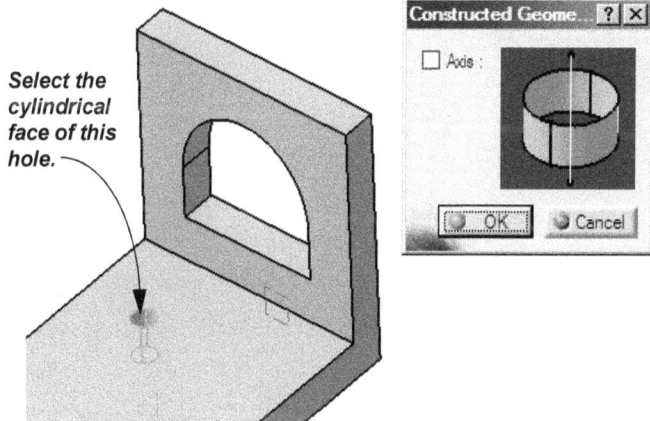

Select the cylindrical face of this hole.

Figure 2–44

3. Select the second hole, as shown in Figure 2–45. This time, the Constructed Geometry dialog box prompts you to create a Plane or Reference cylinder.

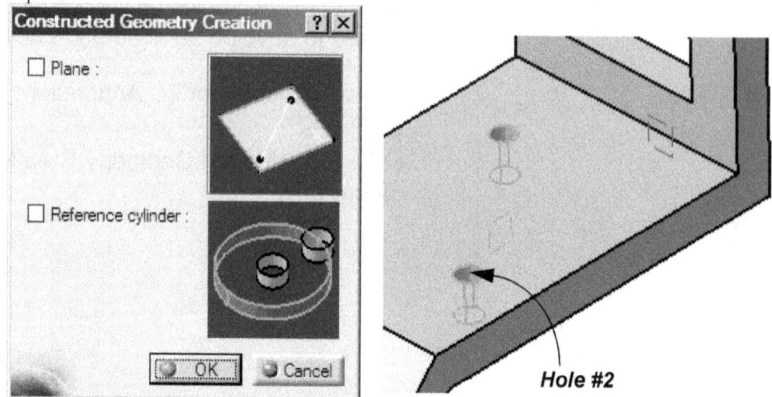

Figure 2–45

4. Select **Plane** and click **OK**. The system adds a Passing Plane to the model and specification tree, as shown in Figure 2–46.

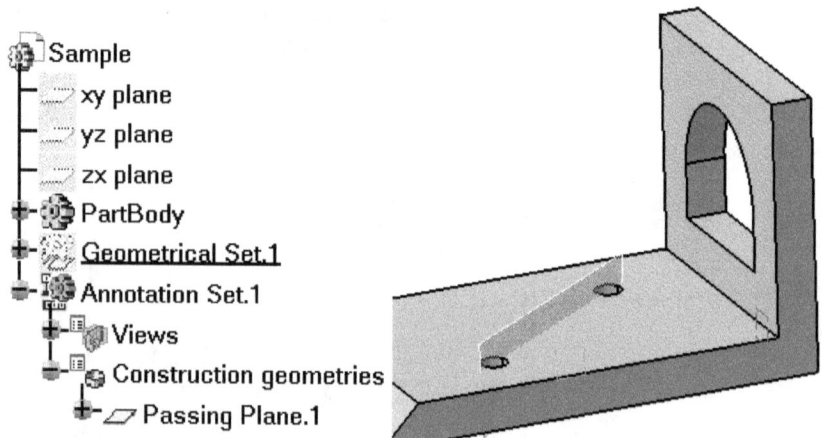

Figure 2–46

Design Considerations

This plane is associative with the geometry selected during its construction. If the position of the holes changes, the plane updates with the new locations.

Task 5 - Create two annotation planes.

1. Select **Tools>Options>Mechanical Design>Functional Tolerancing & Annotation** and select the *View/Annotation Plane* tab.

2. In the *View/Annotation Plane Display* area, enable the **Displayed for current view only** and click **OK**.

3. Click ![icon] (View From Reference) and select **Passing Plane.1** in the model or specification tree.

4. Select **Projection View** in the Type drop-down list, if required. Front View.2 is added to the Views branch of the specification tree

5. Ensure that the axis system matches Figure 2–47.

   - The **Displayed for current view only** option displays the axis as shown in Figure 2–47. In most images in this guide, the axes are toggled off to keep the images uncluttered.

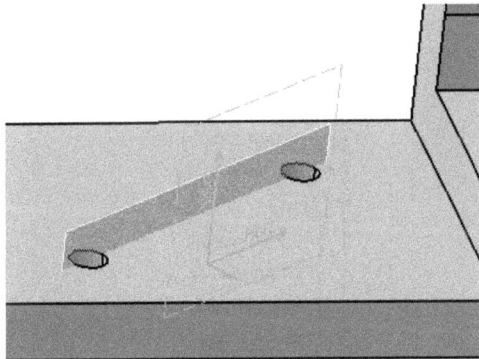

Figure 2–47

6. Click **OK**.

7. Create a final front view annotation plane using the face shown in Figure 2–48.

Select this face.

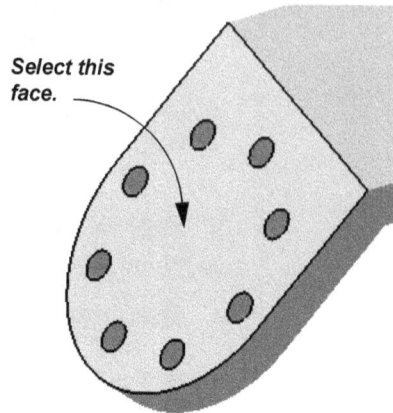

Figure 2–48

The model displays, as shown in Figure 2–49.

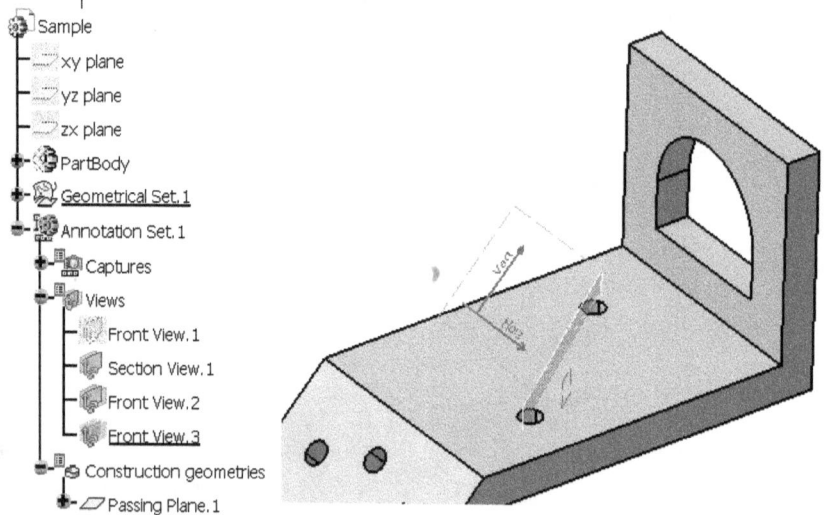

- Sample
  - xy plane
  - yz plane
  - zx plane
  - PartBody
  - Geometrical Set.1
  - Annotation Set.1
    - Captures
    - Views
      - Front View.1
      - Section View.1
      - Front View.2
      - Front View.3
    - Construction geometries
    - Passing Plane.1

Figure 2–49

8. Select **Tools>Options>Mechanical Design>Functional Tolerancing & Annotation** and select the *View/Annotation Plane* tab.

9. In the *View/Annotation Plane Display* area, enable **Displayed for last selected view** and click **OK**.

Task 6 - Create a reference cylinder and axis.

The **Axis** option in the Constructed Geometry dialog box is not displayed until **Cylinder** is selected.

1. Click (Construction Geometry Creation).

2. Expand the PartBody branch in the specification tree and select **CircPattern.1**. The Constructed Geometry dialog box opens, enabling you to create a cylinder.

3. Select **Cylinder**. The system places a cylindrical surface on the model that passes through each instance of the patterned hole. In addition, the system now enables you to create a constructed axis that passes through the center of the patterned holes, as shown in Figure 2–50.

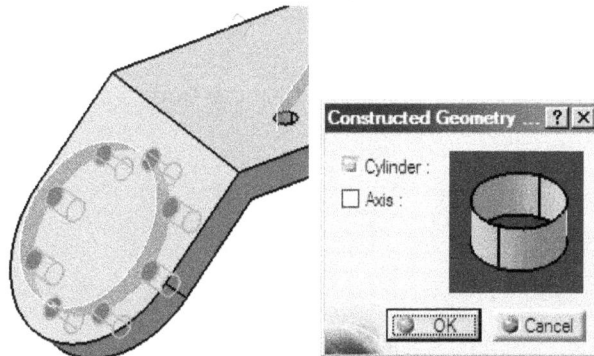

Figure 2–50

4. Select **Axis** and complete the operation. Click **OK**. The model displays, as shown in Figure 2–51.

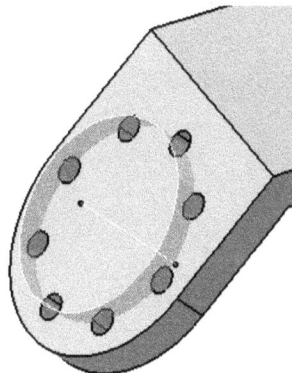

Figure 2–51

Task 7 - Create a constructed axis.

1. Create an additional constructed geometry axis by selecting the face shown in Figure 2–52. Ensure that you select the **Axis** option in the dialog box.

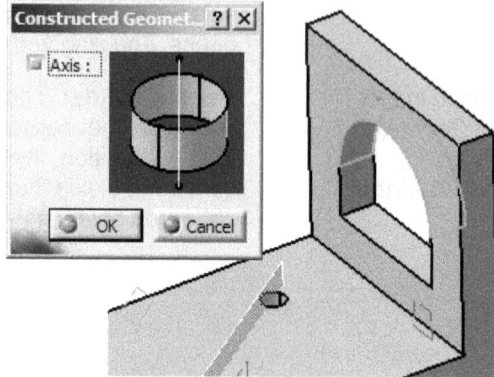

Figure 2–52

2. Save the part. The model displays, as shown in Figure 2–53.

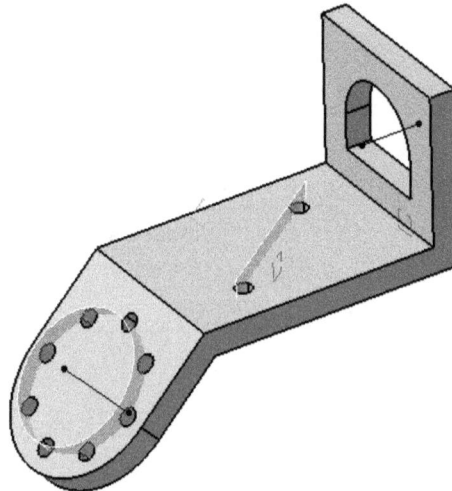

Figure 2–53

Task 8 - (Optional) Drawing view creation.

In this optional task, you develop drawing views using the views created in the part model. Modifications to the annotation set are updated in the drawing views to demonstrate the associativity between FT&A features, the model, and drawing views.

1. Create an empty ASME standard, E size drawing.

2. Click [icon] (View from 3D) and create a view using **Section View.1**. The drawing view displays, as shown in Figure 2–54.

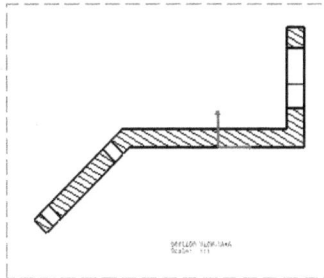

Figure 2–54

Design Considerations

As previously indicated, a section view created in the FT&A workbench automatically generates a section view in the Drafting workbench. The properties of this view can be modified identically to the methods used to modify a section view generated in Drawing mode.

3. Create a second view that references **Front View.2** from Sample.CATPart. The drawing view displays as shown in Figure 2–55.

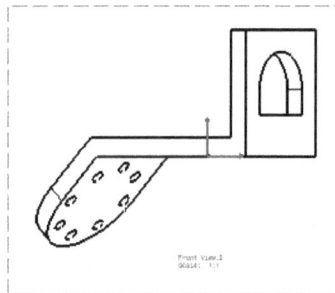

Figure 2–55

Task 9 - Modify the part.

1. Activate Sample.CATPart.

2. Double-click on **Sketch.5** and modify the dimensional values, as shown in Figure 2–56. This sketch is used to position **Hole.4** that was referenced during the construction of **Passing Plane.1** and **Front View.2**.

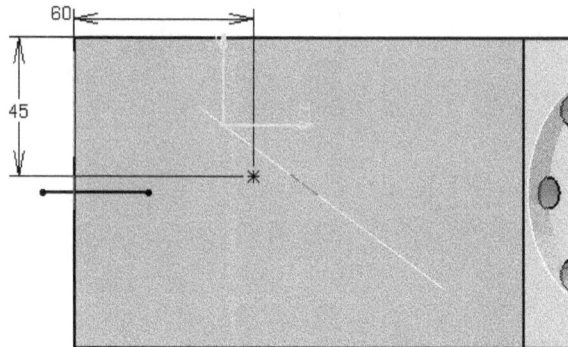

Figure 2–56

3. Click [icon] (Exit workbench) to exit Sketcher.

4. Click [icon] (Update All), if required, to update the model. The model displays, as shown in Figure 2–57.

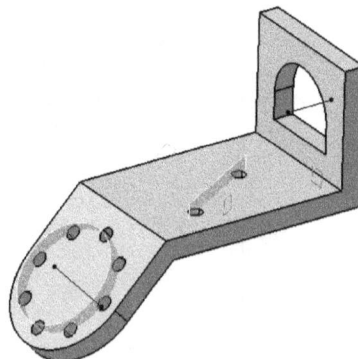

Figure 2–57

Design Considerations

The constructed geometry remains associative to the hole features in the model. In addition, the annotation plane created from the passing plane also updates with the new hole position.

5. Return to the drawing window and update. **Front View.2** changes position based on the modified hole.

Task 10 - Invert the normal for Front View.2.

In this task, you invert the normal for **Front View.2**. When creating an annotation view, you should check the normal direction, indicated by the red arrow, and modify it immediately if it is incorrect. Once an annotation has been added to a view, the normal cannot be modified.

1. Activate the Sample.CATPart window.

2. Activate **Front View.2** by double-clicking on it in the specification tree.

3. Right-click on **Front View.2** and select **Change View Support**.

4. Select **Invert Normal** and click **OK**.

5. Return to the drawing window.

Design Considerations

The view does not change in the drawing. Since the drawing view was oriented before placement, changes to the normal for the front view are not reflected in the drawing. The normal only determines the default orientation of a drawing view. This is demonstrated by placing a second drawing view for **Front View.2**.

6. Create a third drawing view and reference **Front View.2**. The drawing view displays, as shown in Figure 2–58.

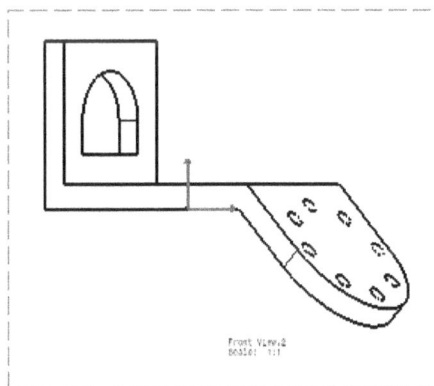

Figure 2–58

Design Considerations

Drawing views can be created as soon as annotation and section views are added to the model. As annotations and other FT&A features are added, they can be updated in the drawing.

This drawing was created for demonstration purposes only and does not need to be maintained.

7. Close the drawing without saving.

8. Save the model and close the window.

Semantic Annotations

This chapter introduces the Semantic Tolerance Advisor. This tool is used to build almost all annotations required for a model, while maintaining the rules defined by the active standard. In addition, this chapter describes the process used to create basic dimensions.

Learning Objectives in this Chapter

- Understand Datum Reference Frames.
- Learn how to use the Tolerance Advisor tool.
- Create Basic dimensions.

3.1 Datum Reference Frames

In CATIA, Datum reference frames are also called Datum systems. The terms are used interchangeably.

Datum reference frames (DRF) provide the basis for all geometrical tolerancing in the model. The DRF defines an origin from which the location or geometric characteristics of all of the geometry of a part or assembly model are established. For example, datums A and B have been defined for the simple part shown in Figure 3–1. The left and bottom sides of the part will be used as an origin to locate the position of the hole using the 0.1mm boundary defined by the geometrical tolerance.

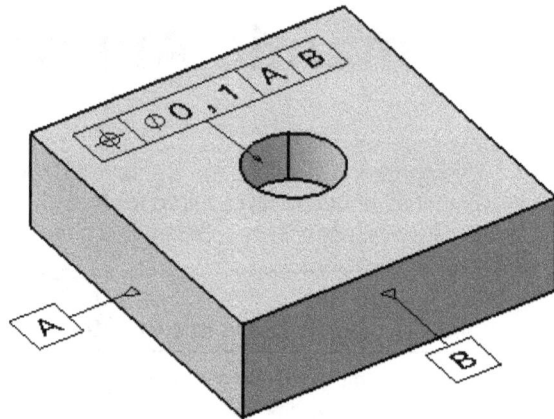

Figure 3–1

General Steps

Use the following general steps to create a datum reference frame for geometrical tolerancing:

1. Activate an annotation plane.
2. Create the semantic datums.
3. Create the required datum reference frame.

Step 1 - Activate an annotation plane.

Double-click on the required annotation plane in the specification tree or directly from the model to activate it. The orientation of the selected annotation plane is used to define the orientation of the text.

Step 2 - Create the semantic datums.

Once you have selected the annotation plane, you must define the semantic datums required to locate your part for geometrical dimensioning and tolerancing. Datums can be created by selecting one of the following types of geometry:

- Point or vertex

- Line, axis, or edge

- Face, surface, or reference plane

The selection of geometry for a datum depends on the geometric shape of the part and the types of tolerances required. You can create as many datums as required to locate the part and all of its geometry in 3D space.

How To: Create a Semantic Datum

1. Select the datum geometry. A face is selected, as shown in Figure 3–2.

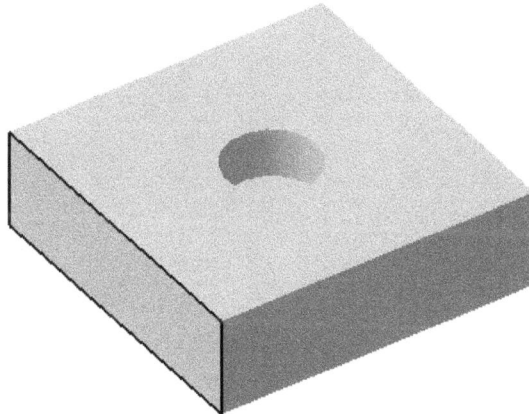

Figure 3–2

2. In the Annotations toolbar, click ▣ (Tolerancing Advisor). The Semantic Tolerancing Advisor dialog box opens, as shown in Figure 3–3.

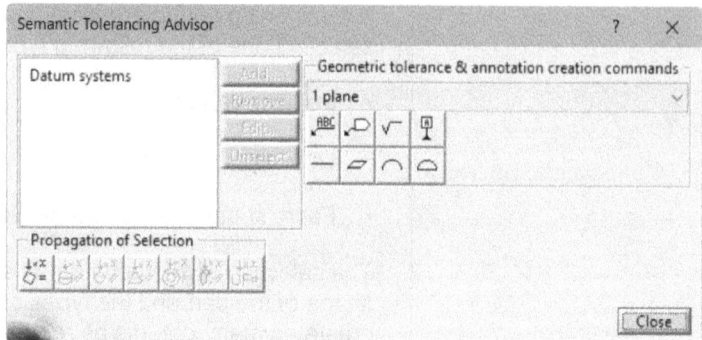

Figure 3–3

3. Click ▣ (Datum Feature). The Datum feature dialog box opens, as shown in Figure 3–4.

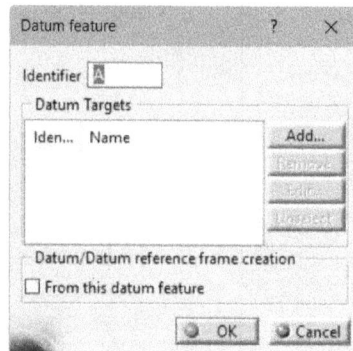

Figure 3–4

4. Enter a name in the *Identifier* field. If the selected geometry is non-planar, you can define the datum targets. These are discussed at the end of this section.

5. Click **OK** once you have defined the datum. The system places a datum flag onto the selected geometry, as shown in Figure 3–5.

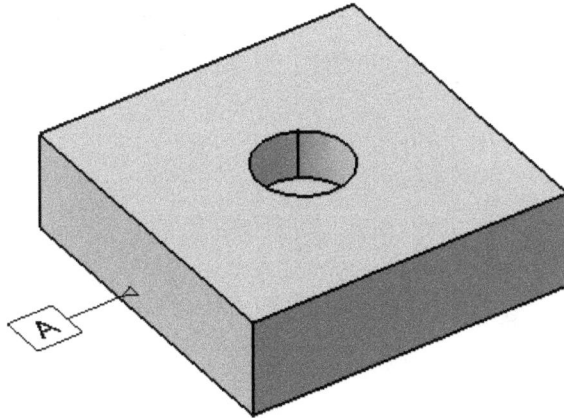

Figure 3–5

6. At this point, the Semantic Tolerancing Advisor dialog box remains open. Selecting additional geometry enables you to define more semantic datums to locate the model in 3D space, as shown in Figure 3–6. Click **Close** once you have completed creating datums.

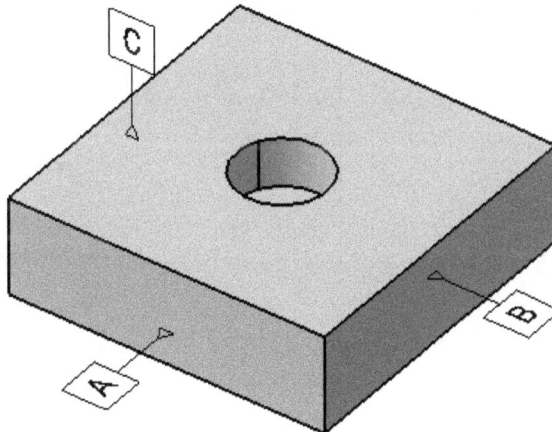

Figure 3–6

Datum Targets

When defining a non-planar or non-linear element as a datum, the system requires you to select datum targets to correctly locate the geometry. For example, the surface shown in Figure 3–7 would require up to three datum targets to correctly define the semantic datum.

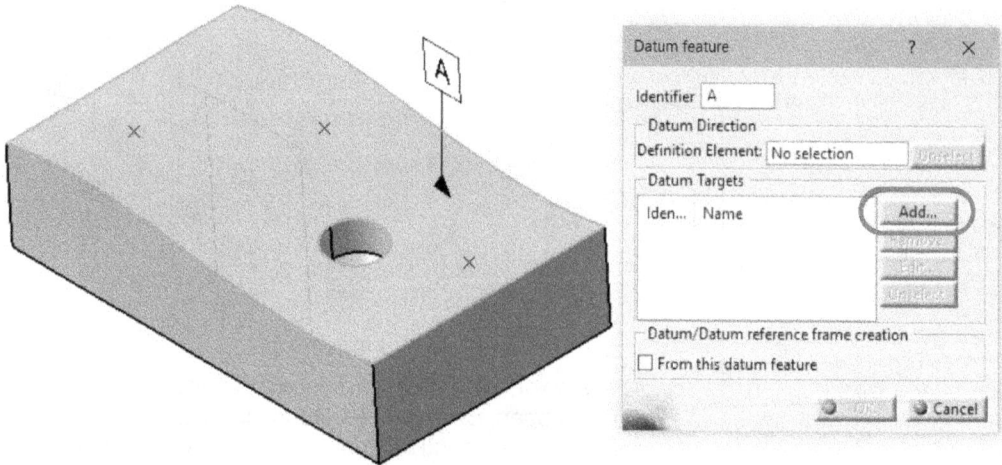

Figure 3–7

Click **Add**. The Datum Target dialog box opens as shown in Figure 3–8.

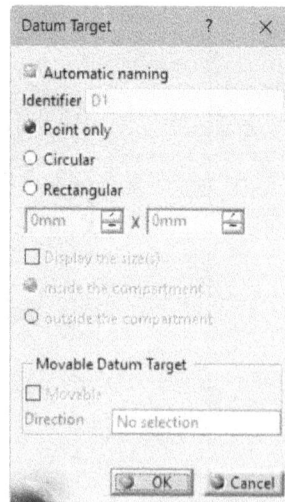

Figure 3–8

This dialog box enables you to create multiple datum target annotations at once by selecting any number of points. Ideally, reference points would be predefined to locate the datum targets; however, you can select anywhere on the datum surface to define a target.

The **Automatic naming** option enables you to meet naming standards (A1, A2, etc.). To manually name the target, clear this option and enter a new name in the *Identifier* field.

Select **Circular** or **Rectangular** to define the size of the target area. You can select the **Display the size(s)** check box. This option enables you to view the sizes:

- Inside the compartment

- Outside the compartment

The **Display the size(s)** check box is unavailable when the selected datum target feature is a point and the **Point only** option is selected, or neither a rectangular nor a circular face.

Click **OK** once the targets are defined. The model displays, as shown in Figure 3–9.

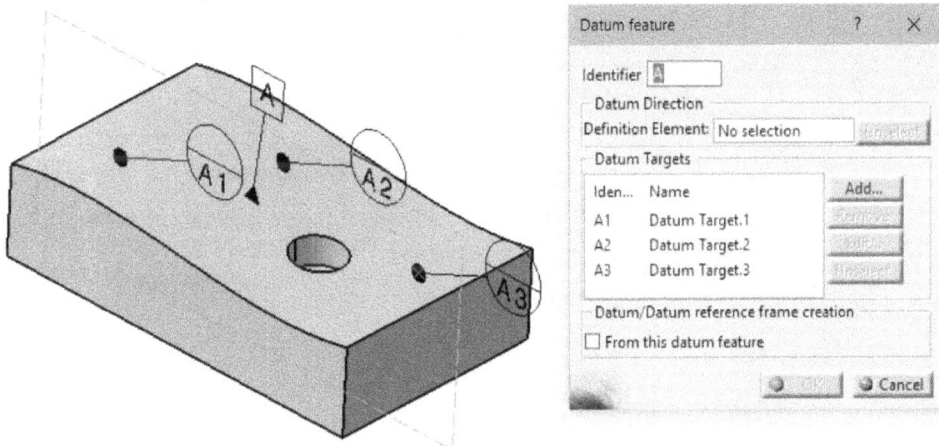

Figure 3–9

Click in the *Datum Direction* field and select a plane that represents the orientation of the datum surface, i.e. the plane's normal direction must be on the external material side.

Step 3 - Create the required datum reference frame.

Although semantic datums have been defined, they cannot yet be used to define a geometrical tolerance. To do this, you must define a datum reference frame for each unique set of datums used in a geometrical tolerance.

How To: Create a Datum Reference Frame

1. Verify that nothing is preselected and then click

   (Tolerancing Advisor). The Semantic Tolerancing Advisor dialog box opens as shown in Figure 3–10.

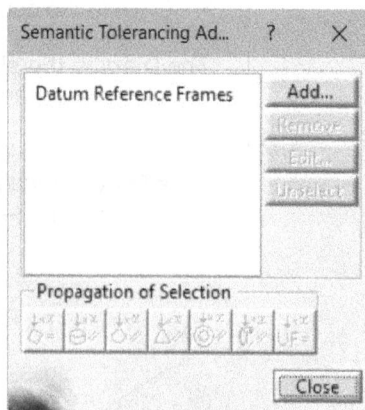

Figure 3–10

2. Click **Add**. The Datums and datum reference frames dialog box opens as shown in Figure 3–11.

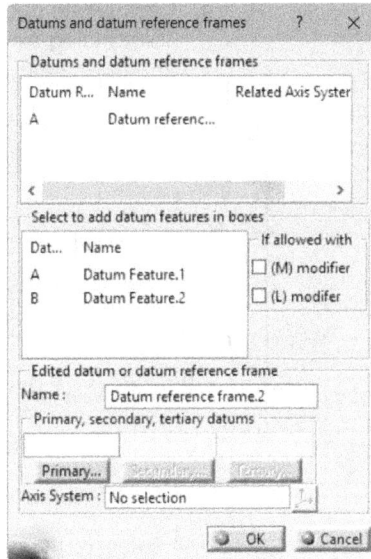

Figure 3–11

3. Select a datum in the list of datum features to add it to the datum frame boxes below. Any combination of datums can be arranged by selecting in the appropriate datum frame boxes field. For example, an A|B datum has been created in Figure 3–12.

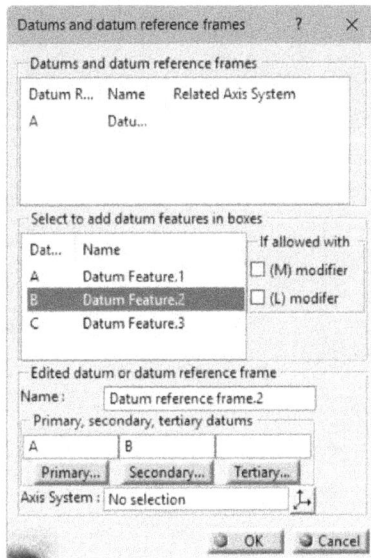

Figure 3–12

4. Click **OK** to complete the operation. The Semantic Tolerancing Advisor and specification tree display, as shown in Figure 3–13.

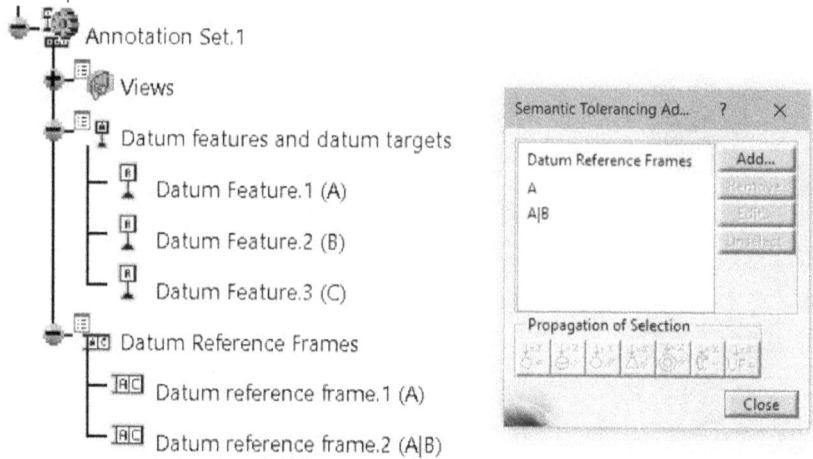

Figure 3–13

If required, select the options highlighted in Figure 3–14 to automatically create a datum reference frame from the semantic datums just created.

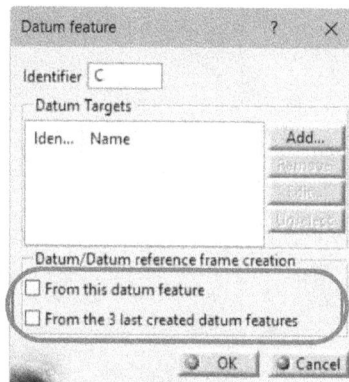

Figure 3–14

3.2 Tolerance Advisor

The Semantic Tolerancing Advisor dialog box is not only used to create semantic datums and datum reference frames. The tolerance advisor enables you to develop almost all of the semantic tolerances required for your model. The following list includes some of the types of annotations that can be created:

- Text with Leader

- Flag Note

- Roughness

- Semantic Datum

- Geometrical Tolerances

- Dimensions

The tolerance advisor only enables you to create an annotation that corresponds to the tolerancing standard based on the selections made. Therefore, as datum reference frames, geometry, or annotations are selected, the options in the Semantic Tolerancing Advisor dialog box change to show only the appropriate annotations.

General Steps

Use the following general steps to create a geometric tolerance:

1. Start the creation of the geometric tolerance.
2. Select the references.
3. Specify and define the annotation.

Step 1 - Start the creation of the geometric tolerance.

In the Annotations toolbar, click (Tolerancing Advisor). The Semantic Tolerancing Advisor dialog box opens, as shown in . Without any preselected elements, the dialog box displays all of the currently defined datum reference frames.

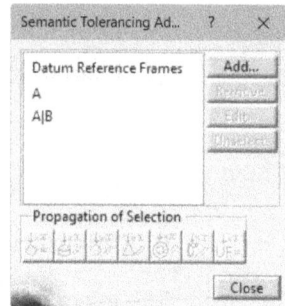

Figure 3–15

Step 2 - Select the references.

If you are defining a geometrical tolerance, select the datum reference frame in the list.

Next, select the geometric entity that is referenced by the annotation. Press and hold <Ctrl> to select multiple entities. The Semantic Tolerancing Advisor dialog box updates with the available annotations. For example, the A|B datum reference frame and a cylindrical face are selected in the dialog box shown in Figure 3–16.

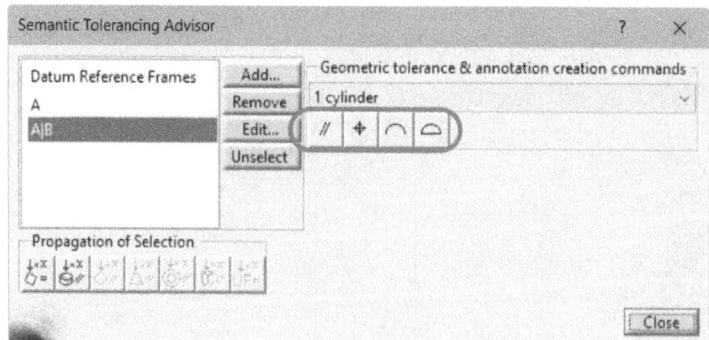

Figure 3–16

If multiple geometric elements are selected, the **Geometric tolerance & annotations creation commands** drop-down list provides additional options, as shown in Figure 3–17.

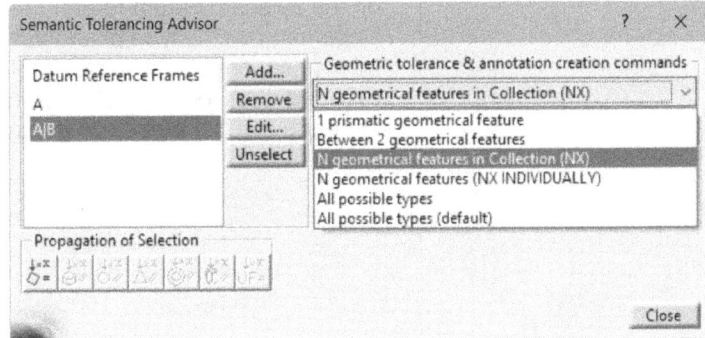

Figure 3–17

Selecting Multiple Items

The propagation selection tools at the bottom of the Semantic Tolerancing Advisor dialog box lets you automatically propagate geometry selection. The tools can be used to select all the faces of the same sphere, plane, cylinder, cone, or torus surface. The three propagation options are as follows.

Options	Description
	The **All same canonicity faces** option selects all the faces of a part that are on the same plane.
	The **All same diameter parallel cylinders** option selects all the faces of a part that have the same cylindrical shape and diameter, and are parallel to the cylindrical face that was selected.
	The **All same diameter parallel sphere** option selects all the faces of a part that have the same spherical shape and diameter as the selected face.
	The **All same user defined features** option selects all the user features or technological results of user features of the same type in the part.
	The **All same diameter, same pitch, parallel CG thread cylinders** option selects all the constructed geometry thread cylinders of a part that have the same diameter and pitch, and have an axis parallel to the Constructed Geometry Thread Cylinder that was selected.

Step 3 - Specify and define the annotation.

Click an icon from the list of annotations that are available based on the selected datum reference frame and geometry.

Depending on the type of annotation selected, a Definition dialog box opens, enabling you to completely define the annotation. For example, the Geometrical Tolerance dialog box opens, as shown in Figure 3–18, if a position geometrical tolerance is created.

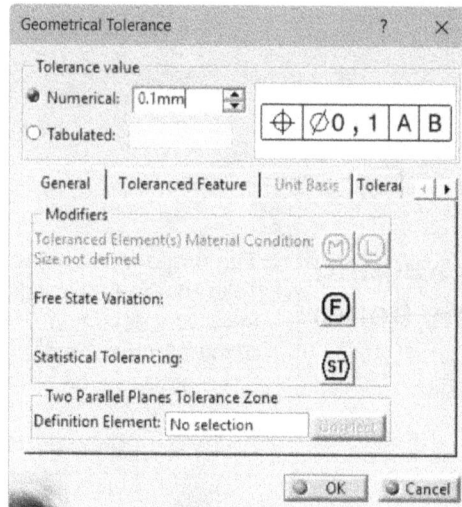

Figure 3–18

A variety of tolerance parameters can be defined in this example, including:

- Tolerance value

- Modifiers

- Unit Basis

- Tolerance Zone

As parameters are defined, the tolerance updates on the model and in the dialog box.

Click **OK** to complete the definition of the annotation. The model displays, as shown in Figure 3–19.

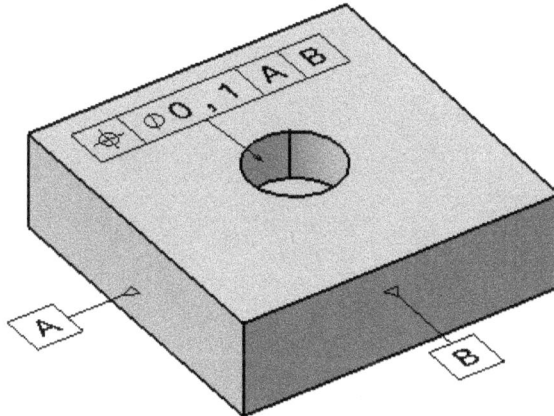

Figure 3–19

Once the annotation has been defined, the Semantic Tolerancing Advisor dialog box remains open for further annotation creation. Click **Close** once you have completed all possible annotations.

3.3 Basic Dimensions

Basic or framed dimensions provide a theoretically exact value that is used to define the size of a feature. Basic dimensions are identified by a rectangle that encloses the value, as shown in Figure 3–20.

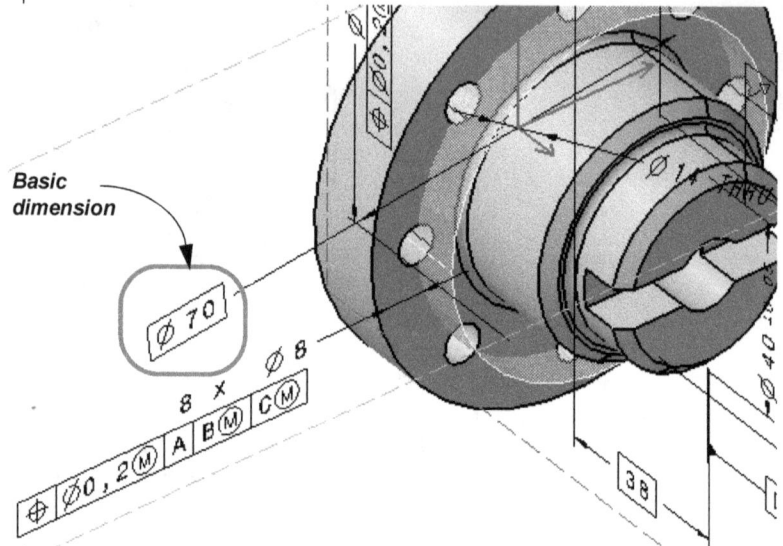

Figure 3–20

General Steps

Use the following general steps to create a basic dimension:

1. Start the creation of a basic dimension.
2. Select a context for the dimension.
3. Start the creation of the dimension.
4. End the creation of the dimension.

Step 1 - Start the creation of a basic dimension.

In the Annotations toolbar, click ⬚ (Framed (Basic) Dimensions). The system prompts you to define a context for the dimension.

Step 2 - Select a context for the dimension.

Since the basic dimension defines a theoretically exact dimension, you must relate the dimension to a specific context. The basic dimension can be related to a datum reference frame, a restricted area, a datum target, or Profile of a Line, Profile of a Surface, Angularity, or Position geometrical tolerances.

Select the appropriate context in the specification tree. The Framed (Basic) Dimensions Management dialog box opens, as shown in Figure 3–21.

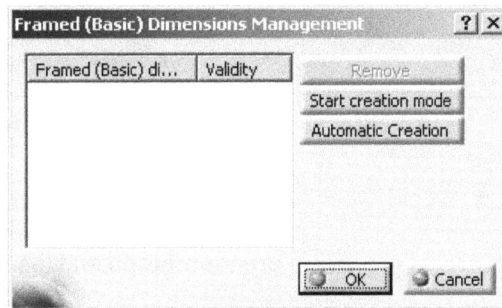

Figure 3–21

Step 3 - Start the creation of the dimension.

Click **Start creation mode** to start the creation of the dimension.

Next, select the geometry to dimension. The system previews the dimension that has been defined, as shown in Figure 3–22.

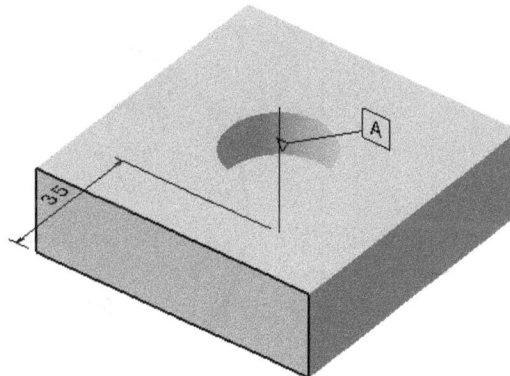

Figure 3–22

Step 4 - End the creation of the dimension.

Select anywhere on the background of CATIA to accept this dimension. The system places a rectangular frame around the dimension and adds it to the dialog box, as shown in Figure 3–23.

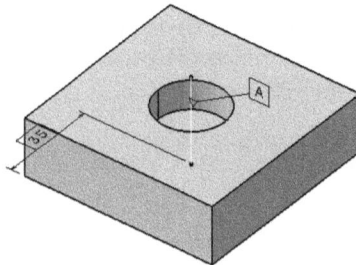

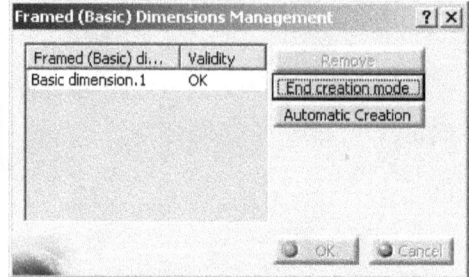

Figure 3–23

At this point, you can continue adding basic dimensions to the model. If you are finished creating basic dimensions, click **End creation mode** and then **OK** to complete the operation.

Automatic Creation

Basic dimensions can be automatically created for patterned features.

How To: Create a Basic Dimension Automatically

1. Click 🖵 (Framed (Basic) Dimensions).
2. Select the context for the dimension. For example, select the position tolerance that was created for the pattern of holes, as shown in Figure 3–24.

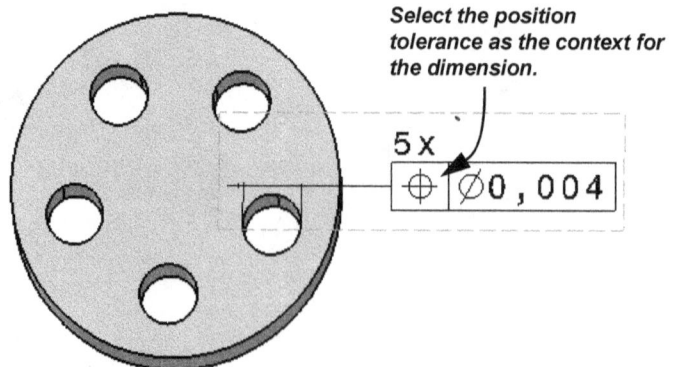

Select the position tolerance as the context for the dimension.

5 x

⊕ ∅0,004

Figure 3–24

The Framed (Basic) Dimensions Management dialog box opens, as shown in Figure 3–25.

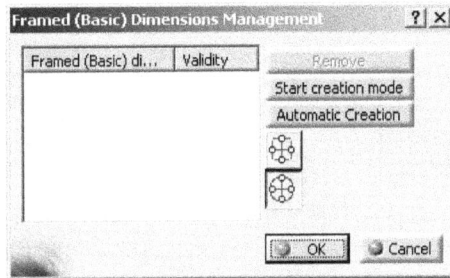

Figure 3–25

3. For circular patterns, two modes are available to define the position of the patterned features. The following describes the two available modes.

Mode	Description
	The position of the patterned features will be defined using rectangular coordinates
	The position of the patterned features will be defined using cylindrical coordinates.

4. Click **Automatic Creation**.
5. The dimensions are automatically generated for the selected feature. Any required construction elements are also created, as shown in Figure 3–26.
6. Click **OK**.

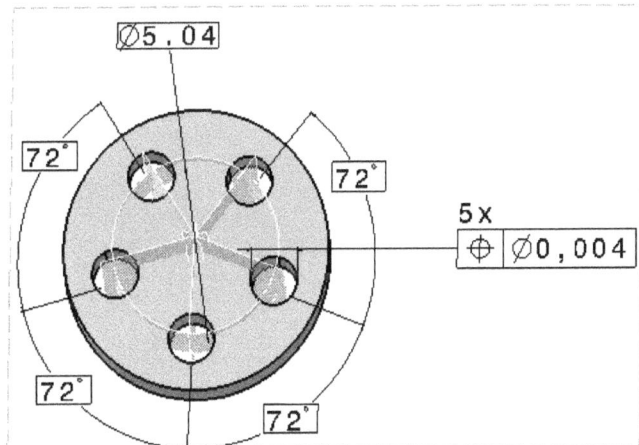

Figure 3–26

Practice 3a

Dimensions and Tolerances

Practice Objectives

- Define the tolerancing standard.
- Create annotation planes.
- Create dimensions with general tolerances and with symmetrical tolerances.

In this practice, you will add annotations to the LockingHub model, as shown in Figure 3–27.

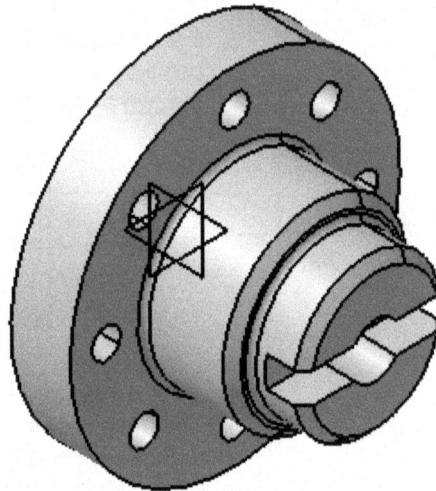

Figure 3–27

Adding dimensions and tolerances to the model should be the first step in any annotation activities, since it enables you to specify material conditions for the geometric tolerances. The completed model displays, as shown in Figure 3–28.

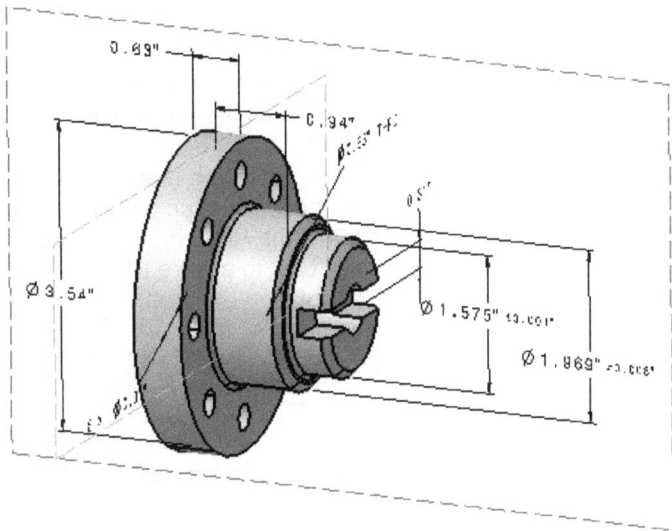

Figure 3–28

Task 1 - Open a part file.

1. Open **LockingHub.CATPart**. The model displays as shown in Figure 3–29.

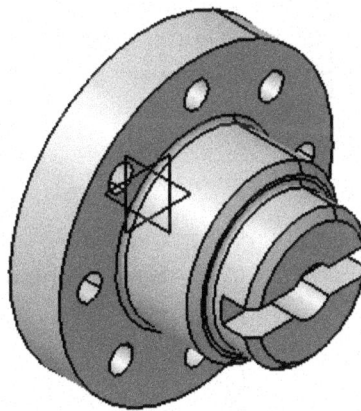

Figure 3–29

Task 2 - Set the tolerancing standard.

Design Considerations

Before you begin the creation of any tolerances and annotations using the FT&A workbench, ensure that the correct tolerancing standard has been defined in the Options dialog box. As annotations are created, they use the standard that has been defined. Although this standard can be changed in the *Standard* tab of the Properties dialog box for the Annotation Set.1 feature, it is best to ensure the correct standard before creating any annotation.

1. Select **Tools>Options>Mechanical Design>Functional Tolerancing & Annotation** and select the *Tolerancing* tab.

2. In the Default standard at creation drop-down list, select **ASME**, as shown in Figure 3–30.

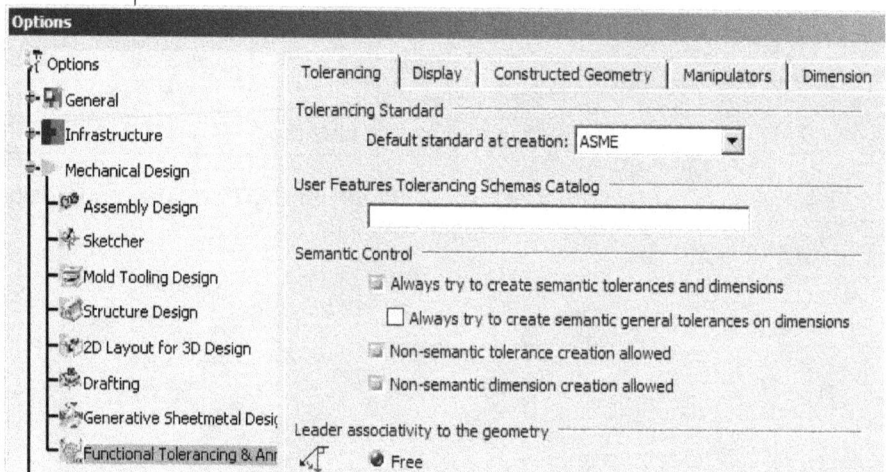

Figure 3–30

3. Select **General>Parameters and Measure** and select the *Units* tab.

4. Select **Inch (in)** in the Length drop-down list, as shown in Figure 3–31.

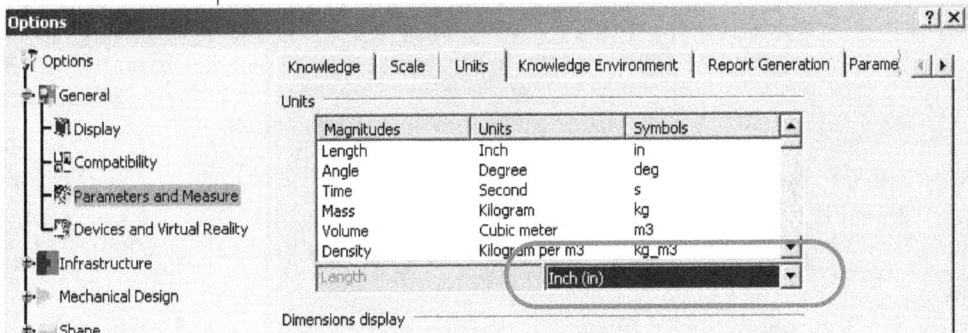

Figure 3–31

5. Click **OK**.

Task 3 - Create annotation planes.

1. Create a Projection View annotation plane on the XY plane with the name **FrontView**.

2. Create a second Projection View annotation plane on YZ plane with the name **SideView**.

3. Ensure that SideView is the active view. The specification tree displays, as shown in Figure 3–32.

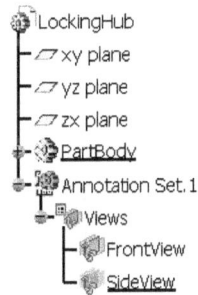

Figure 3–32

4. Hide the three default reference planes to simplify the display of the model.

Task 4 - Create a general tolerance dimension using the Tolerance Advisor.

In the following tasks, you will add a series of dimensions and tolerances to the model. You will use the Tolerance Advisor to ensure that the dimensions conform to the ASME standard defined at the beginning of this practice.

*Note that the View axis is hidden in the following images for clarity. It can be controlled in the **Tools>Options> Mechanical Design> Functional Tolerancing and Annotation>**View/Annotation Plane tab.*

1. In the Annotations toolbar, click 🎓 (Tolerancing Advisor). The Semantic Tolerancing Advisor dialog box opens, as shown in Figure 3–33.

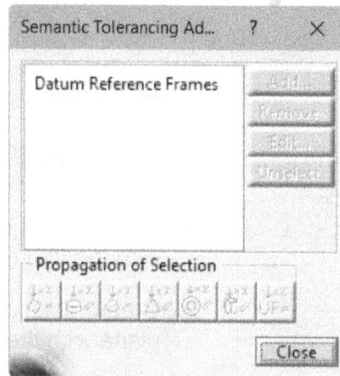

Figure 3–33

2. Select the cylindrical face highlighted in Figure 3–34. The Semantic Tolerance Advisor dialog box updates with annotation options for the selected face.

Select this cylindrical face.

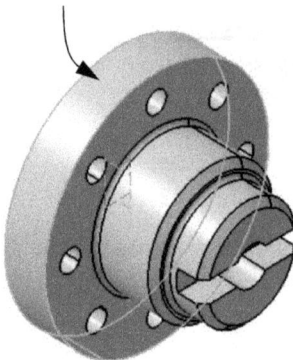

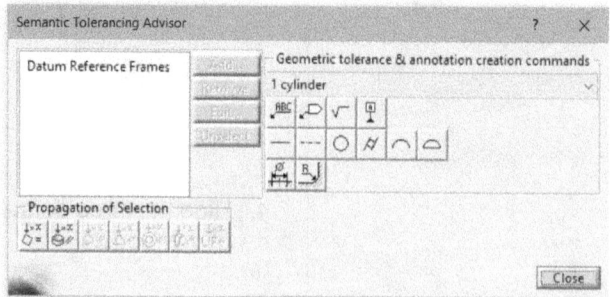

Figure 3–34

3. Click ⬚ (Diameter) in the dialog box. The system places a 0.3' diameter dimension in a default location on the model. Additionally, the Limit of Size Definition dialog box opens, enabling you to configure a tolerance for the diameter dimension.

4. Select **General Tolerance** and accept default standard, as shown in Figure 3–35. Note that if your system is configured so that the Tolerance can be edited, then you should leave it unchanged.

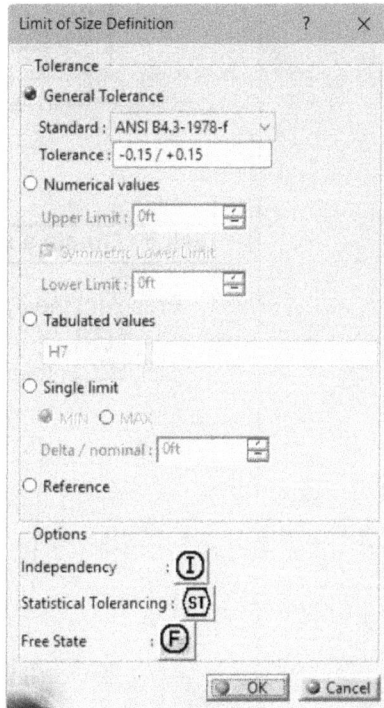

Figure 3–35

5. Click **OK** to return to the Semantic Tolerance Advisor dialog box.

6. Click **Close** to finish the operation.

7. Select the 0.3' diameter dimension and drag it to an appropriate location on the model. The model displays, as shown in Figure 3–36.

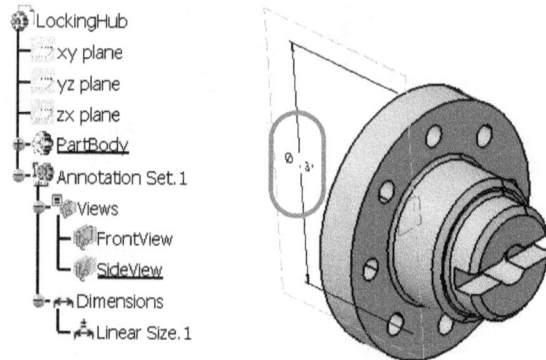

Figure 3–36

Task 5 - Create a symmetric tolerance dimension.

1. Preselect the cylindrical face shown in Figure 3–37 and then click [icon] (Tolerancing Advisor).

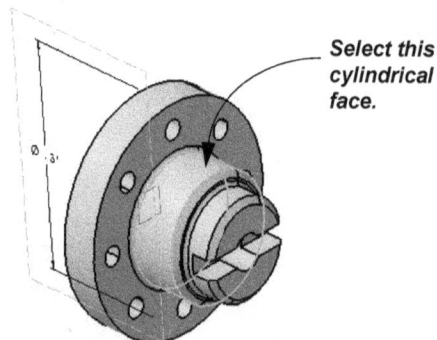

Select this cylindrical face.

Figure 3–37

2. Click [icon] (Diameter) to create a second diameter dimension.

3. Make the following selections in the Limit of Size Definition dialog box, as shown in Figure 3–38.

- Select **Numerical values**.
- *Upper Limit:* **0.008in**
- Select **Symmetric Lower Limit**.

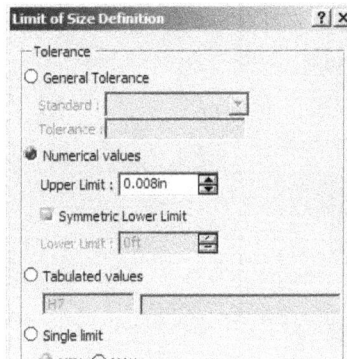

Figure 3–38

4. Click **OK** then move the dimension to an appropriate location, as shown in Figure 3–39.

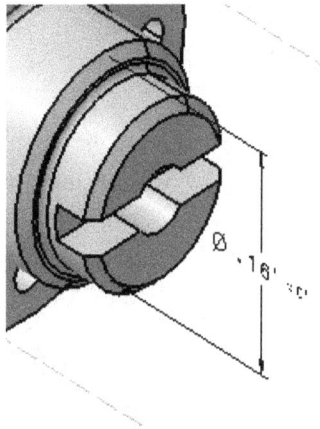

Figure 3–39

5. Click **Close** to close the Semantic Tolerancing Advisor dialog box.

Design Considerations

Note that the tolerance value is 0. This is because the value format is, by default, in Feet. The tolerance is too small. In a later task, you will change all the values to inches at the same time.

Task 6 - Create a dimension for a pattern.

In this task, you create a diameter dimension for the pattern of eight holes. You place this dimension on the FrontView annotation plane.

1. Activate FrontView.

2. Select the surface of the hole shown in Figure 3–40.

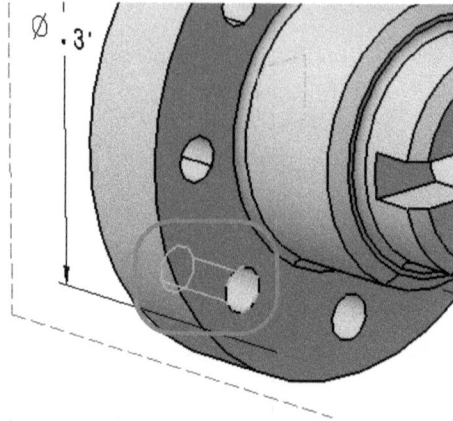

Figure 3–40

3. Click (Tolerancing Advisor).

4. In the *Propagation Selection* area of the Semantic
    Tolerancing Advisor dialog box, click (All same diameter
    parallel cylinders).

5. Note that all eight holes in the pattern highlight and the
    Semantic Tolerance Advisor has **N cylindrical slots/tabs**
    selected in the *Geometric tolerance & annotation creation
    commands* drop-down list, as shown in Figure 3–41.

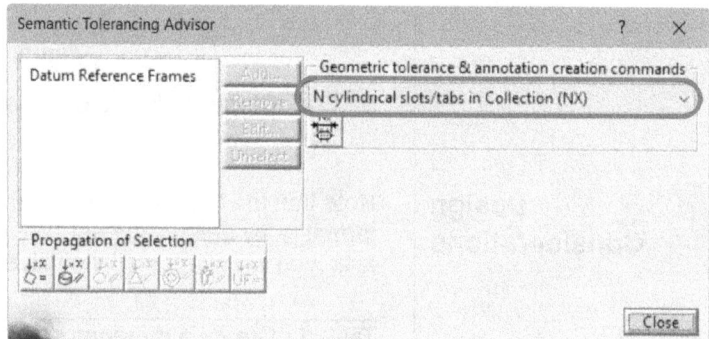

Figure 3–41

6. Select **N cylinders in collection (NX)** in the *Geometric tolerance & annotation creation commands* list, as shown in Figure 3–42.

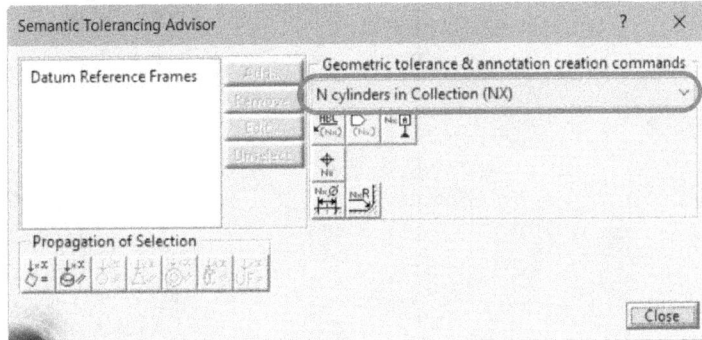

Figure 3–42

7. Click (Pattern Diameter) and apply a **General Tolerance**. Leave *Tolerance* set to the default values.

8. Complete the operation and position the dimension appropriately, as shown in Figure 3–43.

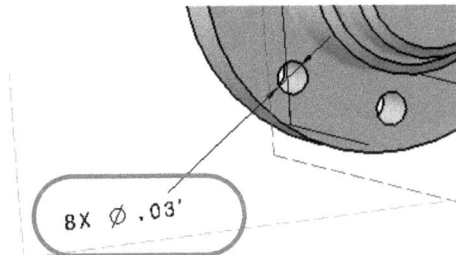

Figure 3–43

Task 7 - Create text with a leader that references a dimension.

In this task, you will need to create a dimension for the center hole. The dimension should be followed with some text that describes the feature as a "thru" hole. You need to modify the properties of the dimension to add additional text.

1. Preselect **Hole.2** in the specification tree and activate the Tolerance Advisor.

2. Create a diameter dimension with a general tolerance. Leave tolerance set to default values.

3. Complete the operation and move it to an appropriate position, as shown in Figure 3–44.

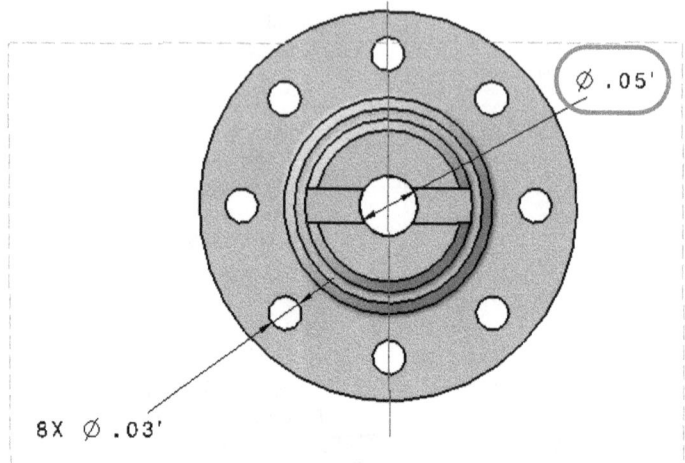

Figure 3–44

4. Right-click on the dimension and select **Properties**. Leave *Tolerance* set to default values.

5. Select the *Dimension Texts* tab and enter **THRU** in the *Associated Texts* field, as shown in Figure 3–45.

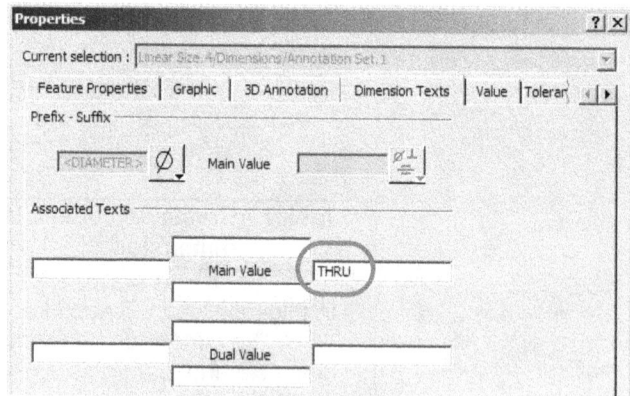

Figure 3–45

6. Click **OK**. The model displays, as shown in Figure 3–46.

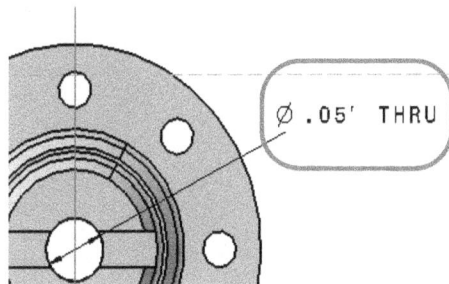

Figure 3–46

Task 8 - Create a distance dimension.

1. Activate SideView.

2. Hold <Ctrl> and select the two parallel faces shown in Figure 3–47.

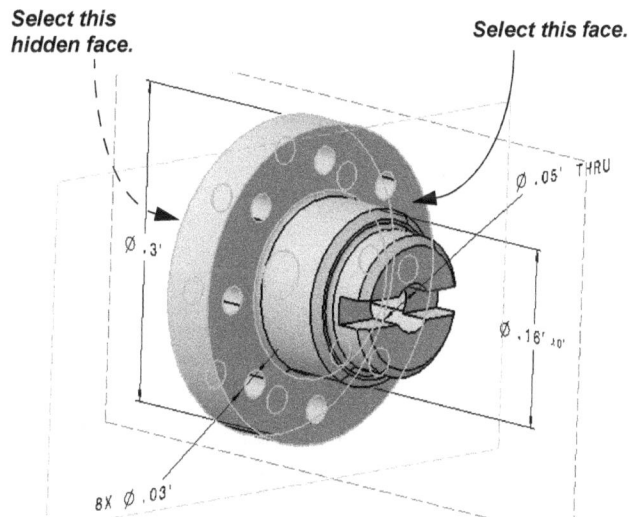

Figure 3–47

3. Activate the Tolerance Advisor. The default Geometric feature type is **1 slot/tab**, as shown in Figure 3–48.

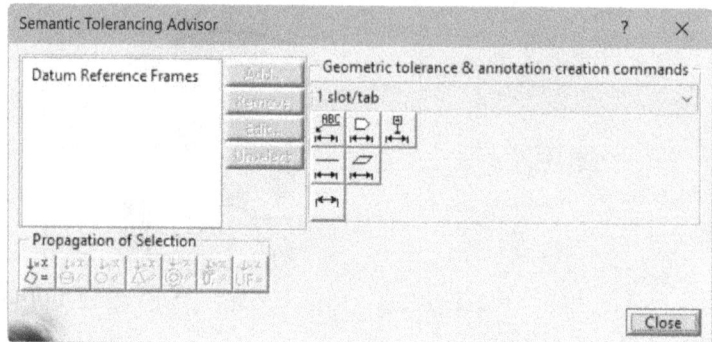

Figure 3–48

4. Click (Distance Creation) to add a distance dimension to the model. Create the dimension using a general tolerance.

5. Complete the operation and move the dimension to an appropriate position, as shown in Figure 3–49.

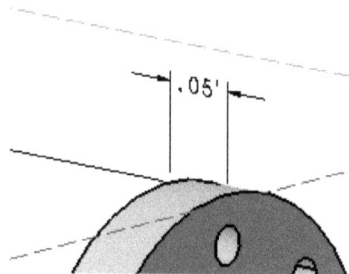

Figure 3–49

Task 9 - Create additional annotations.

1. With the SideView activated and using the Tolerance Advisor dialog box, create the additional annotations shown in Figure 3–50.

   • Create the 0.13' diameter dimension with a +/- 0.001" tolerance.

   • Create the 0.08' dimension shown.

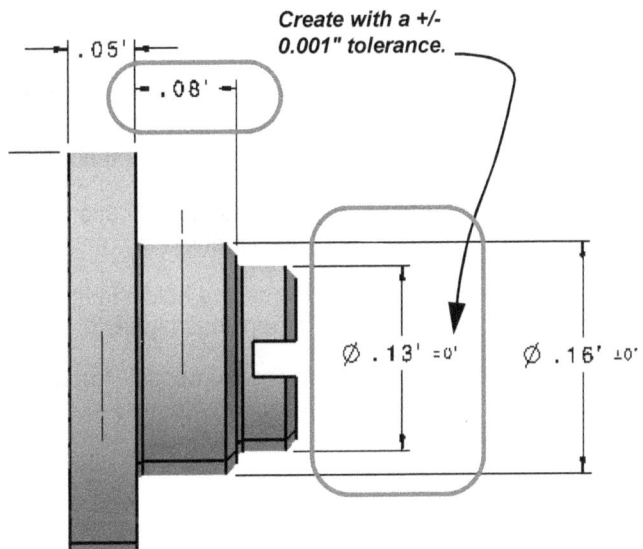

Create with a +/-0.001" tolerance.

.05'

.08'

Ø.13' ±0'

Ø.16' ±0'

Figure 3–50

2. Activate FrontView and create the additional annotation shown in Figure 3–51.

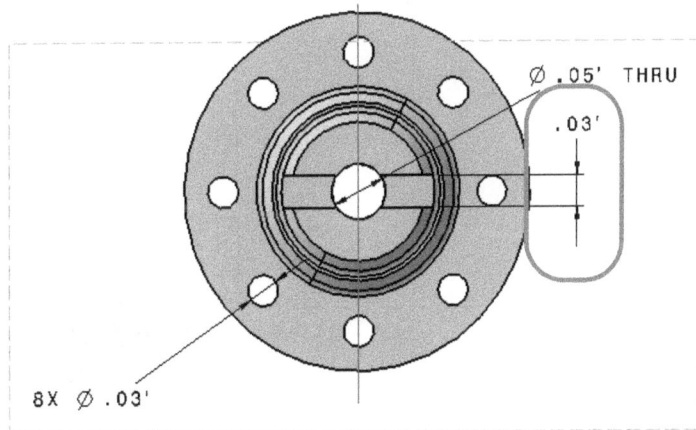

Ø.05' THRU

.03'

8X Ø.03'

Figure 3–51

Task 10 - Change the dimension units.

The tolerances in this model do not display because they are too small for the default units (feet). In this task, you change the units of the dimensions to inches.

1. From the specification tree, select the first dimension under the Dimensions branch.

2. Press and hold <Shift> and select the last dimension. All the dimensions highlight.

3. In the Numerical Properties toolbar, select **DISTINCH**, as shown in Figure 3–52.

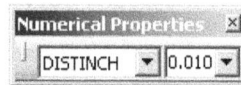

Figure 3–52

The model units update, as shown in Figure 3–53.

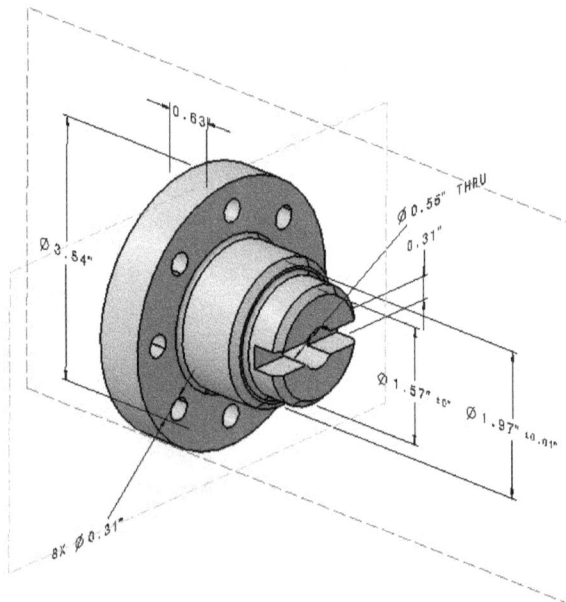

Figure 3–53

4. Note that the tolerances still do not display. To correct this, precision must be increased.

5. Using <Ctrl>, multi-select the 1.57" and the 1.97" dimensions.

6. In the Numerical Properties toolbar, set the precision to **0.0010**. The model units update, as shown in Figure 3–54

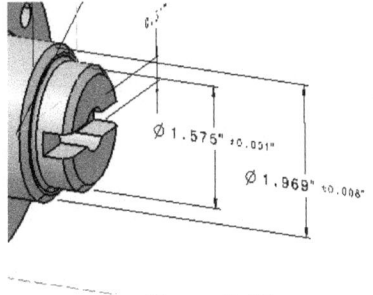

Figure 3–54

7. Save the model.

Practice 3b

Geometric Tolerances

Practice Objectives

- Create a semantic datum.
- Create a datum reference frame.
- Create a geometric tolerance.
- Create a framed (basic) dimension.

In this practice, you will create Datum Reference Frames (DRF), geometric tolerances, and basic (or framed) dimensions. The completed model displays, as shown in Figure 3–55.

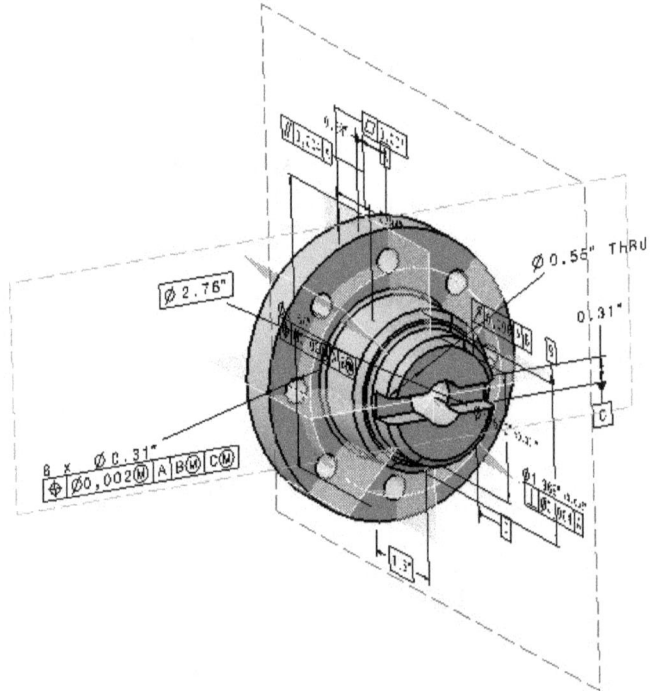

Figure 3–55

Task 1 - Open a part file.

1. Open **LockingHub_Ex3a.CATPart**. The model displays, as shown in Figure 3–56.

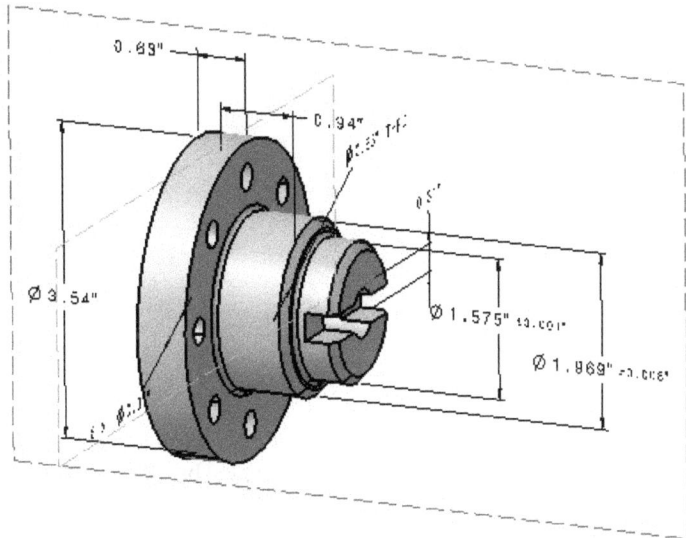

Figure 3–56

Task 2 - Create a semantic datum and datum reference frame.

In this task, you will define the first semantic datum for the model. In addition, you will automatically create a datum reference frame using semantic datum A. This datum reference frame will be referenced during the creation of geometric tolerances for the model.

1. Activate SideView.

2. Preselect the face shown in Figure 3–57.

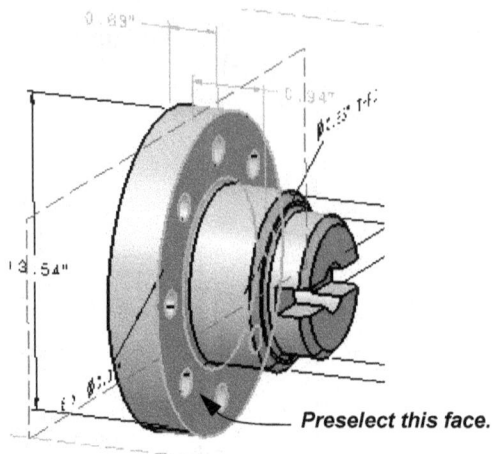

Figure 3–57

3. Click ![graduation cap icon] (Tolerancing Advisor) and then ![datum icon] (Datum Feature). The Datum feature dialog box opens as shown in Figure 3–58.

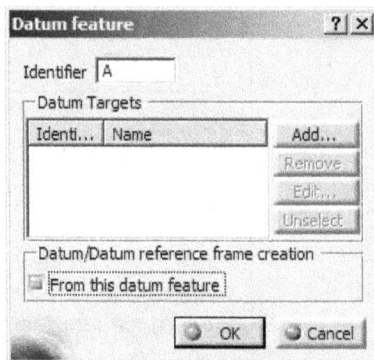

Figure 3–58

4. Ensure that the following selections are made:

   • *Datum Label:* **A**
   • Select **From this datum feature**.

5. Complete the operation. The model displays, as shown in Figure 3–59.

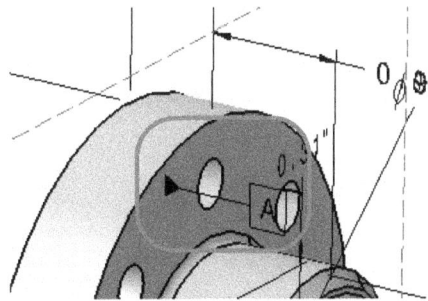

Figure 3–59

Simple **Datum Feature.1** and **Datum reference frame.1** have been added to the specification tree, as shown in Figure 3–60.

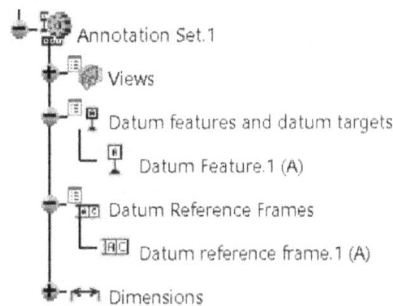

Figure 3–60

Task 3 - Position the semantic datum.

1. Select **Datum A**. The system places a yellow diamond on the datum, enabling you to modify the attachment point.

2. Experiment with positioning the datum and attachment point.

3. Right-click on the yellow diamond and select **Extremity Link>Perpendicular**, as shown in Figure 3–61.

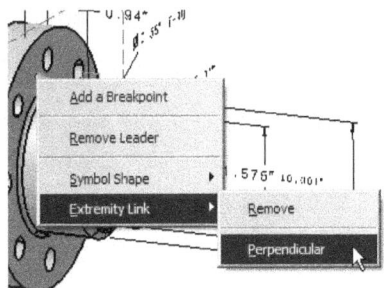

Figure 3–61

4. Drag the datum to the position shown in Figure 3–62.

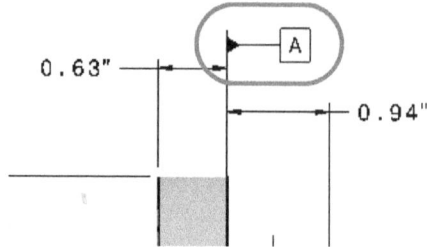

0.63"

0.94"

A

Figure 3–62

Task 4 - Create additional semantic datums.

In this task, you create three more semantic datums to annotate the model. Datum B will reference the 1.969" diameter cylindrical surface. Therefore, you can select the **1.969"** diameter dimension to define this datum.

1. Select the **1.969"** diameter dimension and then click

    (Tolerancing Advisor).

2. Click (Datum Feature) to create a semantic datum. Define the following properties in the Datum feature dialog box:

   - *Datum Label:* **B**
   - Clear the **From this datum feature** option.

3. Complete the operation. The model displays, as shown in Figure 3–63. The datum displays attached to the 1.969" diameter dimension.

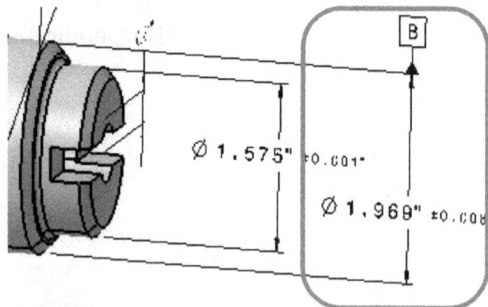

Ø 1.575" ±0.001"

Ø 1.969" ±0.00

B

Figure 3–63

4. Activate FrontView.

5. Create a semantic datum that references the 0.31"
   toleranced dimension. Do not create any datum reference
   frames during this operation. The model displays, as shown
   in Figure 3–64.

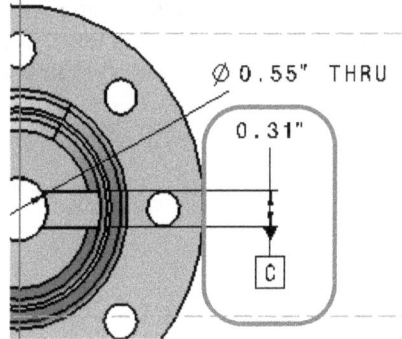

Figure 3–64

6. Activate SideView.

7. Create a final semantic datum named **D** that references the
   planar face shown in Figure 3–65. Do not create any datum
   reference frames during this operation.

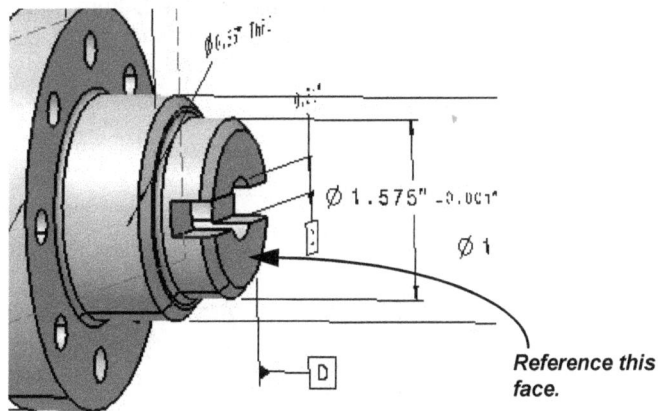

Reference this
face.

Figure 3–65

Task 5 - Manually create a datum reference frame.

In this task, you will manually define the datum reference frame A|B.

1. With nothing preselected, click (Tolerancing Advisor). The Semantic Tolerancing Advisor dialog box opens, as shown in Figure 3–66.

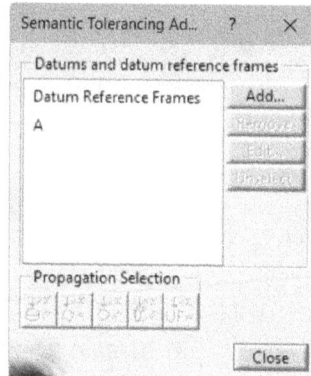

Figure 3–66

2. Click **Add**. The Datum and datum reference frames dialog box opens as shown in Figure 3–67.

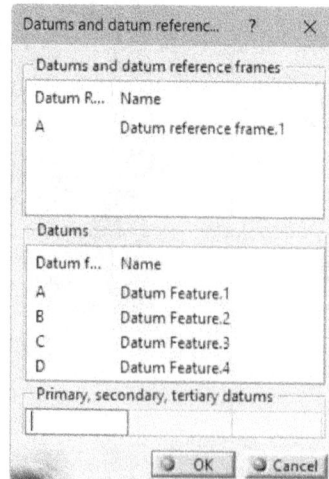

Figure 3–67

3. In the *Datums* area, select **A** and then **B**. The Datum
   Reference Frame dialog box displays, as shown in
   Figure 3–68.

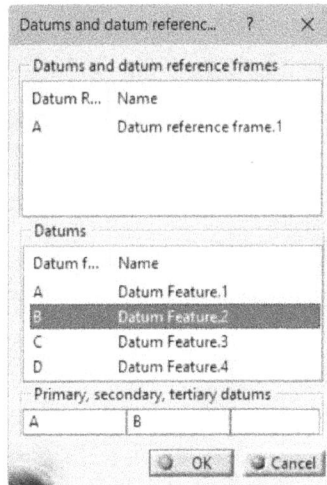

Figure 3–68

4. Click **OK** and then **Close**. The specification tree displays, as
   shown in Figure 3–69.

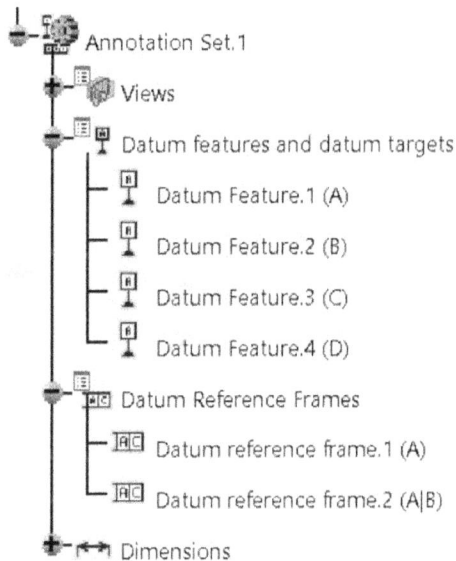

Figure 3–69

5. Save the model.

Task 6 - Change the geometrical tolerance precision.

The model requires geometrical tolerances with a precision of 0.001. By default, CATIA will create them with a tolerance of 0.01. In this task, you increase the global geometric tolerance precision.

1. Select **Tools>Options>Mechanical Design>Functional Tolerancing & Annotation** and select the *Tolerances* tab.

2. Set the Precision to **0.001**, as shown in Figure 3–70.

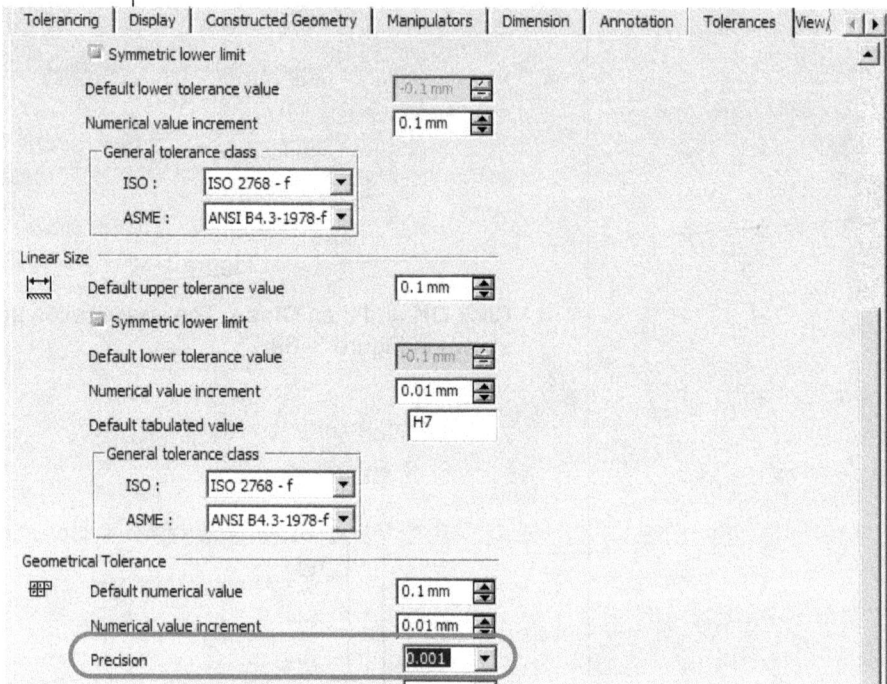

| Tolerancing | Display | Constructed Geometry | Manipulators | Dimension | Annotation | Tolerances | View |

- ☐ Symmetric lower limit
- Default lower tolerance value   -0.1 mm
- Numerical value increment   0.1 mm
- General tolerance class
  - ISO :   ISO 2768 - f
  - ASME :   ANSI B4.3-1978-f

Linear Size
- Default upper tolerance value   0.1 mm
- ☐ Symmetric lower limit
- Default lower tolerance value   -0.1 mm
- Numerical value increment   0.01 mm
- Default tabulated value   H7
- General tolerance class
  - ISO :   ISO 2768 - f
  - ASME :   ANSI B4.3-1978-f

Geometrical Tolerance
- Default numerical value   0.1 mm
- Numerical value increment   0.01 mm
- Precision   0.001

Figure 3–70

3. Click **OK**.

Task 7 - Create a flatness tolerance.

1. Select the model face referenced by datum A and then click

    (Tolerancing Advisor). The Semantic Tolerancing
   Advisor dialog box opens, as shown in Figure 3–71. The
   Semantic Datum icon is highlighted, indicating that a datum
   has already been created on this face.

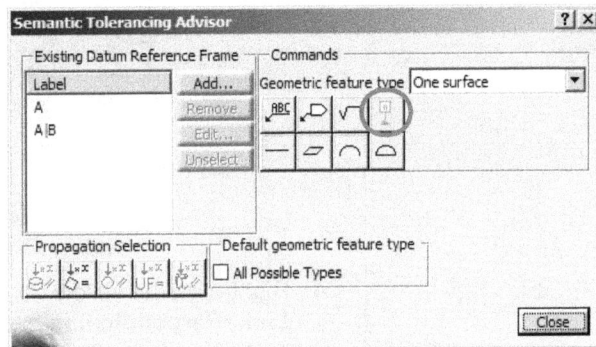

Figure 3–71

2. Click (Flatness Specification). The Geometrical
   Specification dialog box opens, as shown in Figure 3–72.

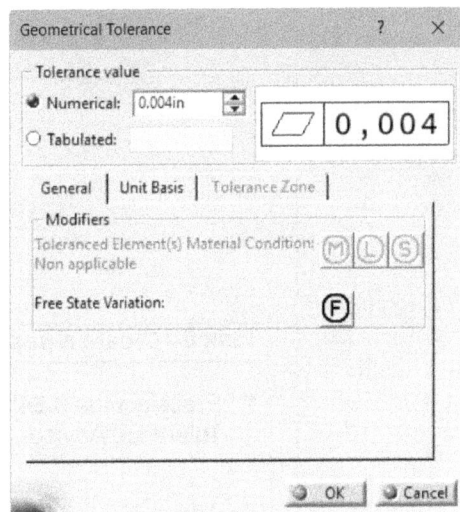

Figure 3–72

3. Enter a numerical tolerance value of **0.001** and complete the operation. **Flatness.1** is added to the **Geometrical Tolerances** branch of **Annotation Set.1,** as shown in Figure 3–73.

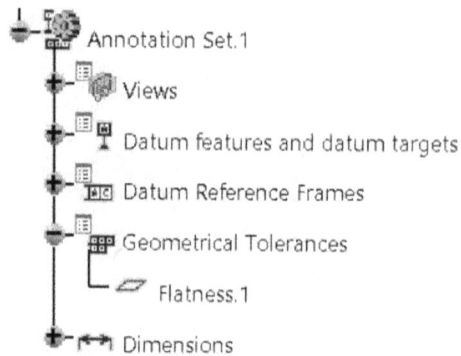

Figure 3–73

4. Right-click the yellow dot on the leader and select **Extremity Link>Perpendicular**, and then position the tolerance as shown in Figure 3–74.

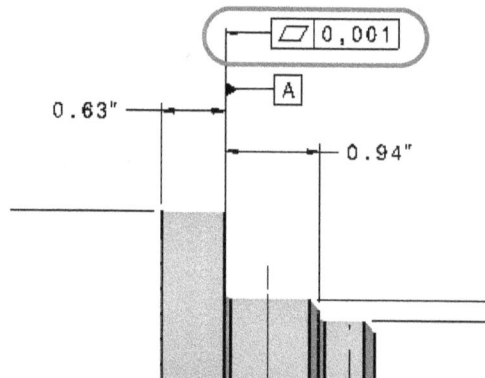

Figure 3–74

Task 8 - Create a positional tolerance.

1. Preselect the **3.54"** diameter dimension and then access the Tolerance Advisor.

2. Select **A|B** in the *Datums and datum reference frames* area. The Semantic Tolerancing Advisor dialog box updates, as shown in Figure 3–75.

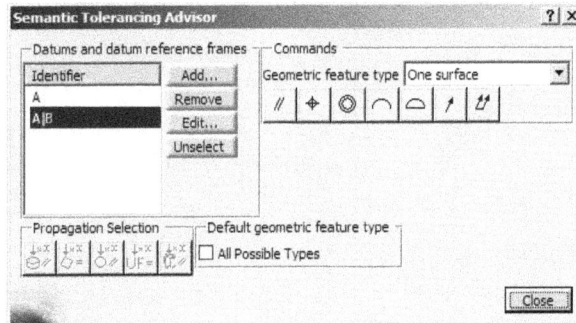

Figure 3–75

3. Click [⊕] (Position-with-DRF Specification). The Geometrical Tolerance dialog box opens.

4. Enter a numerical tolerance of **0.02in** and click Ⓜ to define a maximum material condition for both the toleranced and datum elements. The dialog box displays, as shown in Figure 3–76.

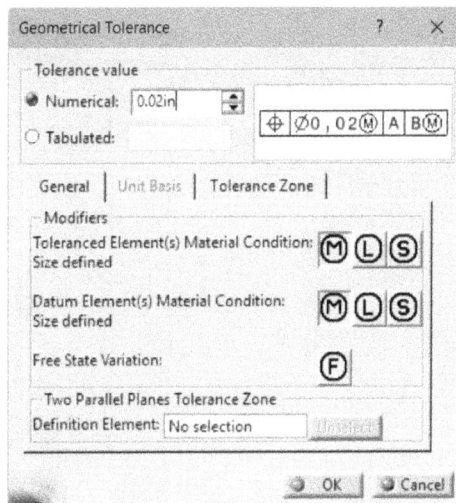

Figure 3–76

5. Complete the operation and appropriately position the tolerance. The model displays, as shown in Figure 3–77.

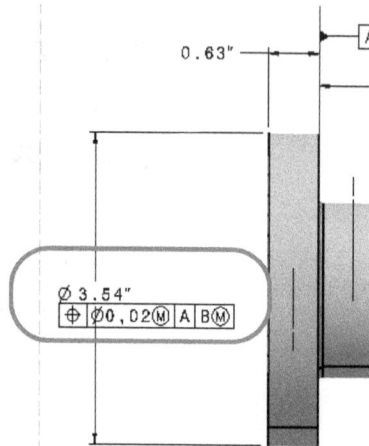

Figure 3–77

Task 9 - Create additional tolerances.

1. With SideView active, create the additional tolerances shown in Figure 3–78, using the information provided as follows:

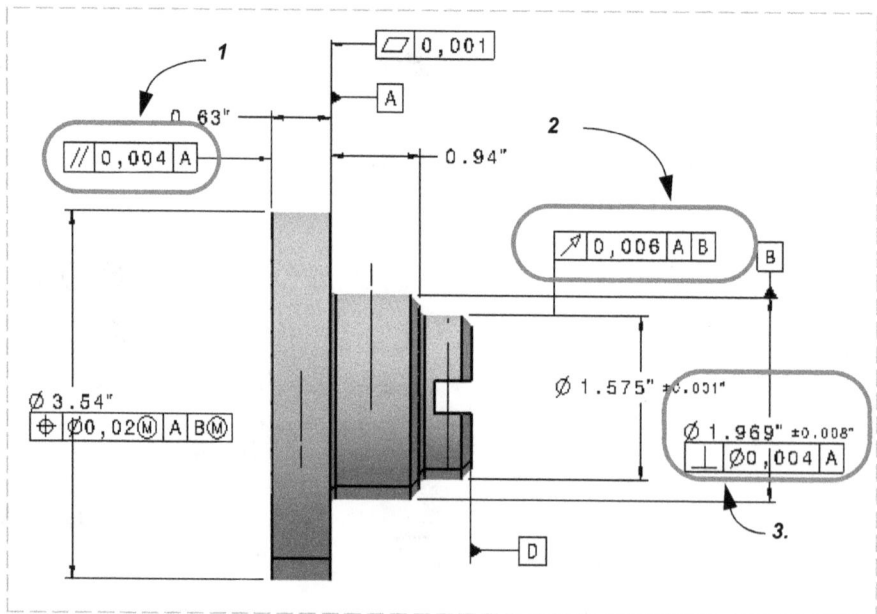

Figure 3–78

Item	Reference	DRF	Type	Tolerance
1.	Back face of part	A	Parallelism	0.004"
2.	Top horizontal leader of the 1.575" diameter dimension	A|B	Circular Runout	0.006"
3.	1.969" diameter dimension	A	Perpendicularity	0.004"

2. Activate FrontView.

3. Access the Tolerance Advisor and define an A|B|C datum reference frame, as shown in Figure 3–79, and then click **OK**.

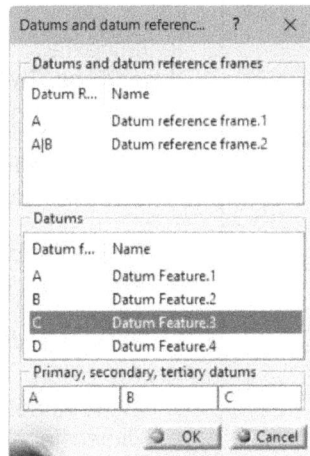

Figure 3–79

4. Select **A|B|C** in the Semantic Tolerancing Advisor dialog box.

5. Select the **8 x 0.31"** diameter dimension from the model.

6. Define the tolerance shown in Figure 3–80.

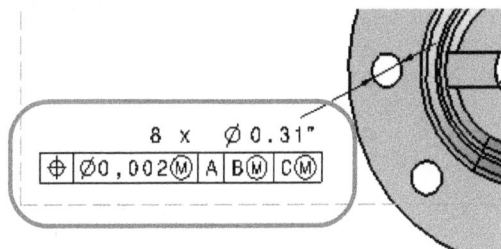

Figure 3–80

7. Complete the operation.

Task 10 - Create a datum reference frame.

In this task, you will manually create the datum reference frame A|D. This datum reference frame is used in the next task to create a basic dimension.

1. Access the Tolerance Advisor.

2. Add a new datum reference frame, select **A** and **D**, and complete the operation.

3. Click **OK** in the Tolerance Advisor dialog box.

Task 11 - Create a basic dimension.

In the next two tasks, you will develop basic or framed dimensions. Two dimensions are created that accomplish the following:

- Locate the front face of the model with respect to the semantic datum A.

- Define the bolt circle diameter with respect to the position tolerance on the holes.

1. Activate SideView.

2. In the Annotations toolbar, click ⬚ (Framed (Basic) Dimensions).

3. The system prompts you to select a context. Select **Datum reference frame.4 (A|D)** in the specification tree. The Framed (Basic) Dimensions Management dialog box opens as shown in Figure 3–81.

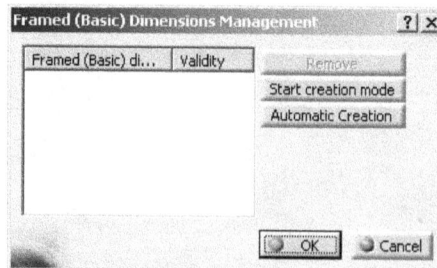

Figure 3–81

4. Click **Start creation mode**.

5. Select the two faces, as shown in Figure 3–82.

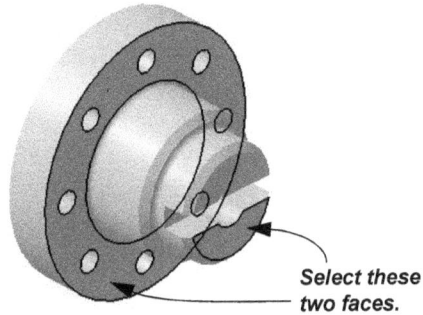

Select these two faces.

Figure 3–82

6. The system places a dimension on the model. if required, right-click on the dimension and select **Dimension Representation>Force Horizontal Dimension in view**, so that the dimension displays as shown in Figure 3–83.

The dimension might appear across the geometry. It can be moved once the operation is complete.

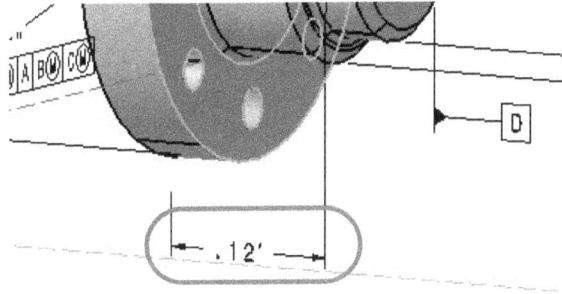

Figure 3–83

7. Select anywhere on the background to frame the dimension. The dimension displays as shown in Figure 3–84.

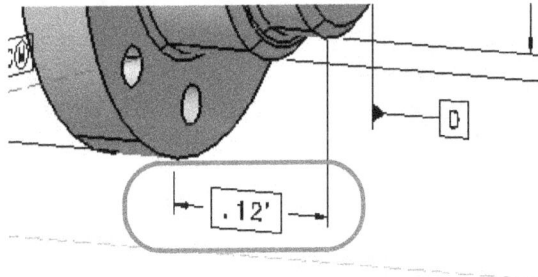

Figure 3–84

8. Click **End creation mode**. The Framed (Basic) Dimensions Management dialog box displays as shown in Figure 3–85.

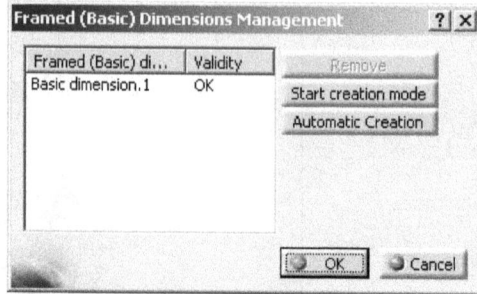

Figure 3–85

9. Click **OK** to complete the operation.

10. Use the Numerical Properties toolbar to set the format of the 12' dimension to **DISTINCH**.

Task 12 - Create a second framed dimension.

1. Activate the FrontView.

2. In the Annotations toolbar, click (Framed **Basic** Dimensions).

3. Select the position tolerance for the pattern of eight holes to set the context.

4. In the Framed (Basic) Dimensions Management dialog box, click **Automatic Creation**.

All associated dimensions display as shown in Figure 3–86.

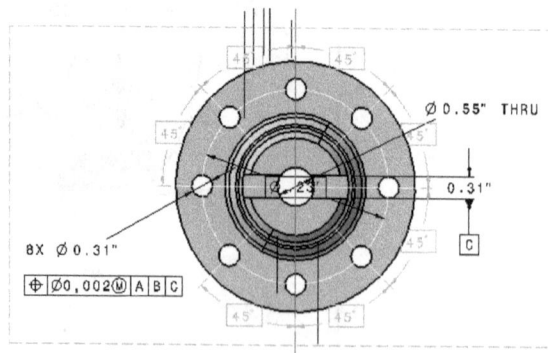

Note that in addition to the dimensions, the system creates reference planes and a reference cylinder. Should you delete these dimensions later, the reference entities will not automatically be deleted.

Figure 3–86

Use <Ctrl> to multi-select the dimensions in the dialog box.

5. Select the dimensions in the dialog box to highlight them on the model.

6. Highlight all of the 45deg dimensions in the dialog box and click **Remove** to remove them from the display.

7. Click **OK**.

8. Change the format of the .23' diameter dimension to **DISTINCH** and position it as shown in Figure 3–87.

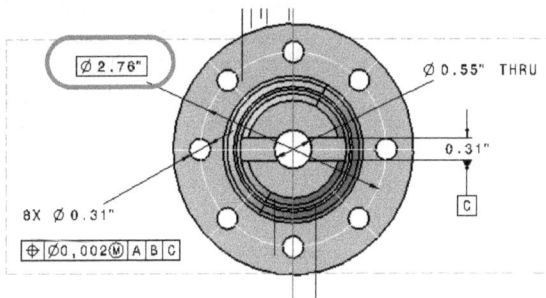

Figure 3–87

9. Save the model and close the window.

Practice 3c | Surface FT&A

Practice Objectives

- Create a semantic datum using datum targets.
- Create a semantic datum on surface geometry.
- Create a positional tolerance on surface geometry.

In this practice, you will add datums and tolerances to a surface part model. The placement of semantic datums and datum reference frames can be challenging due to the complex shapes that can be developed for a surfaced part. Therefore, this practice focuses on the development of these annotations. The completed model displays as shown in Figure 3–88.

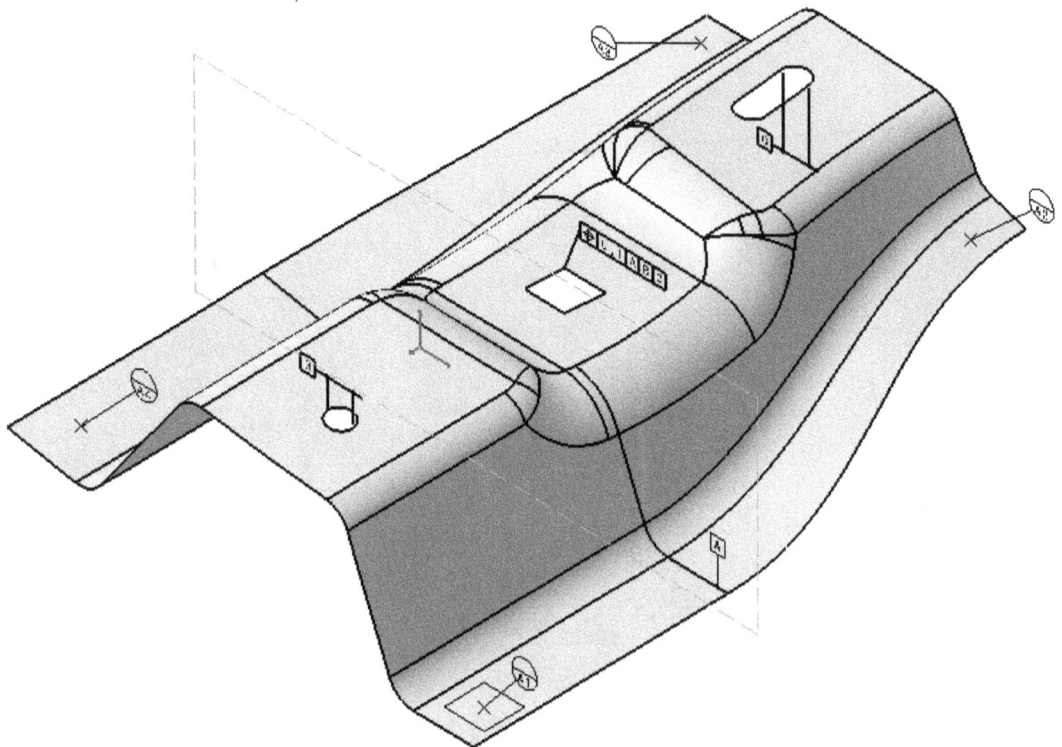

Figure 3–88

Task 1 - Open a part file.

---

1. Open **Skin.CATPart**. The model displays as shown in Figure 3–89.

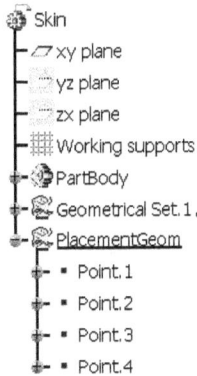

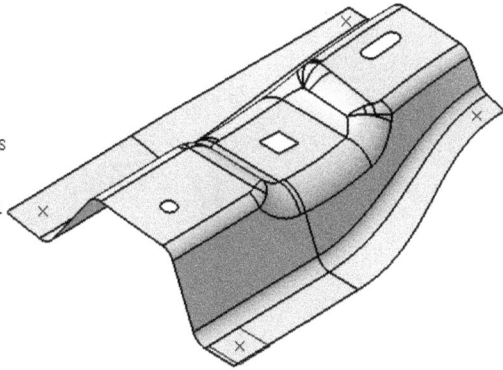

Figure 3–89

2. Expand the **PlacementGeom** geometrical set. It consists of four reference points that lie on the exterior surfaces of the part. These points are used to locate datum targets that define the datum A.

Task 2 - Create Datum A.

1. Hold <Ctrl> and select the four surfaces in the order shown in Figure 3–90.

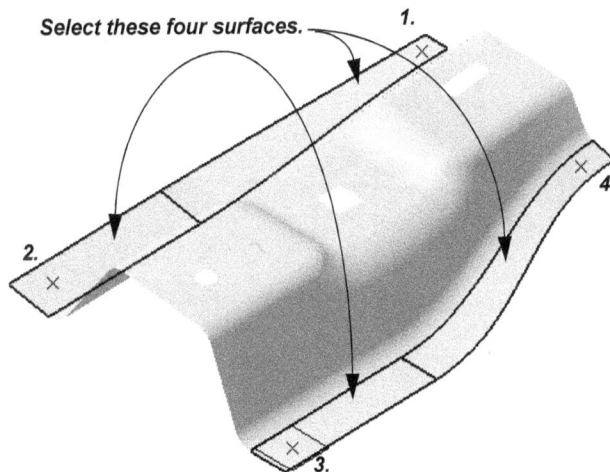

Select these four surfaces.

Figure 3–90

2. Click [icon] (Tolerancing Advisor). The Semantic Tolerancing Advisor dialog box opens.

3. In the *Geometric tolerance & annotation creation commands* drop-down list, select **All possible types**. The dialog box updates as shown in Figure 3–91.

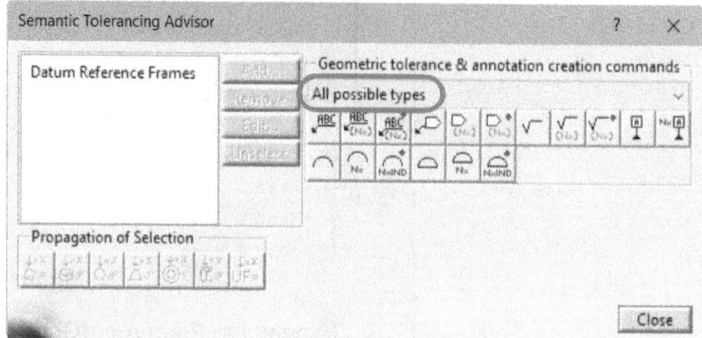

Figure 3–91

4. Click [icon] (Datum Feature). The Datum feature dialog box opens.

Design Considerations

To define a datum on these surfaces, you must define datum targets to position the part. You can add these targets on the fly using the icons in the Datum Targets field.

5. Click **Add**. The Datum Target dialog box opens, as shown in Figure 3–92. This dialog box enables you to create multiple datum target annotations at once.

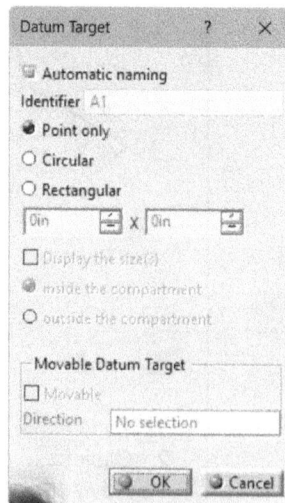

Figure 3–92

6. Select **Point.1** in the model. A datum target is added to the model, as shown in Figure 3–93.

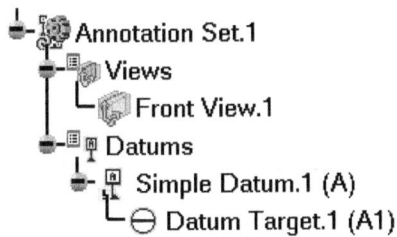

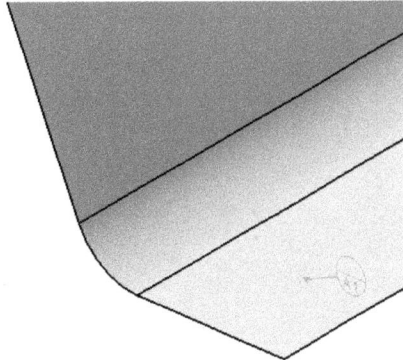

Annotation Set.1
  Views
    Front View.1
  Datums
    Simple Datum.1 (A)
      Datum Target.1 (A1)

Figure 3–93

7. Continue to select **Point.2**, **Point.3**, and **Point.4**. The system creates a target for each point.

8. Click **OK** to close the Datum Target dialog box. The Datum feature dialog box displays as shown in Figure 3–94.

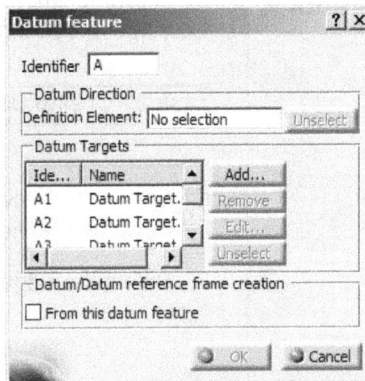

Figure 3–94

9. Click in the Definition Element field and select the XY plane in the specification tree.

10. Verify that the **From this datum feature** option is cleared, and complete the operation. The model displays as shown in Figure 3–95.

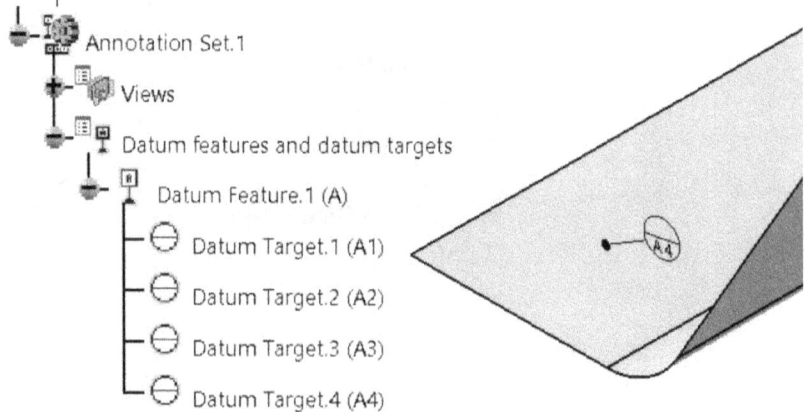

Figure 3–95

Design Considerations

Note the creation of **Front View.1**. Since no annotation plane was created when the datum was defined, the system creates a view that accommodates the selected references.

Task 3 - Create Datum B and C.

1. Click ▦ (View From Reference) and select the yz plane. Rename the view to **SideView** and click **OK**.

2. Select the edge of the hole, as shown in Figure 3–96.

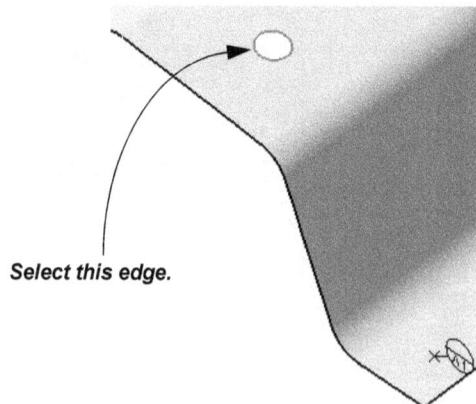

Select this edge.

Figure 3–96

3. Activate the Tolerance Advisor and create a semantic datum. The model displays, as shown in Figure 3–97.

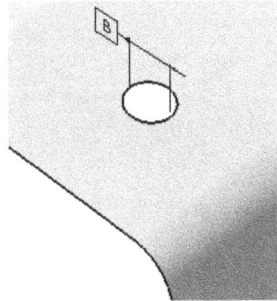

Figure 3–97

4. Preselect the edge shown in Figure 3–98 and access the Tolerance Advisor.

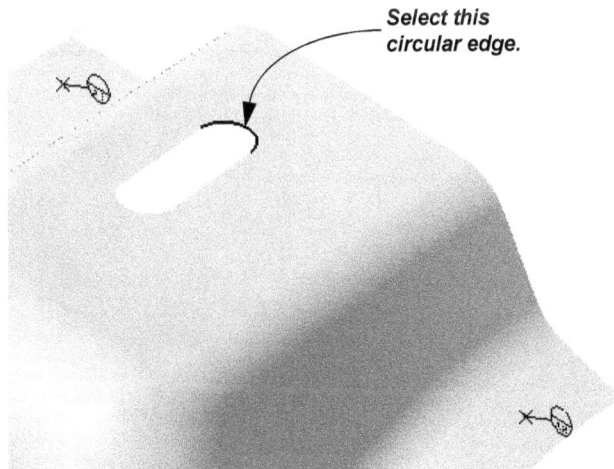

Select this circular edge.

Figure 3–98

5. Create a semantic datum. Verify that the **From the 3 last created datum features** option is enabled, as shown in Figure 3–99, and complete the operation.

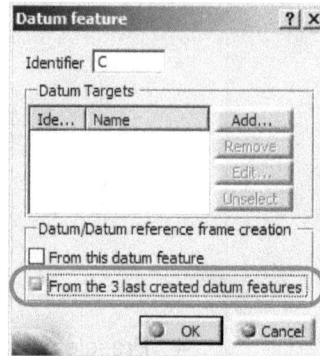

Figure 3–99

Task 4 - Create a position tolerance.

1. Preselect the four edges of the square cutout, as shown in Figure 3–100.

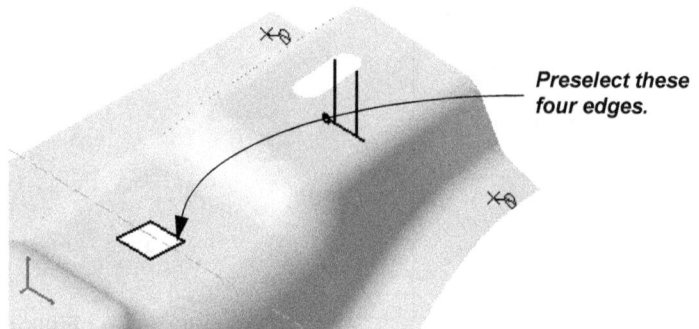

Preselect these four edges.

Figure 3–100

2. Access the Tolerance Advisor and make the following selections to create the position tolerance shown in Figure 3–101.

- **A|B|C**: Select from the *Existing Datum Reference Frame* area

- (Position-with-DRF Specification): Click this icon to create a position tolerance

Accept the default options in the Geometrical Tolerance dialog box and complete the operation. The model displays as shown in Figure 3–101.

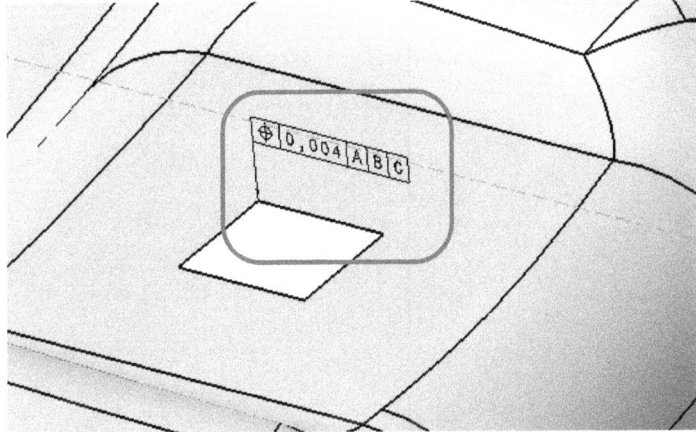

Figure 3–101

3. Save the model and close the window.

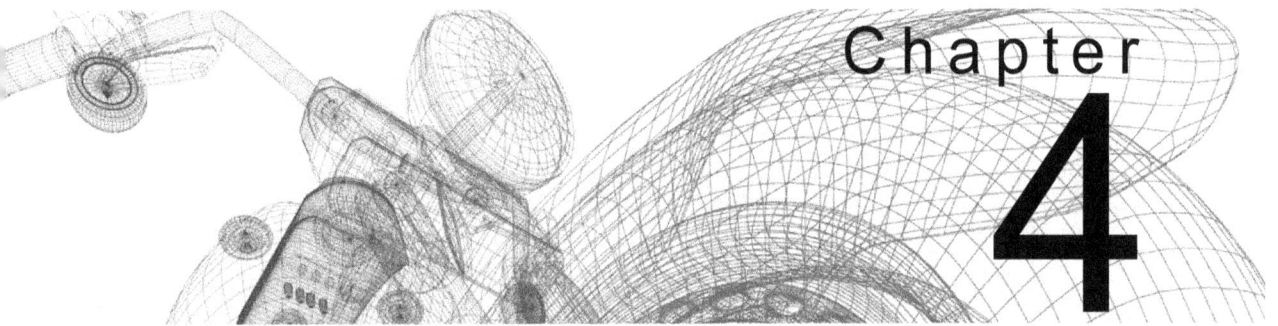

Chapter

4

Non-Semantic Annotations

Non-semantic annotations enable user input that might not meet the defined tolerancing standards. These annotations should be used when the company standard does not match these standards, or the designer has a unique annotation that cannot be made using a semantic annotation. This chapter introduces non-semantic methods of creating annotations.

Learning Objectives in this Chapter

- Create Text and Flag notes.
- Create datum elements and datum targets.
- Create Geometric Tolerances.
- Learn how to place roughness symbols.
- Create dimensions.
- Understand the diagnostic reporting tool.

4.1 Text

Text can be added to 3D models to communicate additional information about the model. You can create three kinds of text annotations:

- Text with Leader

- Text

- Text Parallel to Screen

You have the option to add text with or without a leader. The text in either case is defined on an annotation plane; as a result, the orientation of the text is based on the orientation of the annotation plane you select. If an annotation plane is not parallel to the screen, then all the text created with or without a leader is not parallel to the screen, as shown in Figure 4–1.

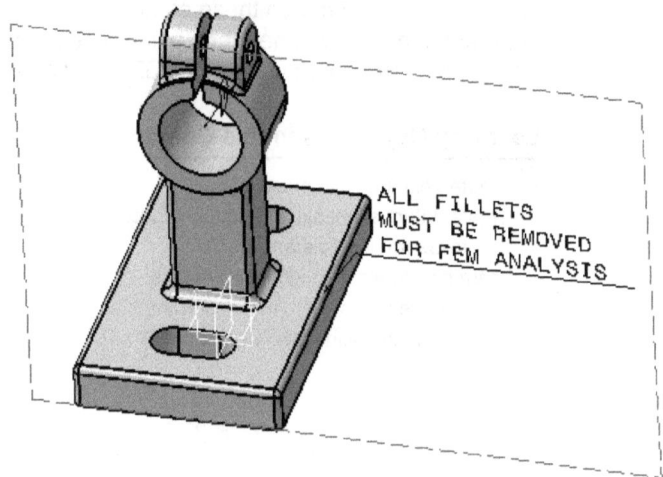

Figure 4–1

If you want some text to remain parallel to the screen, regardless

of the orientation of the annotation plane, use (Text Parallel To Screen).

General Steps

Use the following general steps to create any of the three types of 3D text:

1. Activate an annotation plane.
2. Select the required 3D text icon.
3. Select a reference element.
4. Enter text in the Text Editor.
5. Complete the feature.

Step 1 - Activate an annotation plane.

Double-click on the required annotation plane in the specification tree or directly from the model to activate it. The orientation of the selected annotation plane defines the orientation of the text.

Step 2 - Select the required 3D text icon.

In the Annotations toolbar, click one of the following tools:

*   (Text with Leader)

*   (Text)

*   (Text Parallel To Screen)

Step 3 - Select a reference element.

Select a geometric or annotation element in the specification tree or model. The selected element is used as a reference for the Leader. If the Text tool is being used, you can also indicate a location on the annotation plane to place the text.

Step 4 - Enter text in the Text Editor.

To add multiple lines of text press <Shift> + <Enter>.

The Text Editor opens after a reference element is selected, as shown in Figure 4–2. Enter the required text.

Figure 4–2

Step 5 - Complete the feature.

Click **OK** to complete the creation of the text. The text feature displays under the Notes node in the specification tree, as shown in Figure 4–3.

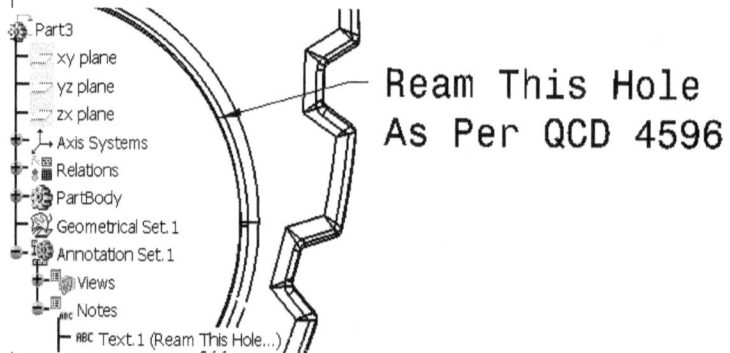

Figure 4–3

Editing Text

Formatting for all text is applied using the Text Properties toolbar, as shown in Figure 4–4.

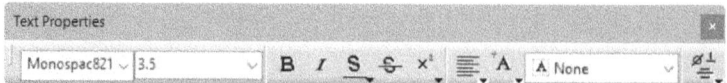

Figure 4–4

Handling Text Features

Select the text and move it using the handles shown in Figure 4–5.

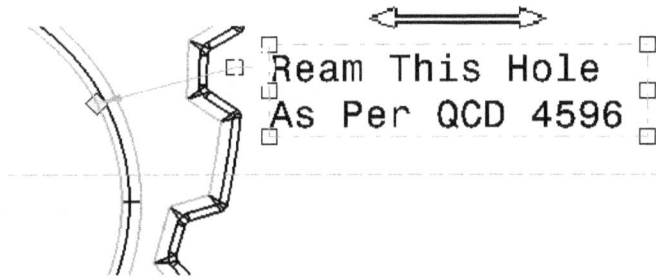

Figure 4–5

Select the yellow diamond and right-click to access the text leader handling options, as shown in Figure 4–6.

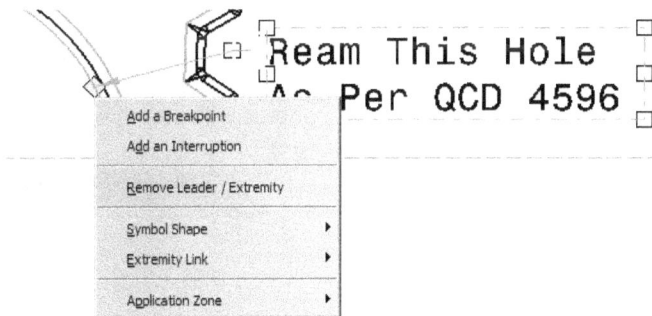

Figure 4–6

Attribute Link

You can associatively add model parameter values to a text note. Right-click in the Text Editor dialog box and select **Attribute Link**, as shown in Figure 4–7.

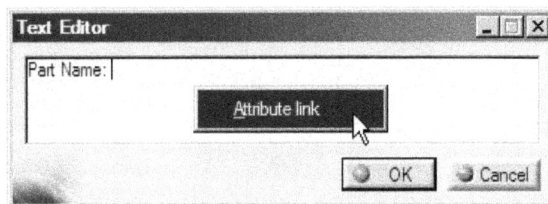

Figure 4–7

Select a feature or body in the specification tree to filter the parameters. The Attribute Link Panel dialog box opens, as shown in Figure 4–8, enabling you to select a parameter from the model.

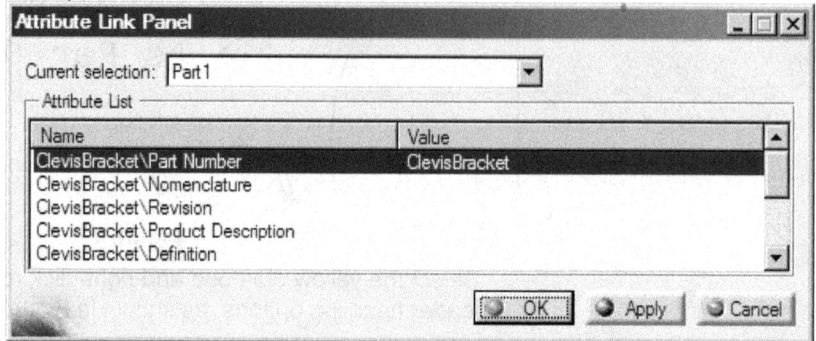

Attribute Link Panel   _ □ ×

Current selection: Part1   ▼
┌ Attribute List ───┐
Name	Value	▲
ClevisBracket\Part Number	ClevisBracket	
ClevisBracket\Nomenclature		
ClevisBracket\Revision		
ClevisBracket\Product Description		
ClevisBracket\Definition		▼

                              OK   Apply   Cancel

Figure 4–8

Once the parameter has been selected, its value is added to the Text Editor, as shown in Figure 4–9. This value is associative, so it updates with changes to the model.

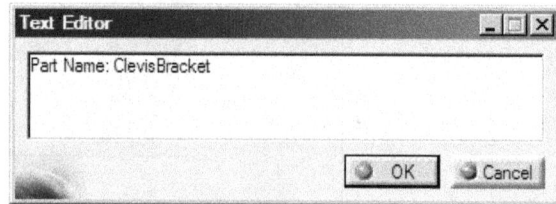

Text Editor   _ □ ×

Part Name: ClevisBracket

                          OK   Cancel

Figure 4–9

4.2 Flag Notes

Flag notes enable you to add a list of files or web links to the document. You can quickly open a related spreadsheet, presentation, or web site from the CATIA document from a flag note. An example displays, as shown in Figure 4–10.

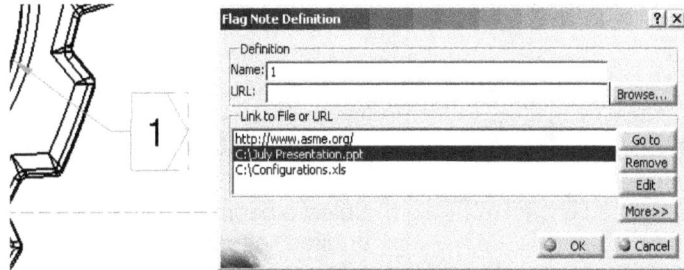

Figure 4–10

You have the option of adding flag notes with or without a leader. The flag note in either case is defined on an annotation plane similar to 3D text.

General Steps

Use the following general steps to create flag notes with or without a leader:

1. Activate an annotation plane.
2. Select the required flag note icon.
3. Select a reference element.
4. Add links in the Flag Note Definition dialog box.
5. Complete the feature.

Step 1 - Activate an annotation plane.

Double-click on the required annotation plane in the specification tree or directly from the model to activate it. The orientation of the selected annotation plane defines the orientation of the flag note.

Step 2 - Select the required flag note icon.

In the Annotations toolbar, click one of the following tools:

- (Flag Note with Leader)

- (Flag Note)

Step 3 - Select a reference element.

Select a geometric or annotation element in the specification tree or directly from the model. The selected element is used as a reference for the Leader.

Step 4 - Add links in the Flag Note Definition dialog box.

The Flag Note Definition dialog box opens after a reference element is selected, as shown in Figure 4–11.

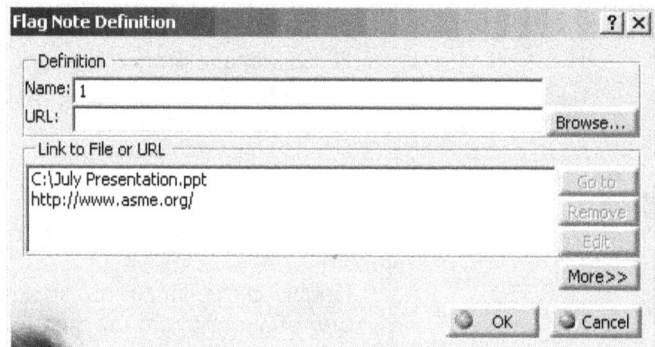

Figure 4–11

Enter a URL in the *URL* field and press <Tab> to add it to the *Link to File or URL* list. Click **Browse** and browse to the file to link from in the File Selection dialog box. Clicking **Open** adds the file path to the Link to File or URL list.

Step 5 - Complete the feature.

Click **OK** to complete the creation of the flag note. The flag note feature displays under the Notes node in the specification tree, as shown in Figure 4–12.

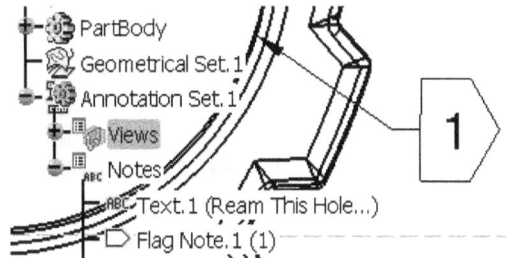

Figure 4–12

Free and Linked Annotations

Any text or flag note annotation that is created by selecting geometry from the model is termed a "linked" annotation. A linked annotation is related to the geometry used to place the annotation. It fails if the associated geometry no longer exists in the model. The symbol for a linked annotation displays in the specification tree, as shown in Figure 4–13.

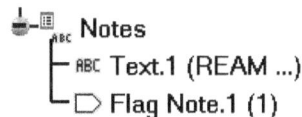

Figure 4–13

A free annotation is created by selecting anywhere in the annotation plane to place the annotation. A free annotation can be created using the following options:

- [ABC] (Text)

- [ABC] (Text Parallel to Screen)

- [▷] (Flag Note)

The symbol for a free annotation displays in the specification tree, as shown in Figure 4–14.

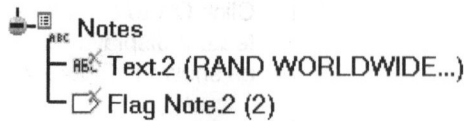

📦 ⊞_{ABC} Notes
 ├ ABC Text.2 (RAND WORLDWIDE...)
 └ Flag Note.2 (2)

Figure 4–14

When transferring free annotations between annotation planes, the system always positions the annotation at the origin of the reference axes of the new view. The annotation might appear lost, because it is no longer positioned relative to the background location selected during creation. Find the annotation by activating the view the annotation was transferred to, and then centering the model on the reference axes.

4.3 Datum Features

Datum features can be added for geometrical tolerancing.

General Steps

Use the following general steps to create datum features:

1. Activate an annotation plane.
2. Start the creation of the Datum feature.
3. Select a reference element.
4. Enter an identifier in the Datum Feature Creation dialog box.
5. Complete the feature.

Step 1 - Activate an annotation plane.

Double-click on the required annotation plane in the specification tree or directly from the model to activate it. The orientation of the selected annotation plane defines the orientation of the datum feature.

Step 2 - Start the creation of the Datum feature.

In the Annotations toolbar, click 🔲 (Datum Feature).

Step 3 - Select a reference element.

Select a geometric element or feature in the specification tree or directly from the model. The selected element is used as a reference for the location of the datum feature.

Step 4 - Enter an identifier in the Datum Feature Creation dialog box.

The Datum Feature Creation dialog box opens after a reference element is selected, as shown in Figure 4–15. Enter an identifier.

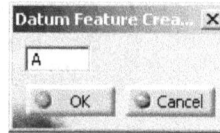

Figure 4–15

Step 5 - Complete the feature.

Click **OK** to complete the creation of the datum element. The datum element feature displays under the Datums node in the specification tree, as shown in Figure 4–16.

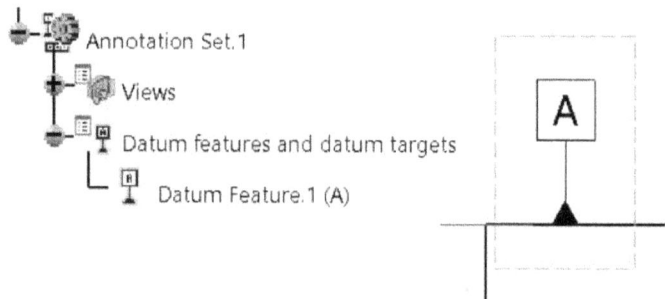

Figure 4–16

Non-Planar Datums

If a non-planar face or surface is selected to define the datum element, you can add datum targets to constrain the datum. To do this, create the datum and then double-click on it in the model or specification tree. The Datum Definition dialog box displays, as shown in Figure 4–17. Click **Add** to create datum targets.

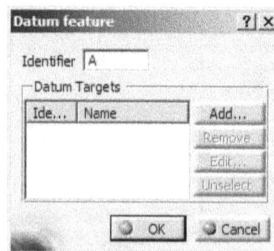

Figure 4–17

DRFs for Non-Semantic Annotation

Once you have defined a simple datum, use the Tolerance Advisor to assign it as a datum reference frame before using it in a geometrical tolerance. The process is identical to defining a semantic datum reference frame.

When non-semantically annotating a model, a datum reference frame is automatically defined when the datum is added to a non-semantic geometrical tolerance.

4.4 Datum Target

A datum target is typically defined using the Datum Feature dialog box. Defining a datum target makes it associative to the datum element. In some cases, this association is undesirable or not possible. In such cases, you can use the Datum Target tool.

General Steps

Use the following general steps to create datum targets:

1. Activate an annotation plane.
2. Start the creation of the Datum Target feature.
3. Select a reference element.
4. Enter the parameters in the Datum Target Creation dialog box.
5. Complete the feature.

Step 1 - Activate an annotation plane.

Double-click on the required annotation plane in the specification tree or directly from the model to activate it. The orientation of the selected annotation plane defines the orientation of the datum target.

Step 2 - Start the creation of the Datum Target feature.

In the Annotations toolbar, click ⊖ (Datum Target).

Step 3 - Select a reference element.

Select a geometric element or feature in the specification tree or directly from the model. The selected element is used as a reference for the location of the datum target.

Step 4 - Enter the parameters in the Datum Target Creation dialog box.

The Datum Target Creation dialog box displays after a reference element is selected, as shown in Figure 4–18.

Select for a square or circular zone.

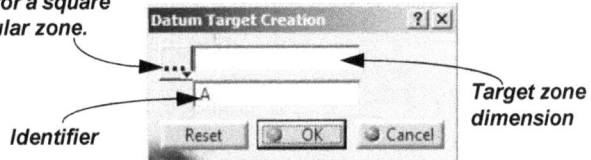

Identifier

Target zone dimension

Figure 4–18

Enter the required parameters in the Datum Target Creation dialog box. An example is shown in Figure 4–19.

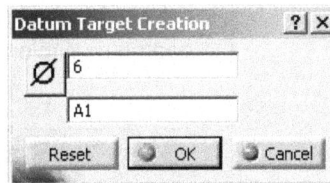

Figure 4–19

Step 5 - Complete the feature.

Click **OK** to complete the creation of the datum target. The datum target feature displays under the Datums node in the specification tree, as shown in Figure 4–20.

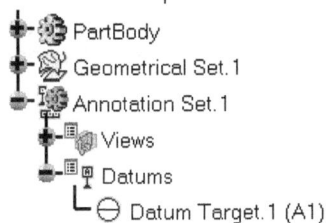

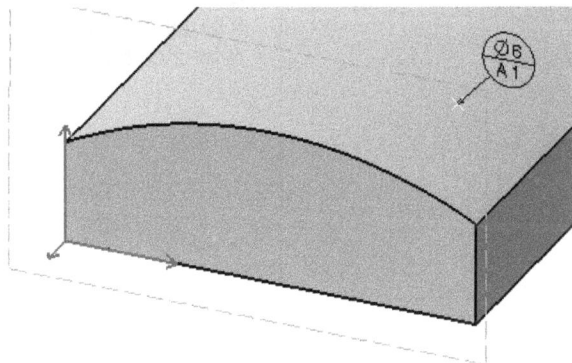

Figure 4–20

4.5 Geometric Tolerances

General Steps

Use the following general steps to create geometric tolerances:

1. Activate an annotation plane.
2. Start the creation of the Geometrical Tolerance feature.
3. Select a reference element.
4. Enter the parameters in the Geometrical Tolerance dialog box.
5. Complete the feature.

Step 1 - Activate an annotation plane.

Double-click on the required annotation plane in the specification tree or directly from the model to activate it. The orientation of the selected annotation plane defines the orientation of the geometrical tolerance.

Step 2 - Start the creation of the Geometrical Tolerance feature.

In the Annotations toolbar, click (Geometrical Tolerance).

Step 3 - Select a reference element.

Select a geometric element or feature in the specification tree or directly from the model. The selected element is used as a reference for the location of the geometrical tolerance.

Step 4 - Enter the parameters in the Geometrical Tolerance dialog box.

The Geometrical Tolerance dialog box opens after a reference element is selected, as shown in Figure 4–21.

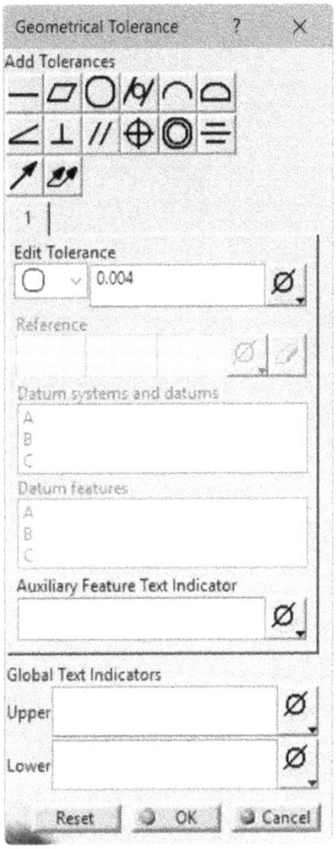

Figure 4–21

Enter the required parameters in the Geometrical Tolerance dialog box. An example is shown in Figure 4–22.

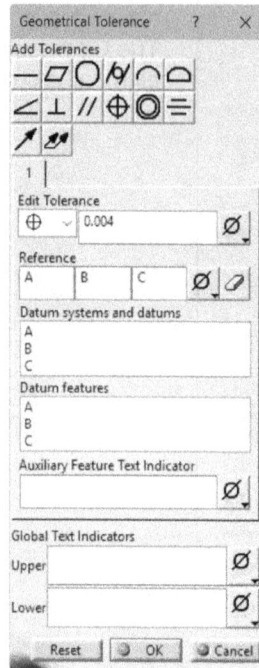

Figure 4–22

Step 5 - Complete the feature.

Click **OK** to complete the creation of the geometrical tolerance. An example of a geometrical tolerance is shown in Figure 4–23.

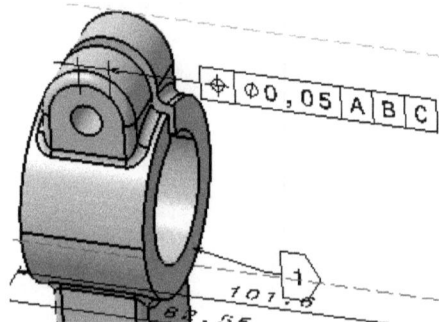

Figure 4–23

The geometrical tolerance feature displays under the Geometrical Tolerances node in the specification tree.

4.6 Roughness Symbols

General Steps

Use the following general steps to create roughness symbols:

1. Activate an annotation plane.
2. Start the creation of the roughness symbol.
3. Select a reference element.
4. Enter the parameters in the Roughness Symbol dialog box.
5. Complete the feature.

Step 1 - Activate an annotation plane.

Double-click on the required annotation plane in the specification tree or directly from the model to activate it. The orientation of the selected annotation plane defines the orientation of the roughness symbol.

Step 2 - Start the creation of the roughness symbol.

In the Annotations toolbar, click √‾ (Roughness).

Step 3 - Select a reference element.

Select a geometric element or feature in the specification tree or directly from the model. The selected element is used as a reference for the location of the roughness symbol.

Step 4 - Enter the parameters in the Roughness Symbol dialog box.

The Roughness Symbol dialog box displays after a reference element is selected, as shown in Figure 4–24.

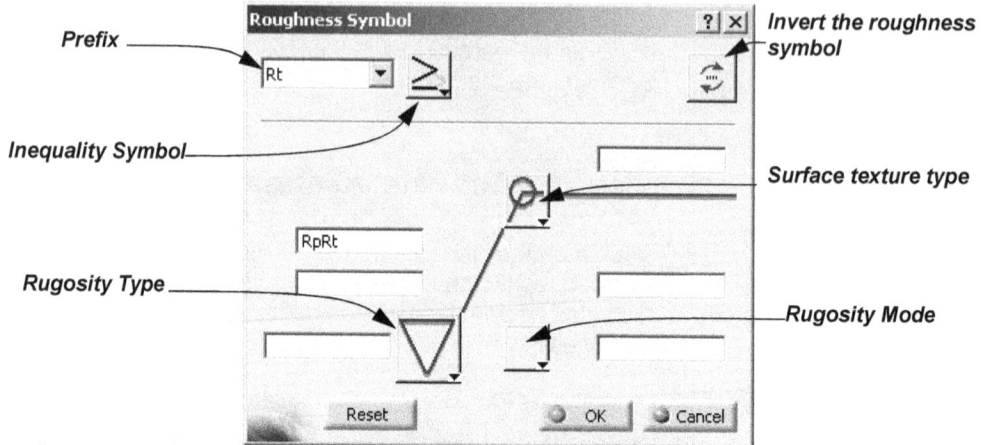

Prefix

Inequality Symbol

Rugosity Type

Invert the roughness symbol

Surface texture type

Rugosity Mode

Figure 4–24

Enter the required parameters in the Roughness Symbol dialog box.

Step 5 - Complete the feature.

Click **OK** to complete the creation of the roughness symbol. An example of a roughness symbol is shown in Figure 4–25.

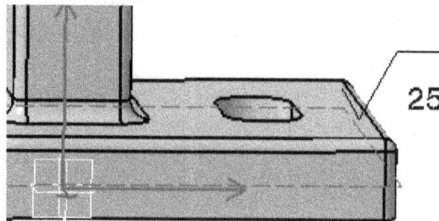

Figure 4–25

The roughness symbol feature displays under the Roughness node in the specification tree.

4.7 Dimensions

General Steps

Use the following general steps to create dimensions:

1. Activate an annotation plane.
2. Start the creation of dimensions.
3. Select the references required to create the required dimension.
4. Place the dimension.
5. Modify the dimension properties, as required.

Step 1 - Activate an annotation plane.

Double-click on the required annotation plane in the specification tree or directly from the model to activate it. The orientation of the selected annotation plane defines the orientation of the dimension.

Step 2 - Start the creation of dimensions.

In the Annotations toolbar, click (Dimensions).

Step 3 - Select the references required to create the required dimension.

Select the references required to create the required dimension. The references selected determine the type of dimension created. For example, select two edges or surfaces that are at an angle to one another to create an angular dimension.

Step 4 - Place the dimension.

When all references have been selected, click anywhere on the CATIA background to place the dimension. An example is shown in Figure 4–26.

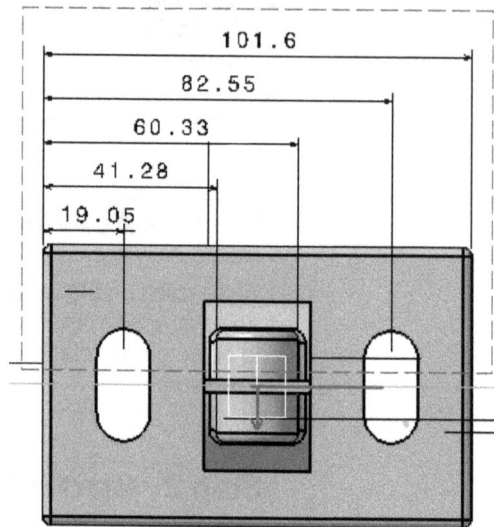

Figure 4–26

Step 5 - Modify the dimension properties, as required.

Modify the line type, tolerance standard, tolerance value, and tolerance precision using the Dimension Properties and Numerical Properties toolbars, as shown in Figure 4–27.

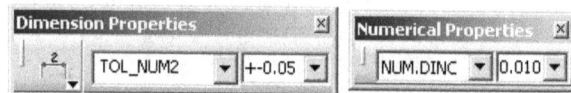

Figure 4–27

Cumulated Dimension

In the Dimensions flyout of the Annotations toolbar, click

[icon] (Cumulated Dimensions) to create a series of cumulated dimensions. The first reference selected is the baseline and further selections are dimensioned from the baseline, as shown in Figure 4–28.

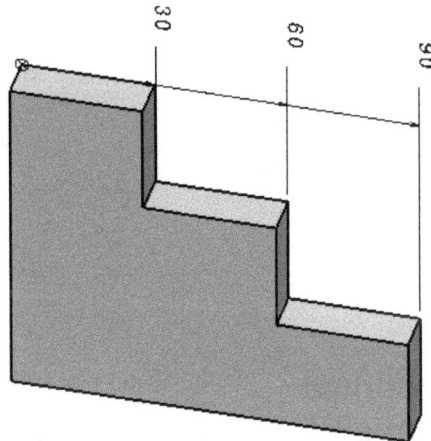

Figure 4–28

Stacked Dimension

In the Dimensions flyout of the Annotations toolbar, click

[icon] (Stacked Dimensions) to create stacked dimensions. An example of stacked dimensions is shown in Figure 4–29.

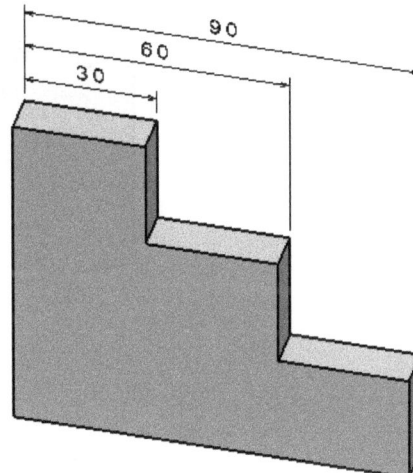

Figure 4–29

Coordinate Dimension

In the Dimensions flyout of the Annotations toolbar, click

(Coordinate Dimensions) to create a coordinate dimension. Select a vertex on the model to display its coordinates, as shown in Figure 4–30.

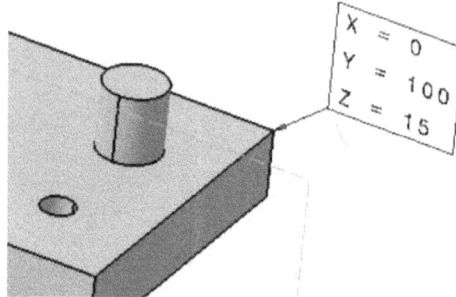

Figure 4–30

Curvilinear Dimension

In the Dimensions flyout of the Annotations toolbar, click

(Curvilinear Dimensions) to create a length dimension for a non-linear edge or curve. Select the edge to display the dimension, as shown in Figure 4–31.

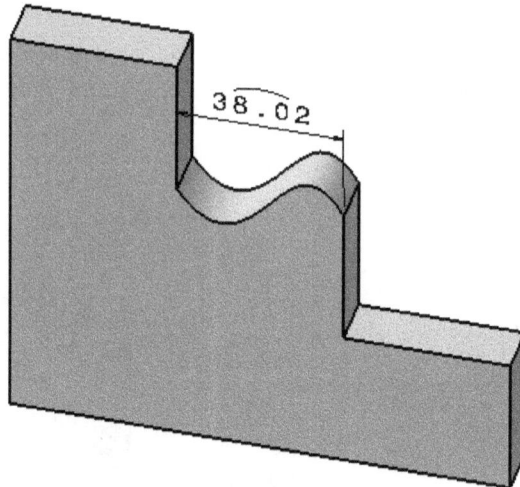

Figure 4–31

4.8 Generative Dimensions

General Steps

Use the following general steps to create generative dimensions:

1. Activate an annotation plane.
2. Start the creation of generative dimensions.
3. Select the features to dimension.
4. Select the dimensions to create.
5. Complete the feature(s).

Step 1 - Activate an annotation plane.

Double-click on the required annotation plane in the specification tree or directly from the model to activate it. The orientation of the selected annotation plane defines the orientation of the text.

Step 2 - Start the creation of generative dimensions.

In the Annotations toolbar, click (Generative Dimension). The Generate 3D Tolerancing dimensions dialog box opens, as shown in Figure 4–32.

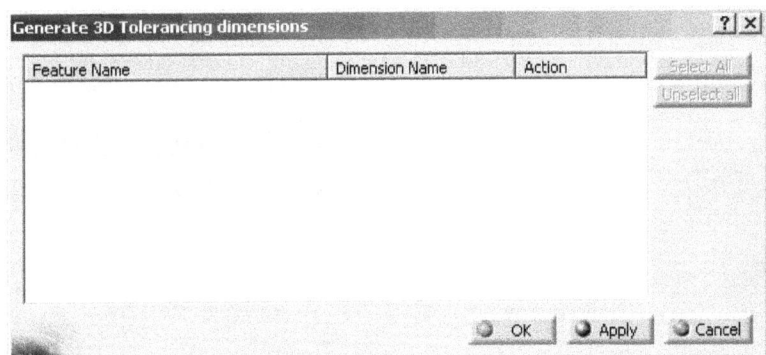

Figure 4–32

Step 3 - Select the features to dimension.

Select the feature(s) to dimension. The dimensions related to each selected feature automatically populate in the Generate 3D Tolerancing dimensions dialog box, as shown in Figure 4–33.

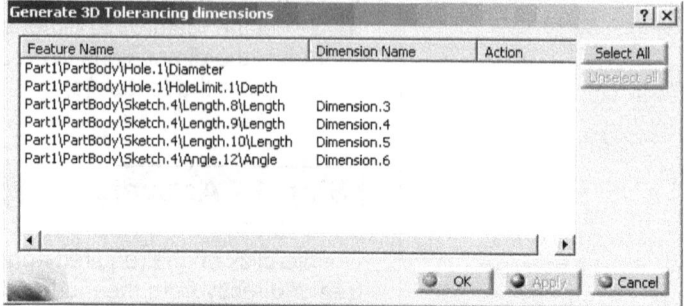

Figure 4–33

The dimensions also display on the model.

Step 4 - Select the dimensions to create.

Not all of the dimensions listed need to be created. Select the dimensions you want to create in the list. The **Create** action displays in the Action column for that dimension, as shown in Figure 4–34.

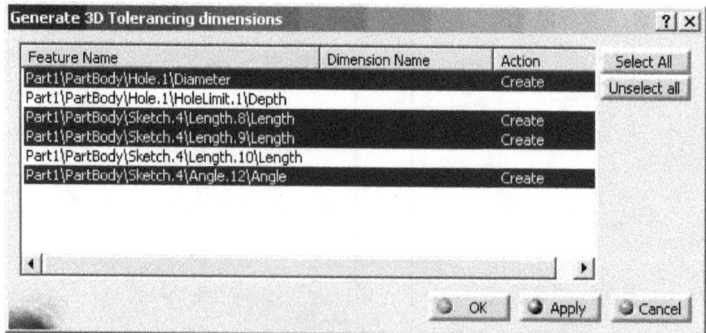

Figure 4–34

Selected dimensions are highlighted in the model. Clear a dimension by selecting it again and the **Create** action is removed from the Action field.

If the dimension already exists on the model, **Delete** is shown in the Action column.

Step 5 - Complete the feature(s).

Once all of the required dimensions have been set with the appropriate action, click **Apply** to preview the created dimensions on the model. Click **Cancel** to return to the model's previous state or **OK** to accept the new dimensions.

The dimensions are created under the Dimensions node in the specification tree.

Semantic Dimensions

If non-semantic annotations are correctly defined, they can conform to the rules of the tolerancing standard that has been defined; however, they are not required to do so.

For example, a tolerance sketched dimension displays with a semantic representation if it is annotated using the Generative Dimension tool. Alternatively, you can create a dimension using the Tolerance Advisor dialog box and then modify it (using the Dimension Properties toolbar) so that it does not conform to the applied standard.

The best method of ensuring that your annotations meet the tolerancing standard is to know the parameters of the standard and to check your annotations to ensure that they conform.

4.9 Reporting Diagnostics

Annotation failures are typically due to a lost reference. If an annotation does fail, you can view a diagnostic report and obtain information to help solve the failure.

The example in Figure 4–35 shows a part that has a text annotation attached to a hole feature. The annotation indicates that this hole feature is used as an indexing reference with a mating part.

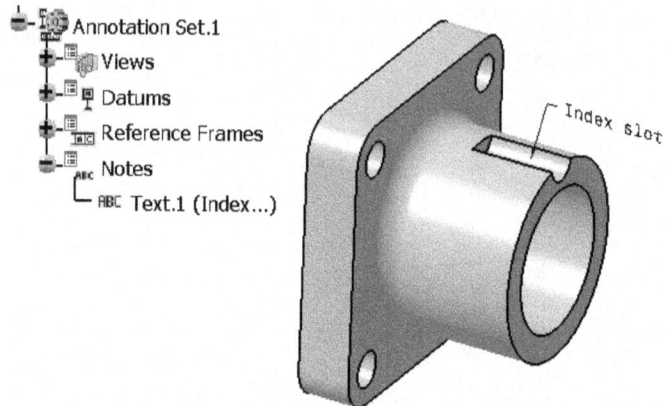

Figure 4–35

If the hole that the annotation references is deleted, the text listed in the specification tree changes by displaying a yellow exclamation mark, as shown in Figure 4–36.

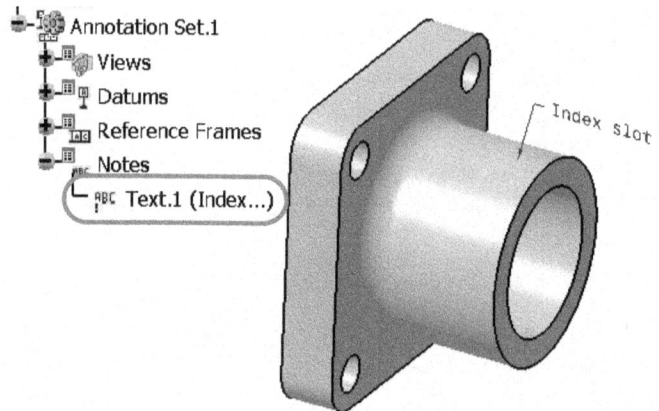

Figure 4–36

You can view the diagnostic report by right-clicking on the failed text in the specification tree and selecting **Diagnostic Report**, as shown in Figure 4–37.

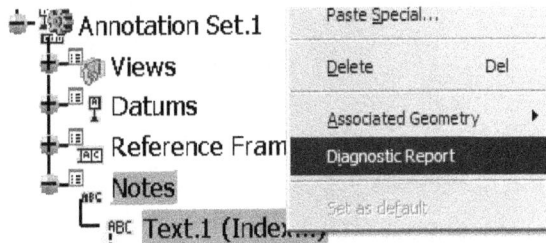

Figure 4–37

In this case, the 3D annotation diagnostics report description reports that a feature has been deleted, as shown in Figure 4–38.

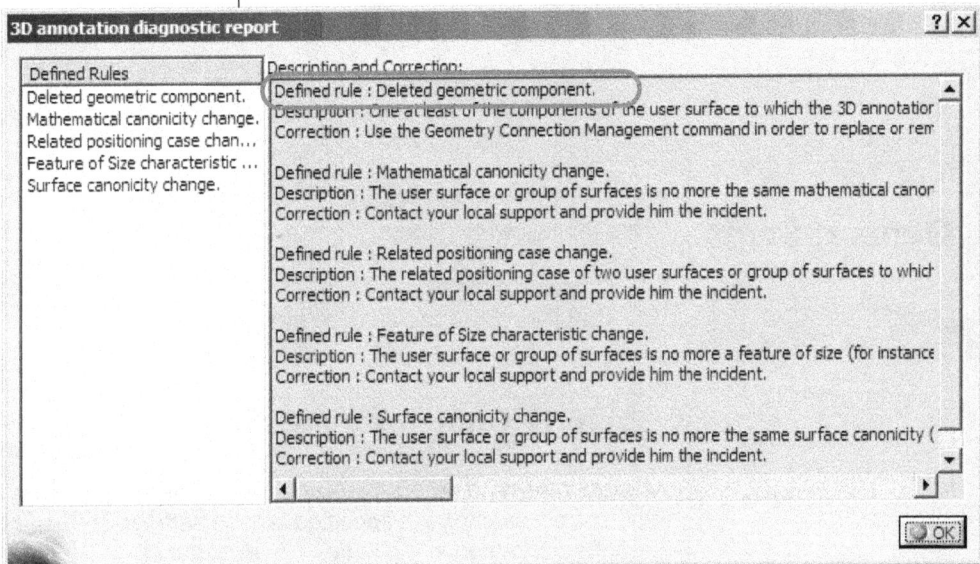

Figure 4–38

The 3D annotation diagnostic report is informational only. No actual changes can be made through this dialog box.

4.10 Reporting

The reporting tool in the FT&A workbench enables you to review the non-semantic tolerances that have been created in the model and to verify that they meet specific tolerancing rules. Since non-semantic tolerances do not need to obey any tolerancing standards, this is a good method of ensuring that mistakes have not been made during the annotation of the model.

The Reporting toolbar consists of two tools, as shown in Figure 4-39.

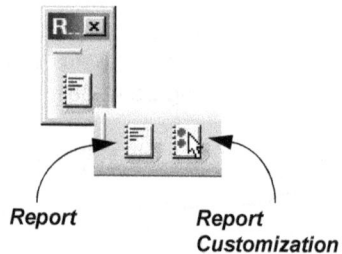

Figure 4-39

General Steps

Use the following general steps to perform a report:

1. Customize the report.
2. Run the report and analyze the results.

Step 1 - Customize the report.

Before running a report, you should customize it to ensure that the correct settings are specified. These settings are used for all reports performed in the active CATIA session.

Click ▨ (Report Customization) in the flyout of the Reporting toolbar. The Tolerancing rule's base Settings dialog box opens, as shown in Figure 4-40.

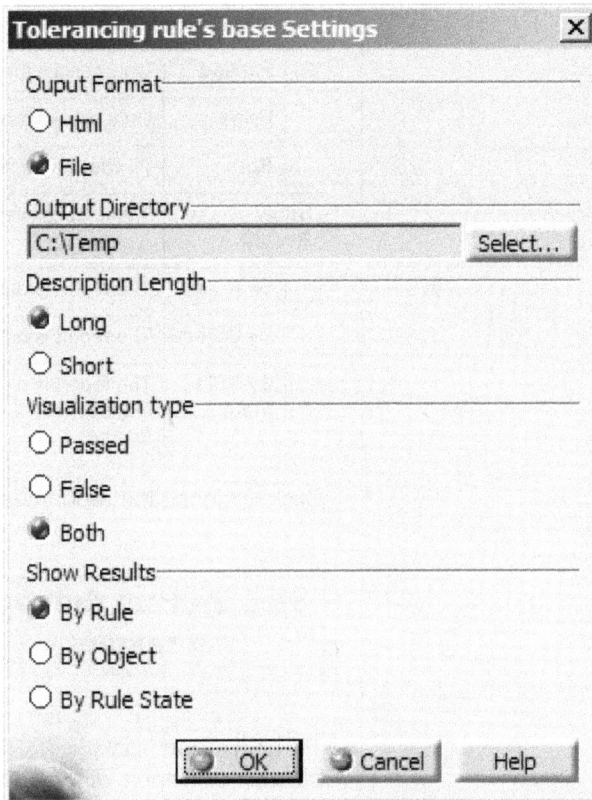

Figure 4–40

The following describes the options in the Tolerancing rule's base Settings dialog box.

Option	Description
Output Format	
Html	The report is generated in an Html format and automatically opened in a web browser.
File	The report is generated in a text format and automatically opened in a Report dialog box.
Output Directory	This field defines the folder in which the report files are stored.
Description Length	
Long	A descriptive help message is added for each check in the report.
Short	Only the check name is reported.

Visualization type

Passed	Only checks that were successful are reported.
False	Only checks that were unsuccessful are reported.
Both	All checks are reported.
Show Results	These options are only available for a file report.
	By Rule	The report is organized by the type of check.
	By Object	The report is organized by annotation feature.
	By Rule State	The report is organized by unsuccessful annotation features, and then followed by successful annotation features.

Click **OK** once the report customization has been completed.

Step 2 - Run the report and analyze the results.

To run a report, click ▤ (Report). Report opens in either a web browser or Report window, depending on the settings made. A sample report displays, as shown in Figure 4–41.

Current Document Name
C:\Functional Tolerancing and Annotation Exercise Files\BarStand.CATPart   1/23/2014

List of Expert Check :

Validity	Hierarchy	Check Name	Percent of Success	Help	Correct Function
✔		datum label unicity	100%	A datum label shall be unique in the tolerancing set	Edit the datum label and replace it with a non-already used label
✗		datum label capital letter	0%	A datum label shall only contain capital letter(s) (upper case)	Edit and Replace the datum-label small letter(s) with the corresponding capital letter(s)
✔		authorized or proposed datum label letter	100%	A datum label should not contain the capital letters I, O or Q, according to ASME Y14.5M-1994 standard.	Edit and Replace the datum label
✔		datum label length	100%	A datum label shall not be composed with more than two letters (ASME standard)	Edit and check the datum label length

Figure 4–41

Read the Validity column to analyze the report. There are three possible values, described as follows:

Validity	Description
✔	The check has completely succeeded.
X	The check has failed. Look at the Percent of Success column to see what percentage of the possible annotation features have failed the check.
Blank	The check did not apply to the model being reported. The Percent of Success column reads "Not Pertinent".

Any check that has failed can be investigated by selecting on the check name. This opens a new browser window and displays the name of the failed annotation feature. For example, the report for the "datum label capital letter" link displays, as shown in Figure 4–42. This window indicates that Datum.1 has failed the check and must be resolved.

Current Document Name

C:\Functional Tolerancing and Annotation Exercise Files\BarStand.CATPart

1/23/2014

Validity	Hierarchy	Check Name	Percent of Success	Help	Correct Function
X		datum label capital letter	0%	A datum label shall only contain capital letter(s) (upper case)	Edit and Replace the datum-label small letter(s) with the corresponding capital letter (s)
			X	Datum.1	

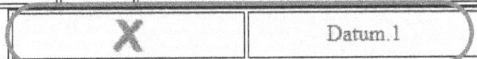

Figure 4–42

Practice 4a

Creating Text Annotations

Practice Objectives

- Add a text annotation.
- Add a coordinate dimension.

In this practice, you will complete the annotation of the LockingHub part model. This includes the creation of annotations to convey the standard titleblock information on the 3D part model. Upon completion of this practice, the model will display, as shown in Figure 4–43.

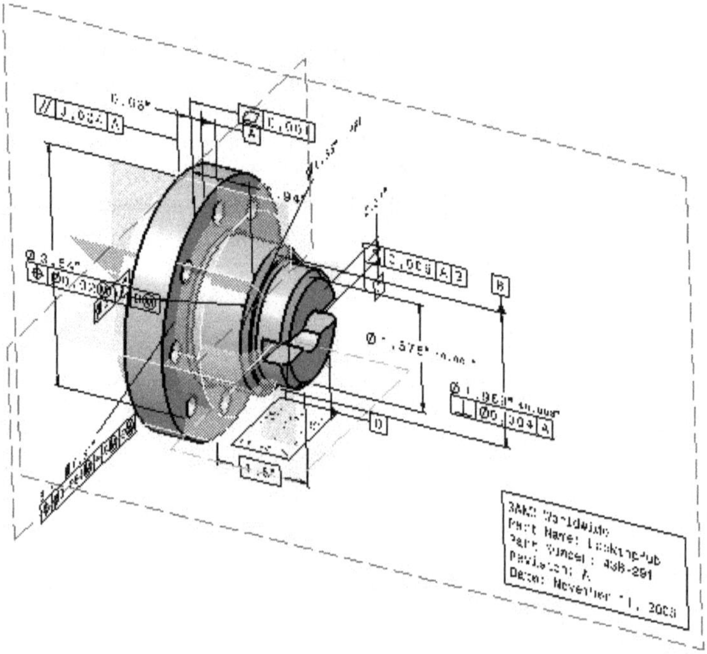

Figure 4–43

Task 1 - Open a part file.

1. Open **LockingHub_Ex3b.CATPart**. The model displays as shown in Figure 4–44.

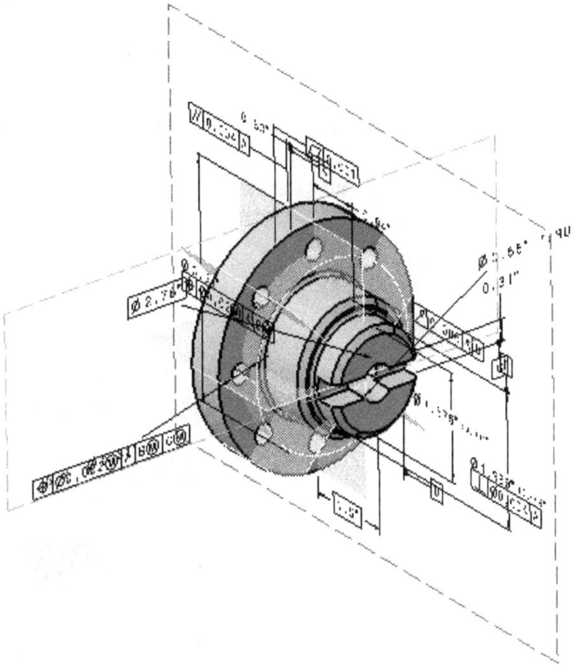

Figure 4–44

2. Activate **SideView**.

Task 2 - Add titleblock notes.

---

1. In the Text flyout of the Annotations toolbar, click [ABC] (Text).

2. Select a location at the bottom right corner of SideView, as shown in Figure 4–45.

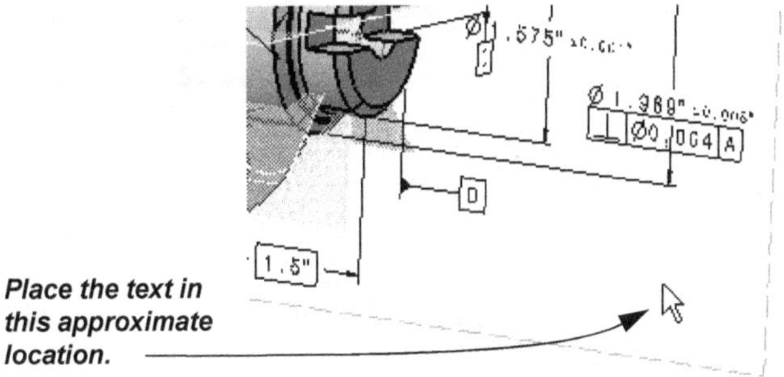

Place the text in this approximate location.

Figure 4–45

---

3. Enter the text shown in Figure 4–46 into the Text Editor dialog box. To add the second line of text, press <Shift> + <Enter>. Do not close the dialog box.

Press <Shift> + <Enter> to add a second line of text.

Figure 4–46

4. Right-click in the Text Editor dialog box and select **Attribute Link**, as shown in Figure 4–47.

Figure 4–47

5. Select **LockingHub** in the specification tree. The Attribute Link Panel dialog box opens.

6. Scroll to the bottom of the list of parameters and select the **LockingHub\PartNumber** parameter that has a value of "LockingHub", as shown in Figure 4–48.

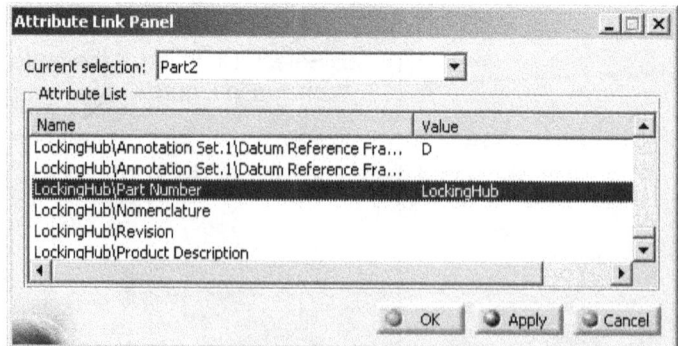

Figure 4–48

7. Click **OK**. The part number is added to the Text Editor dialog box.

Design Considerations

By using the **Attribute Link** option, you are creating associative text in the title block. If the **Part Number** parameter is changed, the text in this annotation updates with the modification.

8. Complete the Text Editor dialog box, as shown in Figure 4–49. **Note:** Do not use the **Attribute Link** option for the remaining three lines in the text.

Press <Shift> + <Enter> to add another line of text in the Text Editor.

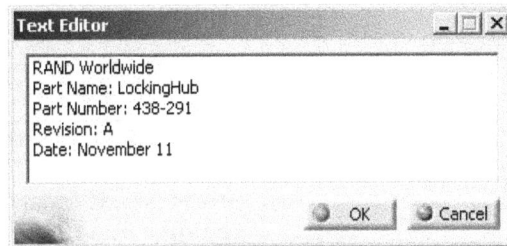

Text Editor

RAND Worldwide
Part Name: LockingHub
Part Number: 438-291
Revision: A
Date: November 11

OK   Cancel

Figure 4–49

9. Click **OK**. The model displays, as shown in Figure 4–50.

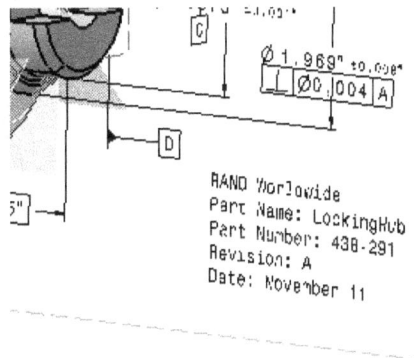

Ø1.969" ±0.008"
Ø0.004 A

RAND Worldwide
Part Name: LockingHub
Part Number: 438-291
Revision: A
Date: November 11

Figure 4–50

10. To add a frame to the title block information, verify that the text is highlighted. In the Frame flyout of the Text Properties toolbar, click ☐ Rectangle as shown in Figure 4–51.

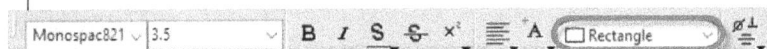

Monospac821 3.5   **B** *I* **S** S x² A ☐ Rectangle

Figure 4–51

The title block displays, as shown in Figure 4–52.

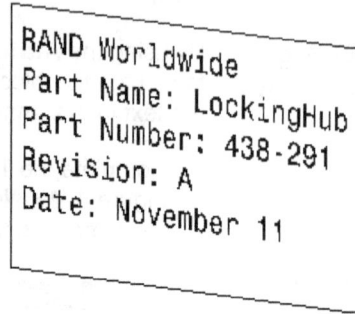

RAND Worldwide
Part Name: LockingHub
Part Number: 438-291
Revision: A
Date: November 11

Figure 4–52

Task 3 - Create a coordinate dimension.

1. Create an additional projection view annotation plane named **TopView** using the ZX plane.

2. In the Dimensions flyout of the Annotation toolbar, click

   (Coordinate Dimensions).

3. Select the vertex shown in Figure 4–53.

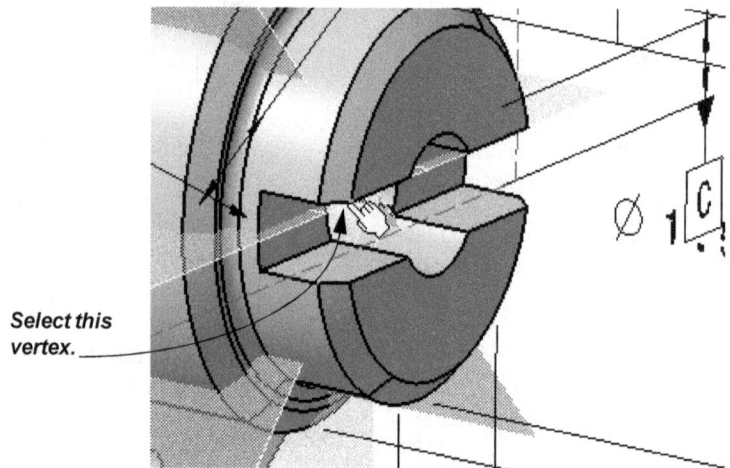

Select this vertex.

Figure 4–53

4. Position the annotation appropriately. The model displays as shown in Figure 4–54.

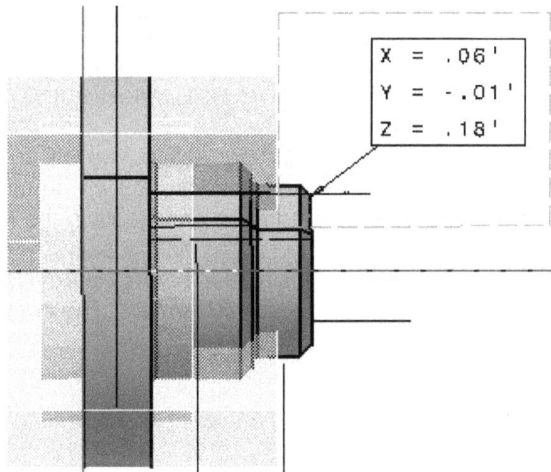

X = .06'
Y = -.01'
Z = .18'

Figure 4–54

5. Hide the three annotation views.

6. Save the model and close the window.

Practice 4b | Non-Semantic Annotations

Practice Objectives

- Add generative and stacked dimensions.
- Add a datum element and tolerance.

In this practice, you will practice creating non-semantic annotations. You will create the annotations using the non-semantic tools in the Annotations toolbar for demonstration purposes only. Ideally, these annotations would be developed using the Tolerance Advisor to ensure that they conform to the applied standard. The completed model displays, as shown in Figure 4–55.

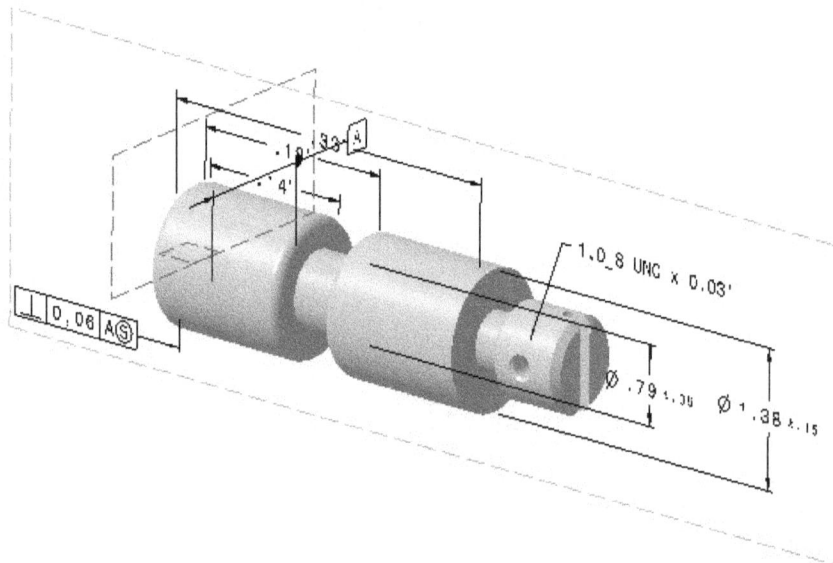

Figure 4–55

Task 1 - Open a part file.

1. Open **StandOff.CATPart**. The model displays as shown in Figure 4–56.

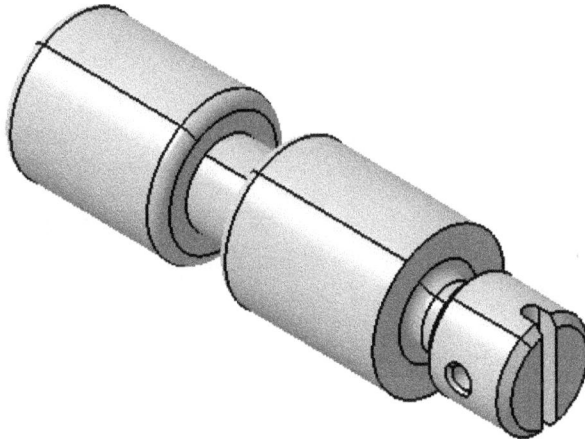

Figure 4–56

2. Toggle on **Annotation Set.1**.

3. Expand the **Annotation Set.1** branch of the specification tree and review the three views that have been established, as shown in Figure 4–57.

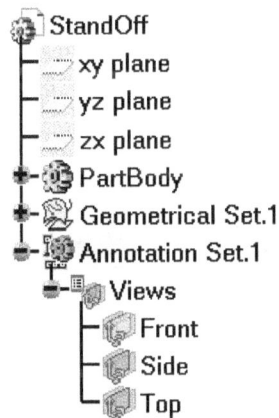

Figure 4–57

4. Activate the view named **Side**.

Task 2 - Add generative dimensions.

In this task, you will use the Generative Dimensions tool to display model dimensions. You will select a feature from the model and the dimensions for this feature can be selected for display as an annotated dimension.

1. In the Annotations toolbar, click ⬚ (Generative Dimension). The Generate 3D Tolerancing Dimensions dialog box opens, as shown in Figure 4–58.

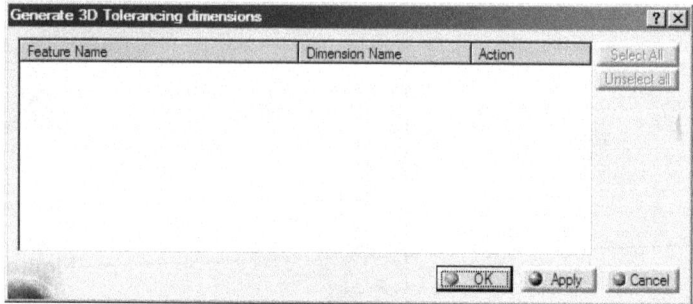

Figure 4–58

2. Expand PartBody and select **Shaft.1** in the specification tree. The dimensions for the shaft feature display on the model. These dimensions are also listed in the Generate 3D Tolerancing Dimensions dialog box, as shown in Figure 4–59.

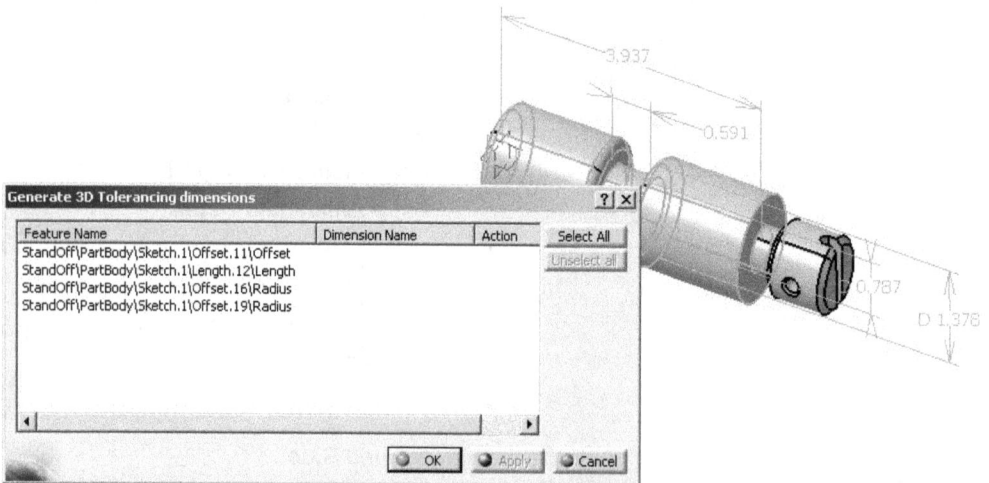

Figure 4–59

3. Select the **0.787in** and **1.378in** diameter dimensions from the model. These dimensions are highlighted in the dialog box and their Action value is set to "Create", as shown in Figure 4–60.

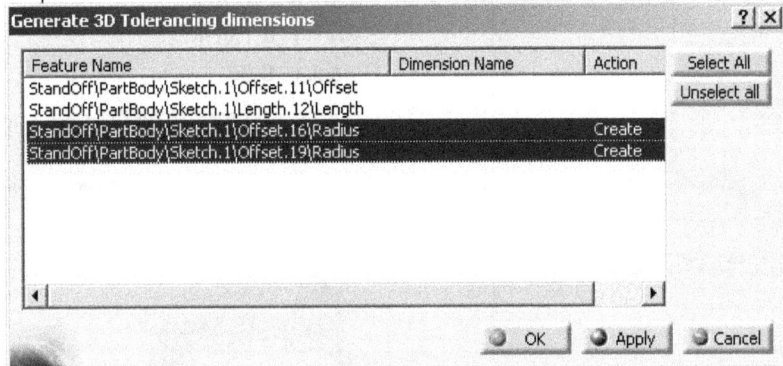

Generate 3D Tolerancing dimensions			? x
Feature Name	Dimension Name	Action	Select All
StandOff\PartBody\Sketch.1\Offset.11\Offset			Unselect all
StandOff\PartBody\Sketch.1\Length.12\Length			
StandOff\PartBody\Sketch.1\Offset.16\Radius		Create	
StandOff\PartBody\Sketch.1\Offset.19\Radius		Create	

OK   Apply   Cancel

Figure 4–60

4. Click **OK** to complete the operation. The system automatically generates annotations for the selected dimensions, as shown in Figure 4–61.

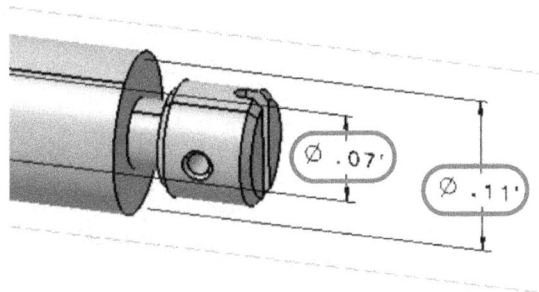

Figure 4–61

Task 3 - Add tolerances to the dimensions.

By default, the dimensions are created with a general tolerance. In this task, you will add specific tolerances to the generated dimensions created in the previous task.

1. Verify that the Dimension Properties and Numerical Properties toolbars display. To display the toolbar, select **View>Toolbars>Dimension Properties** and **Numerical Properties**.

2. Select the **.07ft** diameter dimension.

3. Make the following selections in the Dimension Properties toolbar:

   - Select **NUM.DINC**.
   - Select **TOL_NUM2**.
   - Select **+- 0.05**.

   The toolbar and model display, as shown in Figure 4–62.

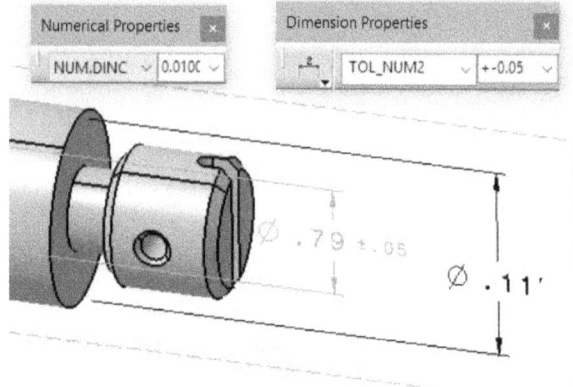

Figure 4–62

4. Repeat this process to add a +/- 0.15 tolerance to the 1.38in diameter dimension. The model displays, as shown in Figure 4–63.

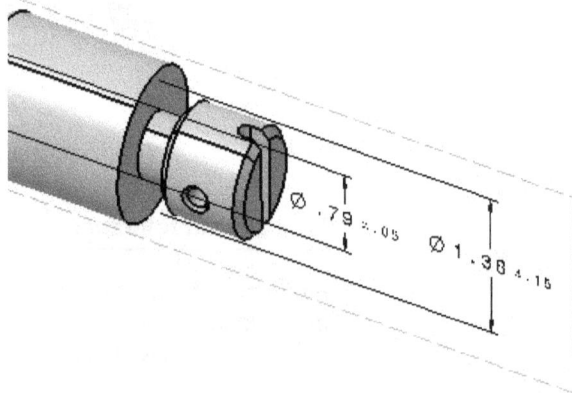

Figure 4–63

Task 4 - Create stacked dimensions.

1. In the Dimensions flyout of the Annotations toolbar, click

    ⬚ (Stacked Dimensions).

2. Select the two faces of the model, as shown in Figure 4–64.
    The system adds a distance dimension between these faces.

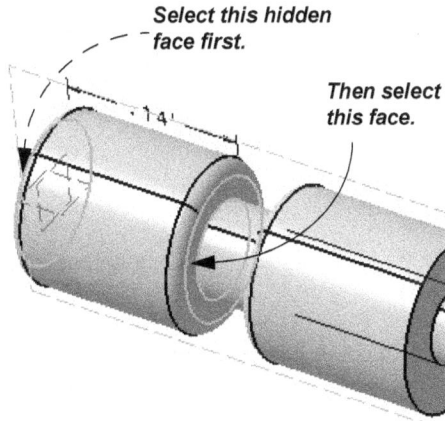

*Select this hidden
face first.*

*Then select
this face.*

Figure 4–64

3. Select the face shown in Figure 4–65. The system adds a
    dimension between this reference and the first face selected.

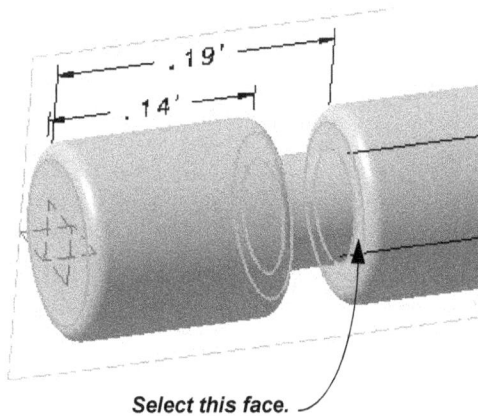

Select this face.

Figure 4–65

4. Select the face shown in Figure 4–66.

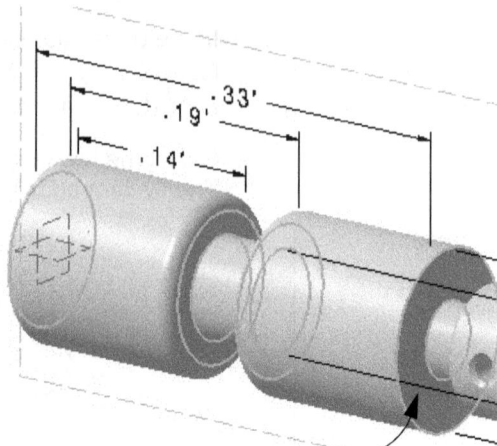

Select this face. —

Figure 4–66

5. Select anywhere on the background to complete the dimension creation. The model displays as shown in Figure 4–67.

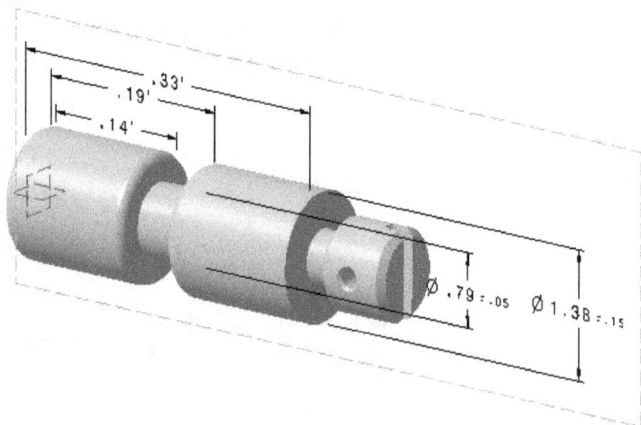

Figure 4–67

Task 5 - Add text with a leader.

1. In the Annotations toolbar, click ![ABC] (Text with Leader).

2. Select the cylindrical face highlighted in Figure 4–68. The Text Editor dialog box opens.

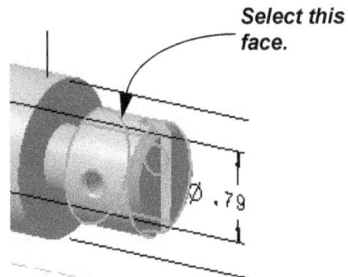

Select this face.

Figure 4–68

3. Enter **1.0_8 UNC x 0.03'** in the Text Editor dialog box and click **OK**. The model displays as shown in Figure 4–69.

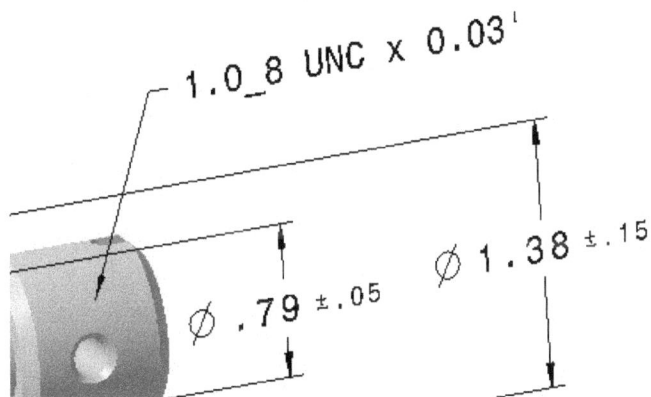

Figure 4–69

Task 6 - Create a datum and tolerance.

1. Activate the view named Front.

2. In the Annotations toolbar, click ![A] (Datum Element).

3. Select the cylindrical face highlighted in Figure 4–70. The Datum Feature Creation dialog box opens.

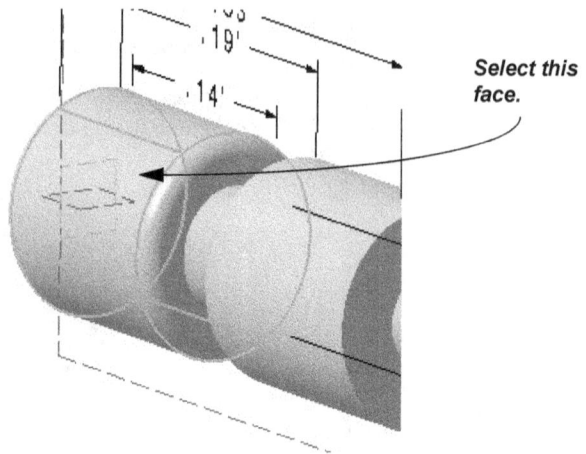

Select this face.

Figure 4–70

4. Accept the default name of **A** and click **OK**. The model displays as shown in Figure 4–71.

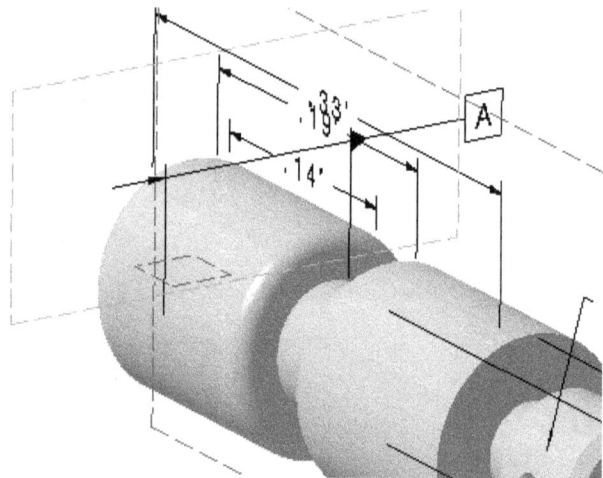

Figure 4–71

5. Activate the view named Side.

6. In the Annotations toolbar, click (Geometrical Tolerance).

7. Select the face, as shown in Figure 4–72.

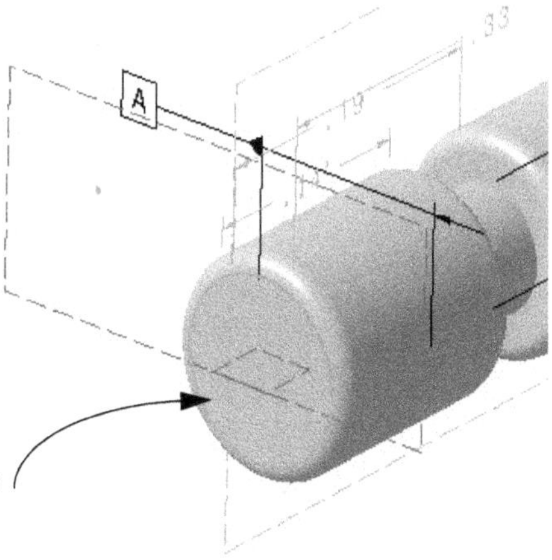

Select this
face.

Figure 4–72

The Geometrical Tolerance dialog box opens, as shown in
Figure 4–73.

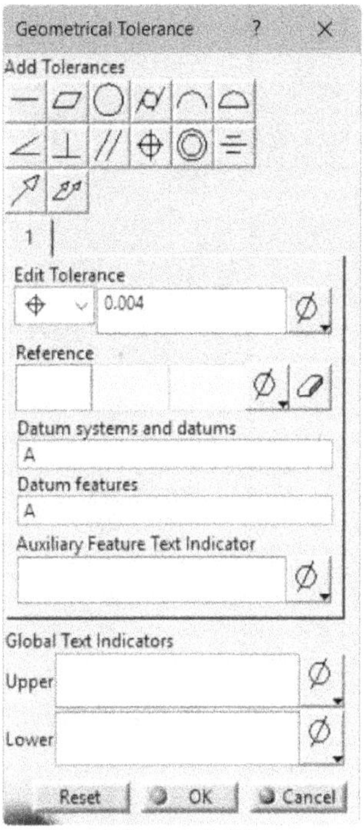

Figure 4–73

8. Make the following selections in the Geometrical Tolerance
    dialog box:

- Select **Perpendicularity** in the Tolerance flyout.
- Enter **0.06** in the *Tolerance* field.
- Enter **A** in the first *Reference* field.

- ⓢ : click this in the Insert Symbol flyout with the cursor in the *Reference* field.

The Geometrical Tolerance dialog box displays, as shown in Figure 4–74.

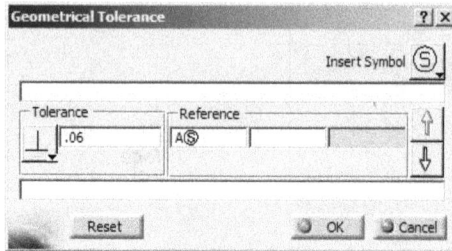

Figure 4–74

9. Click **OK**.

10. Right-click the yellow diamond at the end of the leader and click **Extremity Link> Perpendicular**.

The model displays as shown in Figure 4–75.

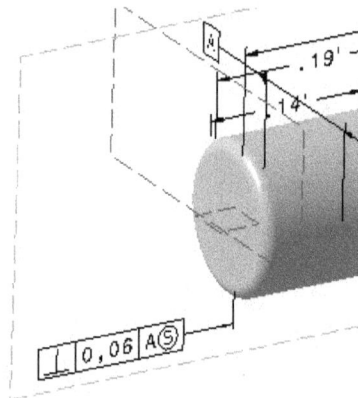

Figure 4–75

11. Save the model and close the window.

Practice 4c | Reporting

Practice Objectives

- Customize a report.
- Run an annotation report.
- Analyze an annotation report.

In this practice, you will analyze a model that contains a number of incorrect non-semantic annotations. You will use the reporting tool to investigate the annotations, identify those that are incorrect, and take corrective action.

Task 1 - Open the part model.

1. Open **BarStand.CATPart**. The model displays, as shown in Figure 4–76.

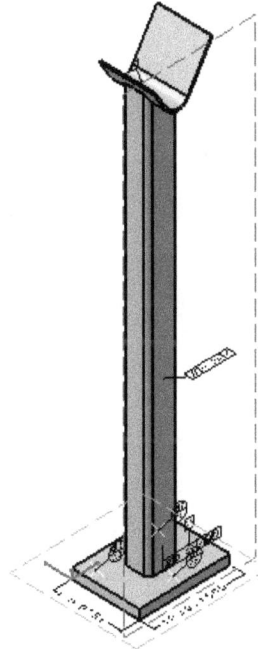

Figure 4–76

2. Expand the annotation set and investigate the different annotations that have been created. All annotations were developed using non-semantic operations.

Task 2 - Customize the report.

Before you run a report for the first time, you should customize it to ensure that its settings are correct. You will customize the report to generate an Html file and only display failed checks.

1. In the flyout of the Reporting toolbar, click (Report Customization). The Tolerancing rule's base Settings dialog box opens, as shown in Figure 4–77.

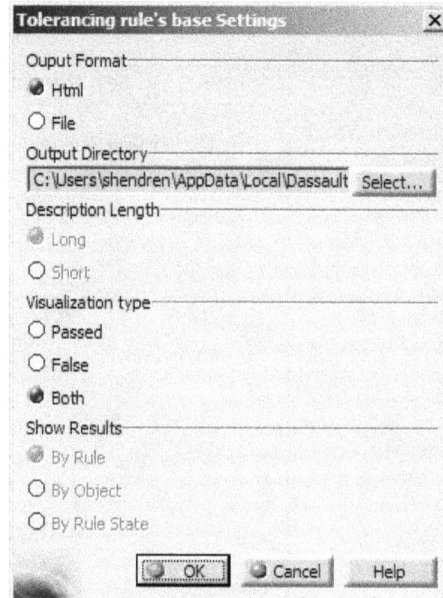

Figure 4–77

2. Make the following selections:

   - *Output Format:* **Html**
   - *Visualization type:* **False**

3. Click **OK**.

Task 3 - Run the report.

1. In the Reporting toolbar, click ⬚ (Report). The system runs the annotation report and opens it in a web browser, as shown in Figure 4–78.

Current Document Name
C:\Functional Tolerancing and Annotation Exercise Files\BarStand.CATPart   1/21/2014

List of Expert Check :

Validity	Hierarchy	Check Name	Percent of Success	Help	Correct Function
X		datum label capital letter	0%	A datum label shall only contain capital letter(s) (upper case)	Edit and Replace the datum-label small letter(s) with the corresponding capital letter(s)
X		sequential datum target numbers	0%	The numbers identifying datum targets shall be sequential and begin with 1	Check the datum target label sequence beginning with 1
X		Modifiers on Toleranced Element	0%	- For any form specification, the Free State Symbol may be applied and specified alone. - For any Form specification, such as linear profile, planar and position specifications, the Maximum/Least Material Condition (M/LMC) may be applied and specified alone. - For any Orientation, Location and Runout specification, several modifiers are allowed on the tolerance zone with following restrictions: * first, MMC or LMC or S (ASME standard only) conditions * second, the free state symbol, if necessary * third, the projected tolerance zone symbol, if necessary * fourth, the statistical tolerancing symbol, if necessary - Only MMC or LMC or S (ASME standard only) conditions shall be specified on datum elements	Edit the GDT and adjust the modifier (s) specification
X		coherence of datums specified in the GDT and datum unicity	0%	- A datum specified in a reference frame//GDT shall be defined in the annotation set. - A datum shall not be specified several times in a the same reference frame//GDT	Edit the annotation to specify an existing datum and//or create the lacking datum

Figure 4–78

2. The report lists four failed checks. Select the link for the name of the first failed check. The system opens the check in a new window and indicates that the check in error is **Datum.1**. The corrective action is described in the last column. You must ensure that **Datum.1** uses only capital letters in its name to resolve the failure.

3. Return to the report to investigate the other failures and identify the associated annotation features. The errors are summarized as follows.

Failed Check	Associated Annotation(s)	Corrective Action
Datum Label Capital Letter	Datum.1	Rename the datum from "b" to "A".
Sequential Datum Target Numbers	Datum Target.1 Datum Target.2 Datum Target.3	Rename the datum targets as follows: • Datum Target.1 = B1 • Datum Target.2 = B2 • Datum Target.3 = B3
Modifiers on Toleranced Element	Geometric Tolerance.1	The Free State symbol must precede the Regardless of Feature Size symbol
Coherence of Datums Specified in the GDT and Datum Unicity	Geometric Tolerance.1 Geometric Tolerance.2	Geometric Tolerance.1 should reference Datum B. Datum B has been misnamed AA. Geometric Tolerance.2 references Datum K. This should be changed to Datum A.

4. Close all report windows and return to CATIA.

Task 4 - Resolve the failed checks.

In this task, you will perform the corrective actions detailed in the annotation report.

1. Double-click on **Datum.1** in the specification tree and rename the datum from **b** to **A**.

2. Double-click on **Simple Datum.1** and rename it from **AA** to **B**

3. With the Datum Feature dialog box open, select **A2** in the list of datum targets and then click **Edit**.

4. Select **Automatic naming** and click **OK**.

5. Repeat this operation to automatically rename the two remaining datum targets.

6. Click **OK** to close the Datum Feature dialog box. The model displays as shown in Figure 4–79.

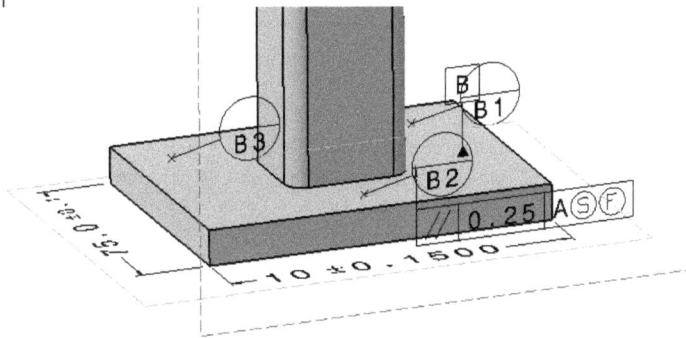

Figure 4–79

7. Double-click on **Geometrical Tolerance.1** in the specification tree.

8. Delete the contents of the Reference field and then select datum **B**, followed by the ⒡ (Free State) symbol, and the Ⓢ (Regardless of Feature Size) symbol.

9. Complete the operation. The model displays, as shown in Figure 4–80.

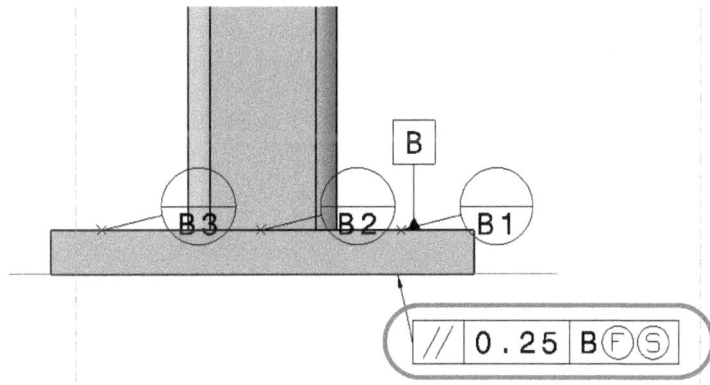

Figure 4–80

10. As the last step, modify **Geometrical Tolerance.2** and change the datum reference frame from K to **A**.

11. Even after performing the corrective actions, if a Report is run again, an error returns. Save the model and close the window.

Annotation Management

This chapter introduces the tools and operations that enable you to manage your annotations.

Learning Objectives in this Chapter

- Create Leader Symbols.
- Learn how to mirror, transfer, and group annotations.
- Understand how to apply annotation filters.
- Learn how to use cameras and captures.
- Learn how to use geometry connection management.

5.1 Leader Symbols

Depending on the leader type and feature being referenced, a particular leader symbol might be required by your company standards, as shown in Figure 5–1.

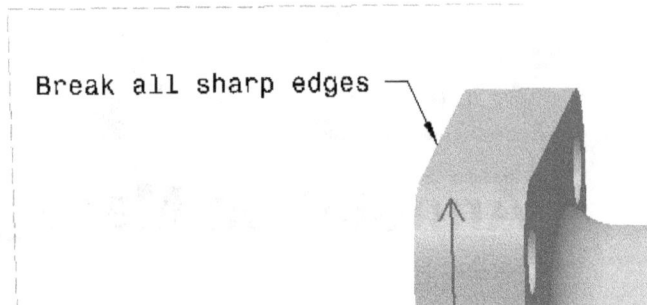

Break all sharp edges

Figure 5–1

General Steps

Use the following general steps to change leader symbols:

1. Select the annotation.
2. Select the end manipulator.
3. Select the symbol.

Step 1 - Select the annotation.

Select the annotation for which you want to change the leader symbol. The handles for the test display and the end manipulator turns yellow, as shown in Figure 5–2.

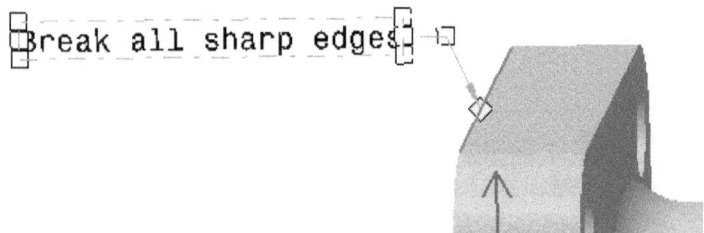

Break all sharp edges

Figure 5–2

Step 2 - Select the end manipulator.

Right-click and select **Symbol Shape**, as shown in Figure 5–3.

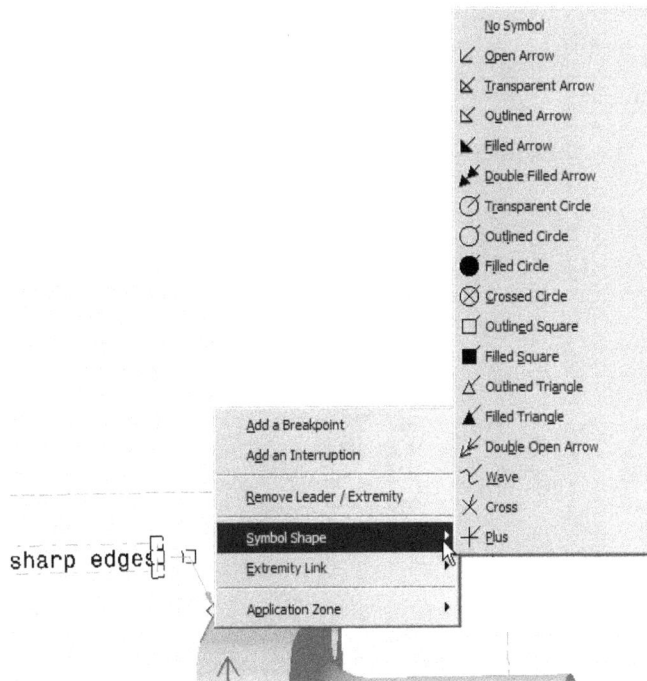

Figure 5–3

Step 3 - Select the symbol.

Select the required symbol shape to complete the change, as shown in Figure 5–4.

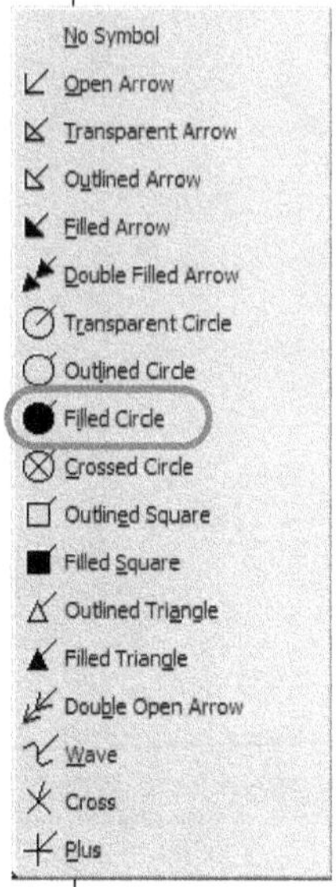

No Symbol
↙ Open Arrow
↘ Transparent Arrow
↖ Outlined Arrow
◤ Filled Arrow
➤ Double Filled Arrow
⊘ Transparent Circle
◯ Outlined Circle
● Filled Circle
⊗ Crossed Circle
☐ Outlined Square
■ Filled Square
△ Outlined Triangle
▲ Filled Triangle
↙ Double Open Arrow
⌇ Wave
✕ Cross
╀ Plus

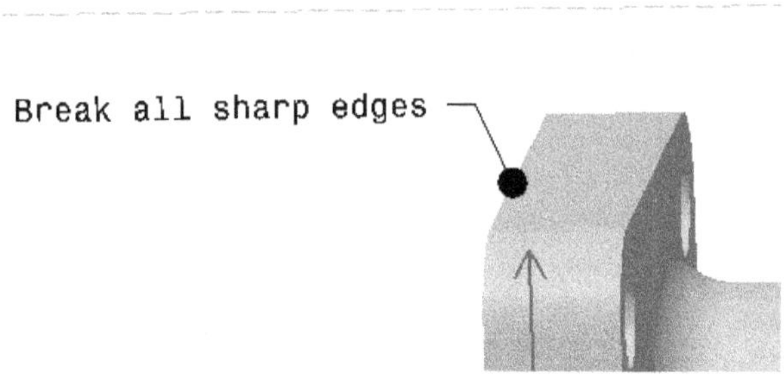

Break all sharp edges

Figure 5–4

5.2 Mirror Annotations

As the model is oriented, the annotations remain fixed and the direction of the text might not display as required. For example, the model shown in Figure 5–5 has been oriented so that the annotated text reads backwards.

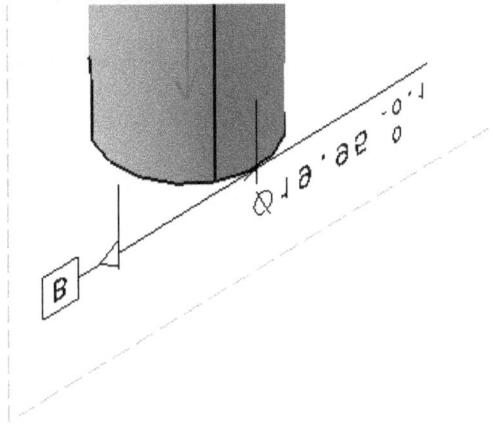

Figure 5–5

At any time, you can flip text using ![icon] (Mirror Annotations) in the Visualization toolbar. All reversed annotations are mirrored, as shown in Figure 5–6.

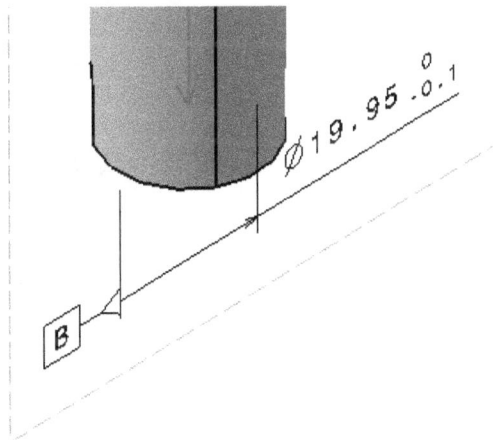

Figure 5–6

5.3 Transferring Annotations

Each annotation is placed in a particular view to better organize and display the information. This view can easily be changed to improve the organization of the model.

General Steps

Use the following general steps to transfer annotations:

1. Select the annotation to be transferred.
2. Transfer the annotation.
3. Select the destination view.

Step 1 - Select the annotation to be transferred.

Select the parent annotation. In this case, the geometric tolerance frame follows the selected semantic diameter dimension, as shown in Figure 5–7.

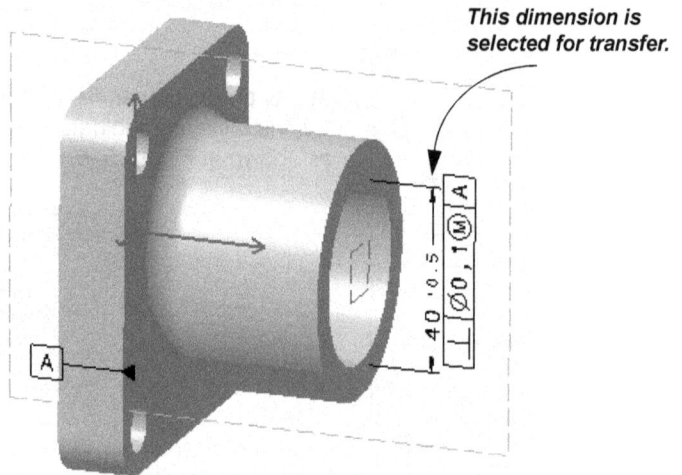

This dimension is selected for transfer.

Figure 5–7

Step 2 - Transfer the annotation.

Right-click and select **Transfer to View/Annotation Plane**, as shown in Figure 5–8.

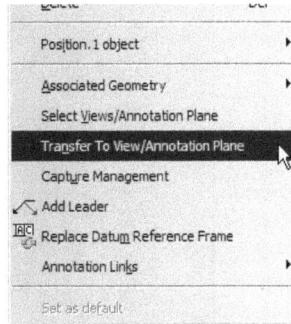

Figure 5–8

Step 3 - Select the destination view.

Select the destination view. The annotation is transferred, as shown in Figure 5–9.

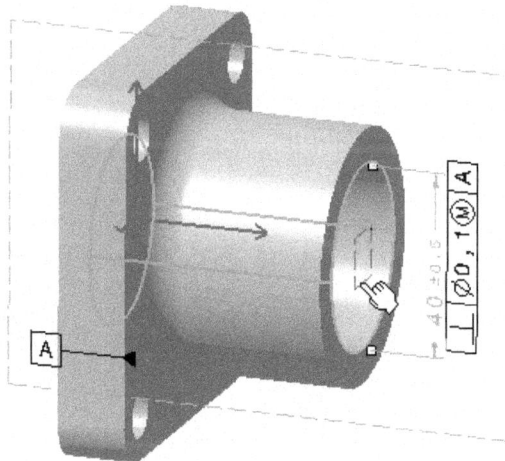

Figure 5–9

The annotation plane must exist before performing the transfer operation, as shown in Figure 5–10.

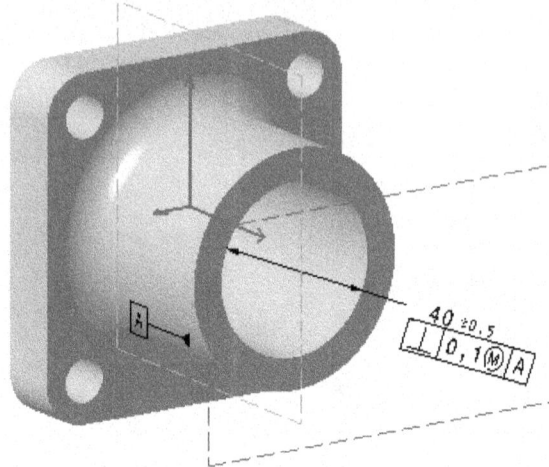

Figure 5–10

5.4 Grouping Annotations

One element of a model can have many different annotations. It might have a text note, a surface condition, and a geometrical tolerance. To simplify the display of information, these elements can be grouped together.

A new annotation can be grouped with an existing annotation by preselecting the existing annotation during the creation of the new annotation. This section focuses on the manual grouping of existing annotations.

General Steps

Use the following general steps to group annotations:

1. Start the grouping operation.
2. Select the annotations to group.
3. Specify the positioning options.
4. Group additional annotations, if required.
5. Complete the grouping.

Step 1 - Start the grouping operation.

In the Grouping toolbar, click [icon] (Manual Grouping). CATIA prompts you to select annotations. In this example, the annotations shown in Figure 5–11 are grouped.

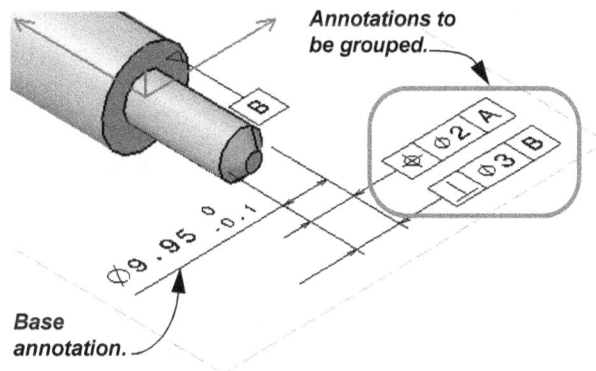

Figure 5–11

Step 2 - Select the annotations to group.

Multiple annotations can be grouped in one operation. The system always groups the selected annotation with the previously selected annotation. For example, if annotations are selected in the order shown in Figure 5–12, the following groups are formed:

- Group 1: toleranced dimension and position geometrical tolerance

- Group 2: position and perpendicular geometrical tolerances

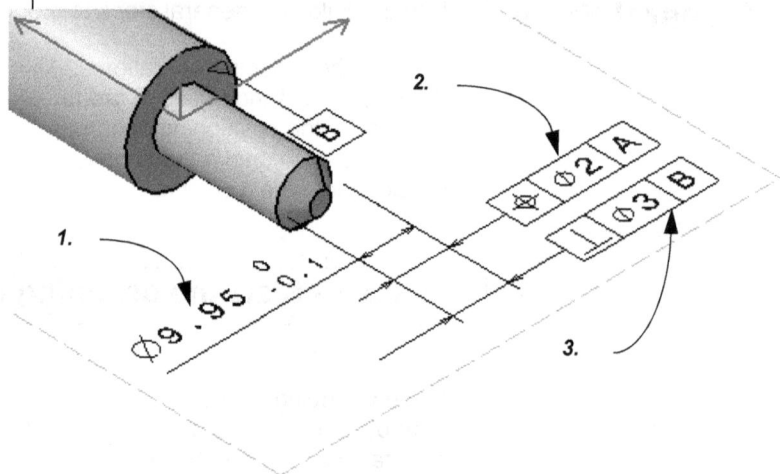

Figure 5–12

As a result, all three annotations move if the toleranced dimension is moved. Likewise, the perpendicular tolerance moves if the position tolerance is moved.

When you need to group more than one annotation, you must define the positioning options for each annotation before continuing to the next one. Start by selecting the base annotation, and then the first annotation to group. The system groups the annotations in a default position after you finish selecting them, and the Positioning dialog box opens, as shown in Figure 5–13.

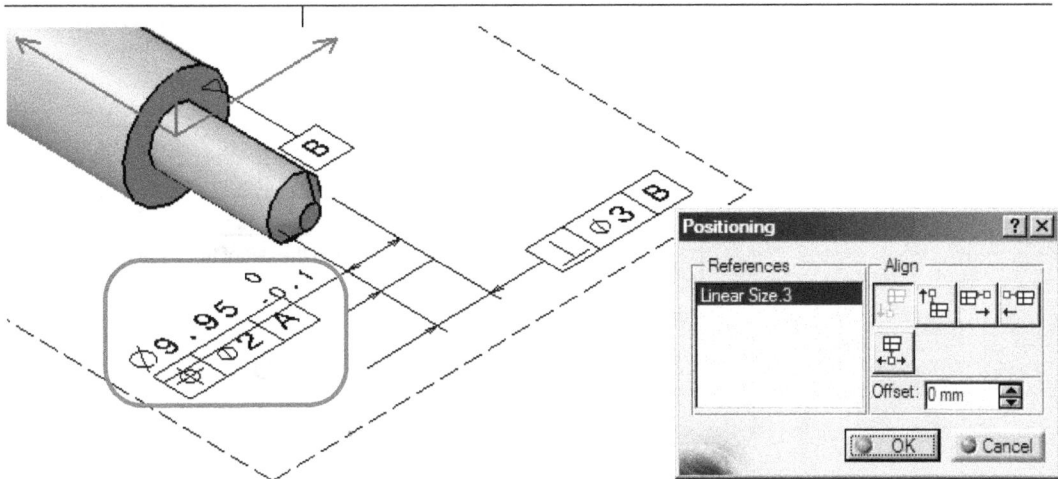

Figure 5–13

Step 3 - Specify the positioning options.

Use the Positioning dialog box to specify the alignment and offset parameters for the active annotation. The options are described as follows:

Option	Description
Align	
Align Bottom	Position the annotation beneath the base annotation, as shown below.
Align Top	Position the annotation above the base annotation, as shown below.

Align Right	Position the annotation to the right of the base annotation, as shown below. $\varnothing 9.95 \begin{smallmatrix} 0 \\ -0.1 \end{smallmatrix}$ ⊕ Φ2 A
Align Left	Position the annotation to the left of the base annotation, as shown below. ⊕ Φ2 A $\varnothing 9.95 \begin{smallmatrix} 0 \\ -0.1 \end{smallmatrix}$
Center Horizontally	Position the left side of the annotation at the center of the base annotation. This option can be used in conjunction with the other four alignment options. A bottom-center alignment is shown below. $\varnothing 9.95 \begin{smallmatrix} 0 \\ -0.1 \end{smallmatrix}$ ⊕ Φ2 A
Offset	Move the annotation by the specified distance in the alignment direction. A bottom alignment that is offset by 4mm is shown below. Since a bottom alignment is used, the annotation is offset downwards. $\varnothing 9.95 \begin{smallmatrix} 0 \\ -0.1 \end{smallmatrix}$ ⊕ Φ2 A

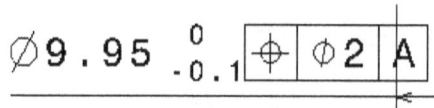

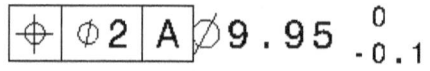

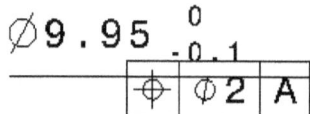

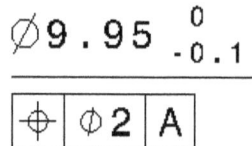

Once the positioning options have been specified, you can group additional annotations to the base annotation.

Step 4 - Group additional annotations, if required.

To group further annotations to the base annotation, select them in the model. The annotation is added to the References list and the **Alignment** and **Offset** options now apply to the last annotation selected.

In the example shown in Figure 5–14, the position tolerance is grouped to the toleranced dimension using a bottom alignment and offset of 4mm. The perpendicular tolerance is grouped using a bottom alignment and 0mm offset.

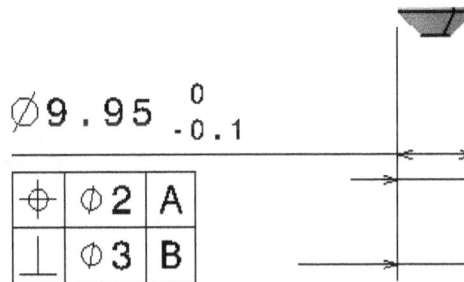

Figure 5–14

Step 5 - Complete the grouping.

Click **OK** to complete the grouping operation.

Once the annotations are successfully grouped, you might have to delete any detached leaders that were left behind when an annotation was grouped. This can be done by selecting the leader lines and pressing <Delete>.

5.5 Annotation Filters

When viewing a detailed part with many annotations, it can be helpful to use a filter to clear up the display. This enables you to hide unwanted annotations and only display those annotations that are applicable to the current model view or application.

General Steps

Use the following general steps to filter annotations:

1. Start the filter operation.
2. Define the Filter options.
3. Apply the filter.

Step 1 - Start the filter operation.

In the Visualization toolbar, click ⊞→ (Filter). The Filter dialog box opens, as shown in Figure 5–15.

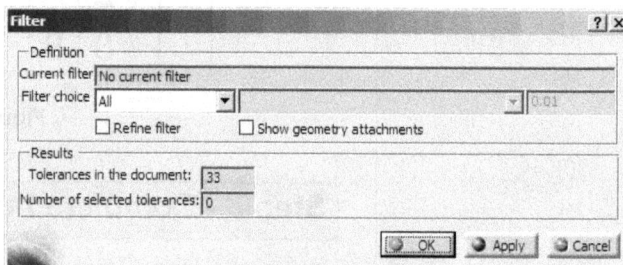

Figure 5–15

Step 2 - Define the Filter options.

The *Current filter* field lists the name of the filter if one has already been applied to the model, as shown in Figure 5–16.

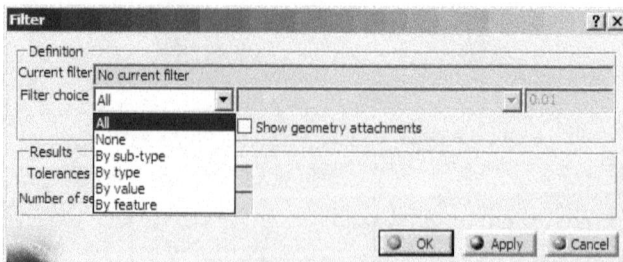

Figure 5–16

Specify the Filter options by selecting an option in the Filter choice drop-down list. The options are described as follows:

Filter Choice	Description
All	The system displays all annotations.
None	The system displays none of the annotations.
By sub-type	Enables you to select a specific sub-type of annotation to display. The list is limited to the sub-types of annotations that have been created in the model. Examples are: • Simple Datum • Linear Size • Perpendicularity
By type	Enables you to select a specific type of annotation to display. The list is limited to the types of annotations that have been created in the model. Examples are: • Datum • Size • Position Orientation and Runout
By value	Enables you to define the value of the tolerance that displays. Non-toleranced annotations are automatically hidden. To define this type of filter, select an operator in the drop-down list and enter a value. The following operators are available: • > greater than • < less than • = equal to • >= greater than or equal to • <= less than or equal to For example, the filter shown below only displays annotations that have a tolerance value greater than or equal to 2.

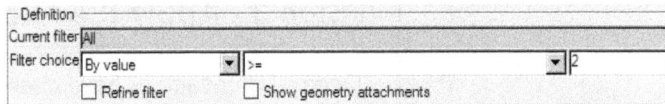

Definition
Current filter All
Filter choice By value   >=   2
☐ Refine filter   ☐ Show geometry attachments

By feature	Enables you to select the specific annotations that are shown in the specification tree. To select more than one annotation, press and hold <Ctrl>.
By capture	Displays the selected capture and any annotations associated with it.

Refine filter

The **Refine filter** option enables you to specify multiple conditions to a single filter. These conditions are applied using an AND operator. For example, you can display all annotations with positional geometrical tolerances that have a tolerance value greater than 2mm.

How To: Refine a Filter

1. Enter the first filter and click **Apply**. The filter is added to the *Current filter* field, as shown in Figure 5–17.

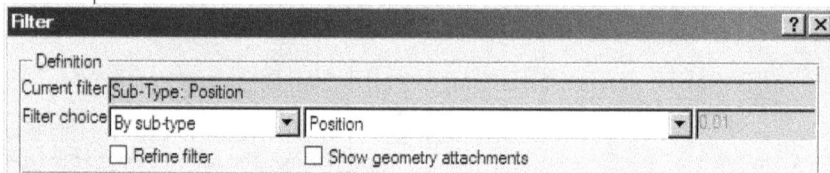

Figure 5–17

2. Select **Refine filter**.
3. Enter the next filter and click **Apply**. The system lists the new conditions in the *Current filter* field, as shown in Figure 5–18.

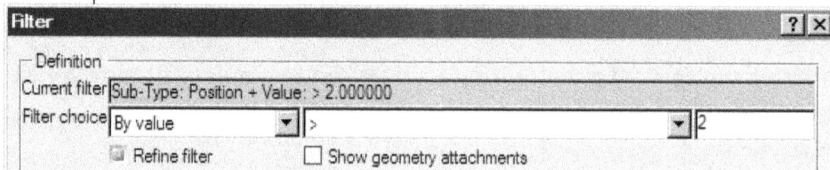

Figure 5–18

Show Geometry Attachments

The **Show geometry attachments** option enables you to show any annotations that have been grouped to the annotations displayed by a filter.

Step 3 - Apply the filter.

Once all filter settings have been made, click **OK** to complete the filter operation.

5.6 Cameras

Cameras show a particular viewpoint of the part. They are useful for revealing detail on complex parts by showing a unique view.

How To: Save a Camera View

1. Adjust the orientation and position of the model using the following methods:
   - Dynamically orienting the model using the mouse.
   - Applying an existing named view.
   - Clicking (Normal View) and then selecting a view.

2. Once the model has been oriented, in the Quick View flyout in the Views toolbar, click (Named Views). The Named Views dialog box opens, as shown in Figure 5–19.

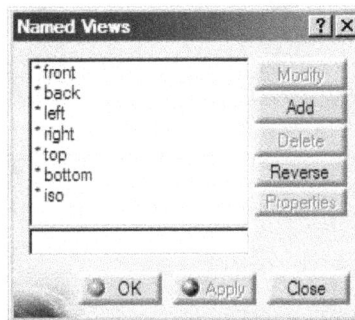

Figure 5–19

3. Click **Add** to add a new view. The view is named Camera1 by default and you can modify it by entering a new name and pressing <Enter>.

   Retrieve named views by accessing the Named Views dialog box, selecting a view, and clicking **Apply**.

5.7 Captures

Captures enable you to save different views of an annotated part. The following parameters can be customized for a capture:

- Annotation filters

- Cameras

- Clipping plane

- Mirror annotations

The captures are stored in the specification tree and can be displayed using the shortcut menu, as shown in Figure 5–20.

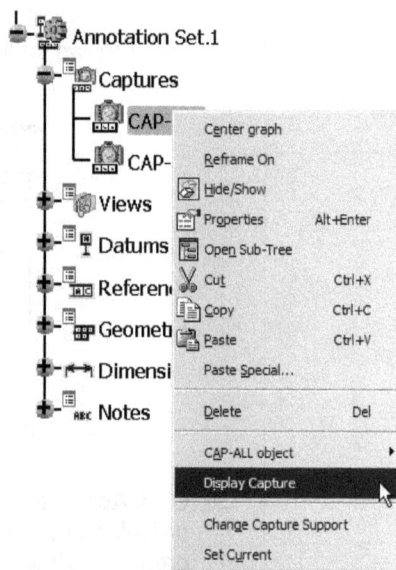

Figure 5–20

Prior to creating a capture, you must customize one or more of the following properties of the annotated model. You use these tools to specify the required display configurations for your capture.

- Annotation Filters

- Cameras

- Clipping Plane

- Mirror Annotations

- Active View State

- Current State

Annotation Filters

Click ⬚ (Filter) to filter out specific annotations from the display. You can apply multiple filters. The capture uses the last annotation display status that was set before exiting from the Tolerancing Capture workbench.

Cameras

You can save a camera that has not been saved using

⬚ (Named Views). Reorienting the model into a new position without applying a camera does not successfully save the orientation with the capture.

Mirror Annotations

Depending on the model orientation, you might need to click

⬚ (Mirror annotations) to display the annotations correctly.

Current State

By default, new annotations that are added after a capture has been defined are not shown when the capture displays.

Right-click a capture in the Specification Tree and select **Set Current**. When the Current State tool is toggled on, the system places a record symbol on the capture icon in the specification tree, as shown in Figure 5–21. Consider this capture to be recording all new annotations made to the model until the Current State mode is disabled.

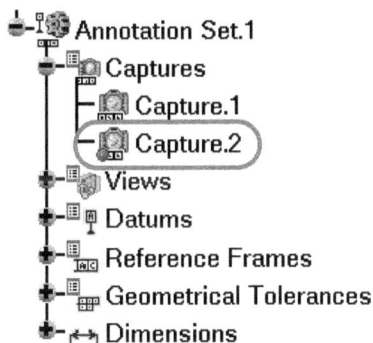

Figure 5–21

You can place more than one capture in Current State mode so that they all display the new annotations added to the model. You can access the **Current State** option by right-clicking on a capture in the specification tree and selecting **Set Current** (enable) or **Unset Current** (disable).

Visibility Status

With Captures, you can use the **Hide/Show** option to control the visibility of bodies and geometrical sets in parts and components in an assembly. By default, the visibility status of a part body, geometrical set, or component is not saved with a capture. However, these settings can be retained by right-clicking on the Capture in the specification tree and selecting **Properties**. In the *Visualizations* tab in the Properties dialog box, select the **Manage the visibility of Part instances, bodies and geometrical sets** option, as shown in Figure 5–22.

*This option can be set for all future captures by selecting **Tools> Options>Mechanical Design>Functional Tolerancing & Annotation**. In the View/Annotation Plane tab, select the **Manage the visibility of Part instances, bodies and geometrical sets** option.*

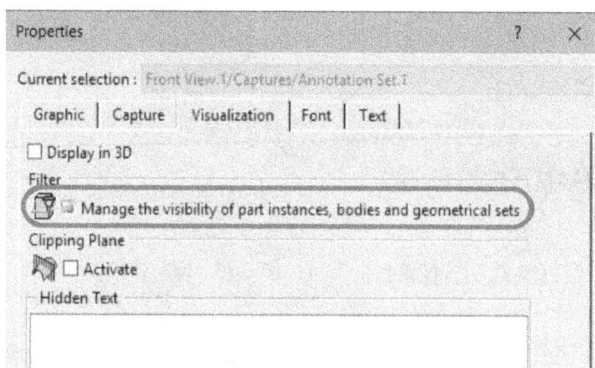

Figure 5–22

Once the view settings are applied, click **Insert>Capture> Capture**. The Capture Creation dialog box opens, as shown in Figure 5–23.

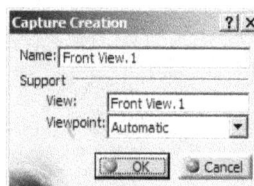

Figure 5–23

A capture is always associated with a view/annotation plane. If your model does not contain any view/annotation plane, a projection view/annotation plane is created parallel to the xy plane, passing through the origin.

When the model contains a view/annotation plane, the active view/annotation plane is selected by default. However, you can select another view/annotation plane by selecting the **View** field and selecting a view/annotation plane from the specification tree or from the model.

By default, the capture name and viewpoint is the same as the associated view/annotation plane, but you can edit the **Name** field and Viewpoint as required. The Viewpoint is selected from the list of existing cameras.

Enter a name for the capture and click **OK**.

Clipping Plane

In order for the system to display a section in a capture, you have to enter the Filter workbench. After a capture is created, double-click it in the Specification Tree. Click (Clipping Plane), then click (Exit from capture).

Capture Management

By default, annotations are not included if they are created when there is no current capture in the model. You can manually associate or disassociate an annotation from a capture using the Capture Management tool.

You can automatically add new annotations to an existing capture using the Current State tool.

How To: Add Annotations to a Capture(s)

1. Select the annotations to be added the capture(s).
2. Right-click and select **Capture Management**. The Capture Management dialog box opens, as shown in Figure 5–24. The left side of the dialog box displays all captures in the model that do not currently contain the selected annotations. The right side of the dialog box displays any captures that do currently contain the selected annotations.

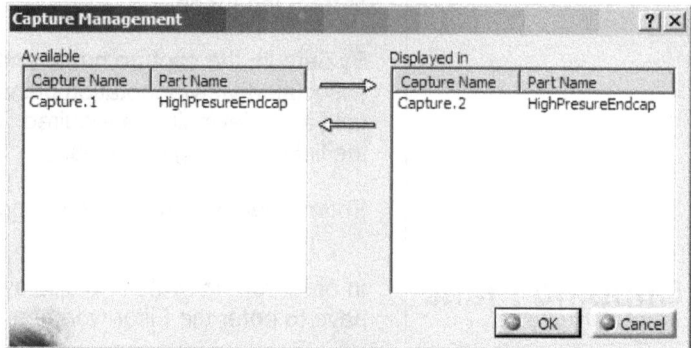

Figure 5–24

3. To add the selected annotations to a capture, select the capture in the Available list, and click ⟹. To remove an annotation from a specific capture, select the capture in the Displayed in list, and click ⟸.
4. Click **OK** to close the Capture Management dialog box and apply the change.

Default Capture

When a capture is applied to the model, you cannot automatically restore the model to its default display status. Therefore, you should create a default capture (recommended) as the first capture in the model.

1. Ensure that all annotations display.
2. Create a camera with an appropriate orientation.
3. Select **Insert>Capture>Capture**.
4. Edit the *Name* and set the View Point to the appropriate camera.
5. Click **OK**.

   This creates a capture that shows all annotations and displays the model in a default position.

5.8 Geometry Connection Management

The Geometry Connection Management tool enables you to investigate, change, add, and rename geometric references that have been selected to create an annotation. This is useful when executing design changes, since modifications to the underlying geometry might cause annotations to lose their references and fail.

This section describes how to change a reference using the model shown in Figure 5–25. This model contains a toleranced dimension (Dimension.1) and a simple datum. The hole position is currently dimensioned to the incorrect face and must be modified to reference Datum A.

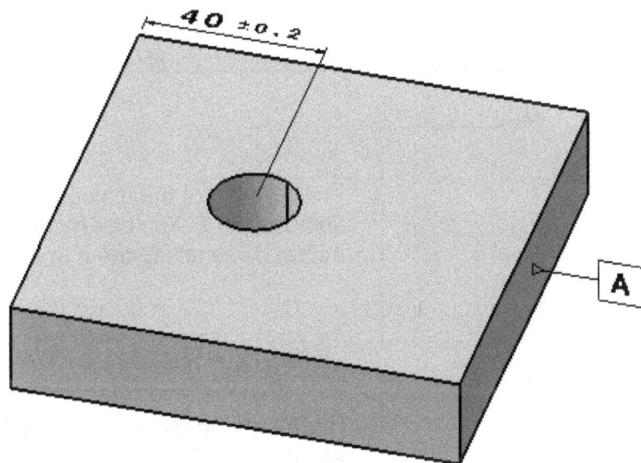

Figure 5–25

General Steps

Use the following general steps to modify an annotation reference:

1. Start the Connection Management operation.
2. Replace the reference.
3. Check the validity and complete the operation.

Step 1 - Start the Connection Management operation.

Select **Dimension.1** in the tree and in the Geometry for 3D Annotations toolbar, click (Geometry Connection Management). The Connection Management dialog box opens, as shown in Figure 5–26.

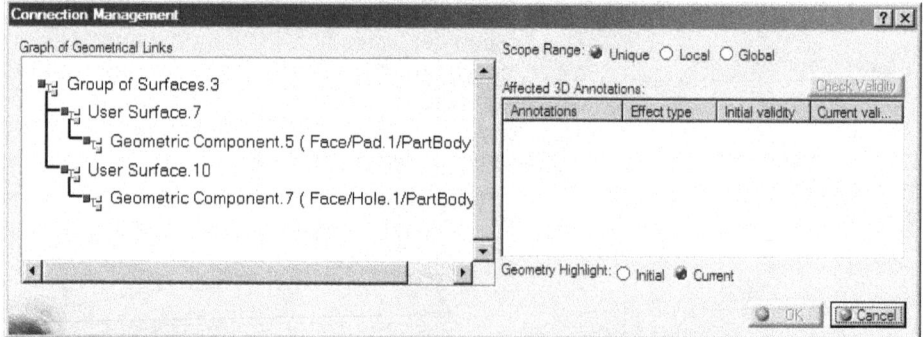

Figure 5–26

The left side of the dialog box displays references that belong to **Dimension.1**. You can highlight these references on the part model by selecting them in the dialog box.

Step 2 - Replace the reference.

Right-click on the reference to be modified and select **Connect**, as shown in Figure 5–27.

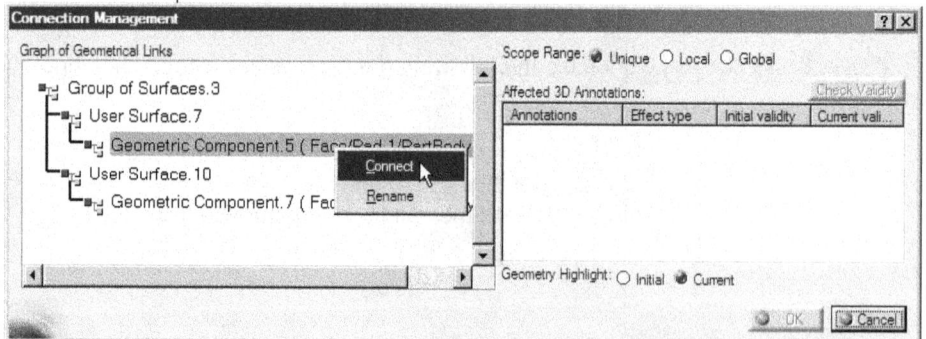

Figure 5–27

When this is done, the icon for the surface changes, as shown in Figure 5–28, indicating that a new reference can be selected.

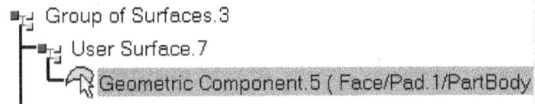

■ Group of Surfaces.3
■ User Surface.7
Geometric Component.5 (Face/Pad.1/PartBody

Figure 5–28

Select the new reference in the model. In this example, the Datum A face is selected. The Connection Management dialog box updates, as shown in Figure 5–29.

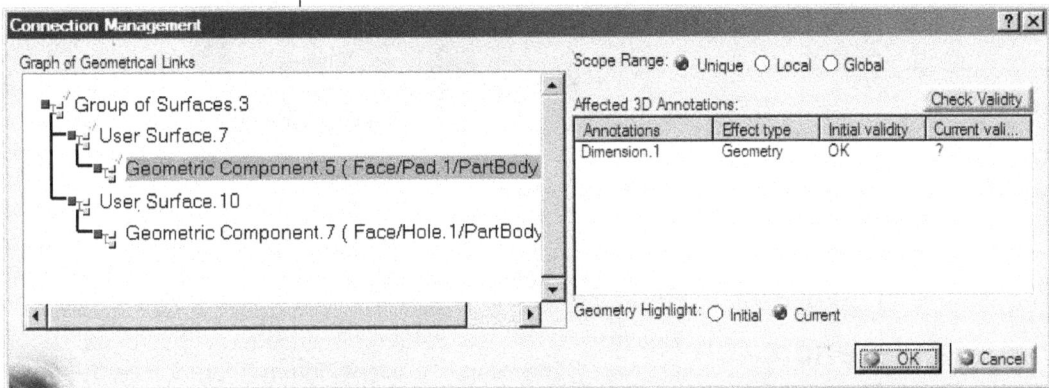

Connection Management

Graph of Geometrical Links

■ Group of Surfaces.3
■ User Surface.7
■ Geometric Component.5 (Face/Pad.1/PartBody
■ User Surface.10
■ Geometric Component.7 (Face/Hole.1/PartBody

Scope Range: ● Unique ○ Local ○ Global

Affected 3D Annotations: Check Validity

Annotations	Effect type	Initial validity	Current vali...
Dimension.1	Geometry	OK	?

Geometry Highlight: ○ Initial ● Current

OK   Cancel

Figure 5–29

Step 3 - Check the validity and complete the operation.

Click **Check Validity** to confirm that the selected reference did not cause a failure in the annotation. If the reference causes a failure, the Current validity column changes to KO. If the reference is successful, the Current validity column changes to OK, as shown in Figure 5–30.

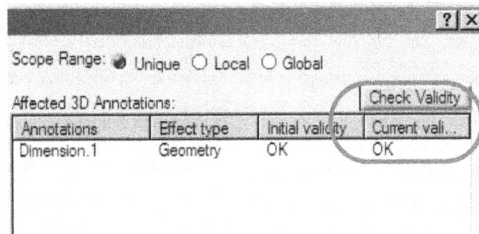

Scope Range: ● Unique ○ Local ○ Global

Affected 3D Annotations: Check Validity

Annotations	Effect type	Initial validity	Current vali...
Dimension.1	Geometry	OK	OK

Figure 5–30

Once the reference has been successfully checked, click **OK** to complete the operation. With the new reference for the dimension, the model displays, as shown in Figure 5–31.

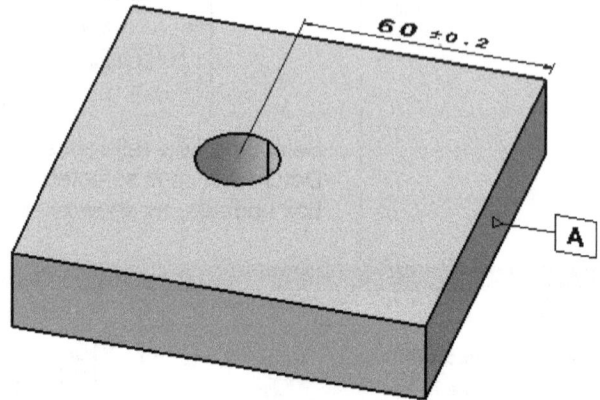

Figure 5–31

Replacing a Datum Reference Frame

You can change the datum reference frame that was used to construct a geometrical tolerance.

1. Ensure that the new datum reference frame has been created. For example, the new datum reference frame A|B|C has been created, as shown in Figure 5–32.

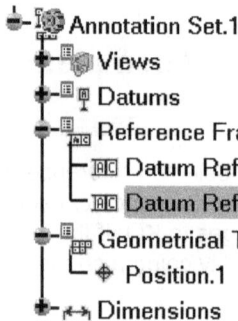

Annotation to be modified.

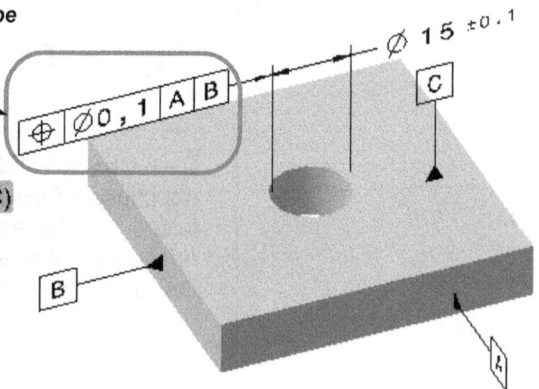

Figure 5–32

2. Right-click on the geometrical tolerance and select **Replace Datum Reference Frame**, as shown in Figure 5–33.

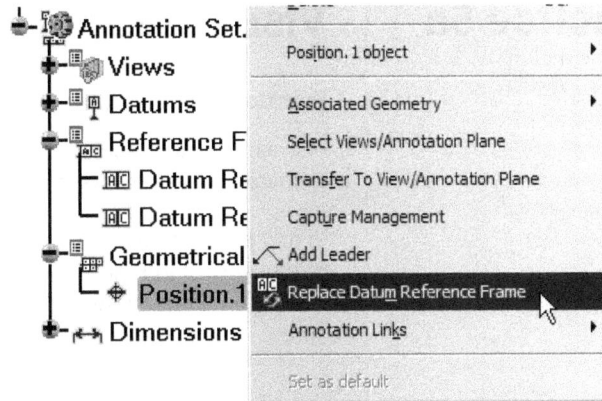

Figure 5–33

3. Select a new datum reference frame. The system updates the tolerance to reference the new datum reference frame, as shown in Figure 5–34.

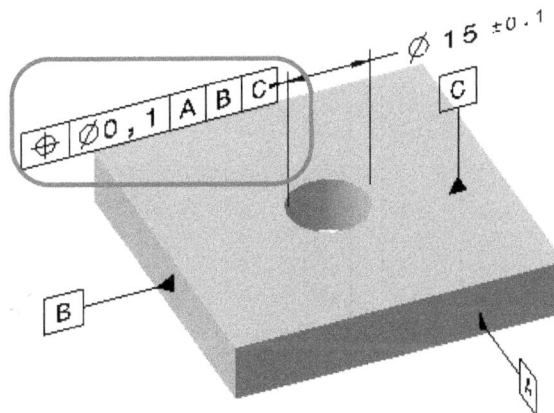

Figure 5–34

Practice 5a

Visualization

Practice Objectives

- Create a default capture.
- Create various captures to manage the model display.

In this practice, you will create a variety of captures from the model shown in Figure 5–35. These captures use annotation filters and cameras during their creation.

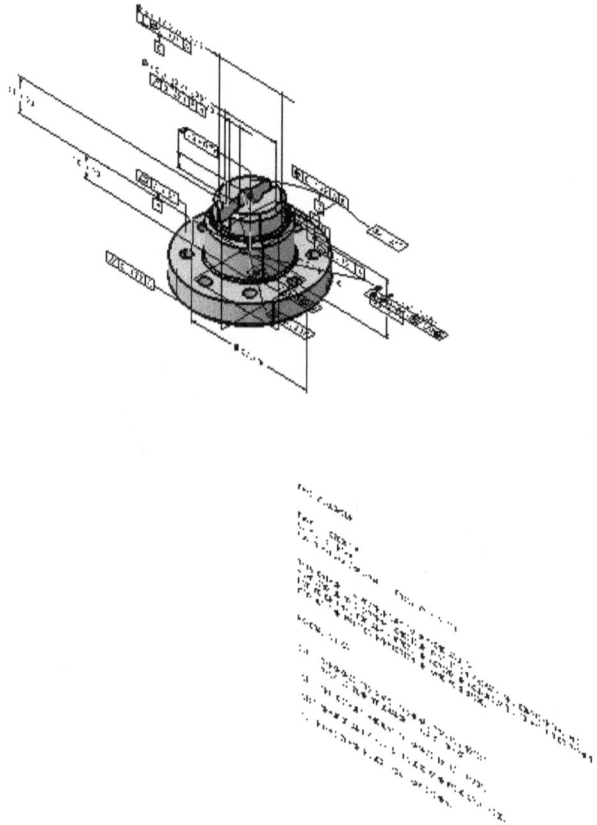

Figure 5–35

Task 1 - Open a part that contains tolerancing and annotations.

1. Open **LockingHub_Finished.CATPart**. The part displays, as shown in Figure 5–36.

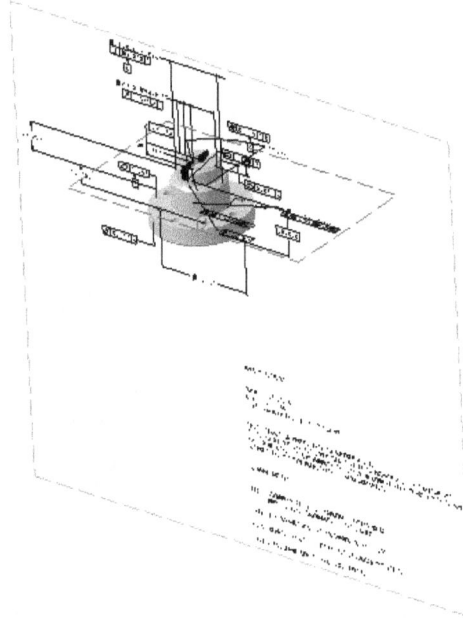

Figure 5–36

Task 2 - Create a default capture.

Design Considerations

In this task, you will use the capture functionality to create a capture of the native state of the model. Since you cannot reset a capture, the default capture enables you to return to the display properties of the original model. In this task, the default capture is called CAP-ALL.

1. In the View toolbar, expand ⬛ (Isometric) and select ⬛ (Named views).

2. Click **Add** and edit the name to **CAP-ALL**.

3. Click **OK**.

4. Select **Insert>Capture>Capture**.

5. Edit the *Name* to **CAP-ALL** in the Capture Creation dialog box.

6. In the Viewpoint drop-down list, select **CAP-ALL**.

7. Click **OK**. The capture displays in the specification tree, as shown in Figure 5–37.

Figure 5–37

Task 3 - Create a filtered capture.

1. In the Visualization toolbar, click (Filter). The Filter dialog box opens as shown in Figure 5–38.

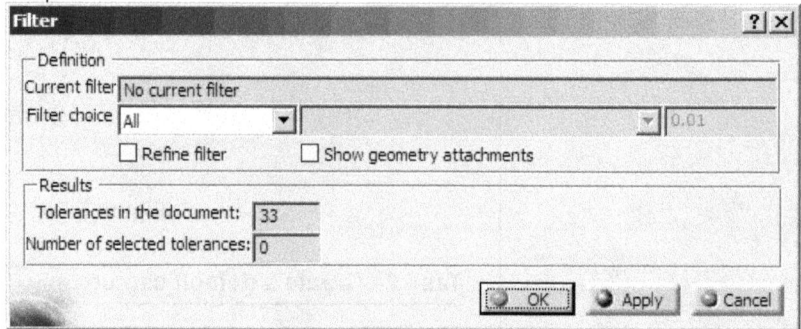

Figure 5–38

2. While pressing <Ctrl>, select the following dimensions in the specification tree, as shown in Figure 5–39:

    *   **Linear Size.5**
    *   **Linear Size.6**
    *   **Linear Size.8**

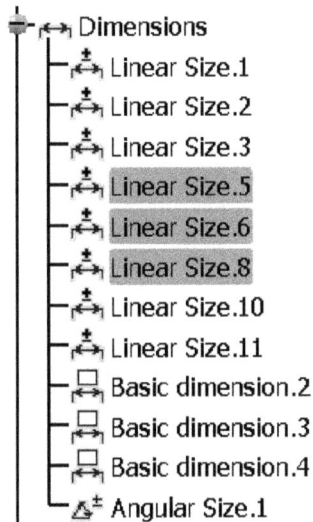

Figure 5–39

- The Filter dialog box automatically selects the Filter choice **By feature**.

3. Click **Apply**. The Filter dialog box displays, as shown Figure 5–40.

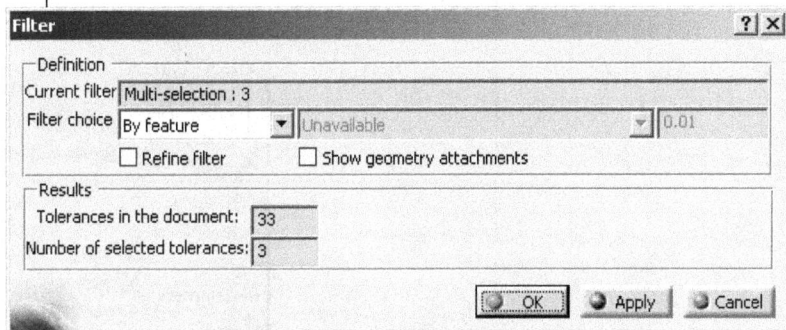

Figure 5–40

4. Click **OK** to complete the filter.

5. Select **Insert>Capture>Capture**.

6. Enter **CAP-FEATURE_001** in the Capture Creation dialog box.

7. Leave the View as **Front.View.1** and the Viewpoint as **Automatic**.

8. Click **OK** to complete the capture. The model displays as shown in Figure 5–41.

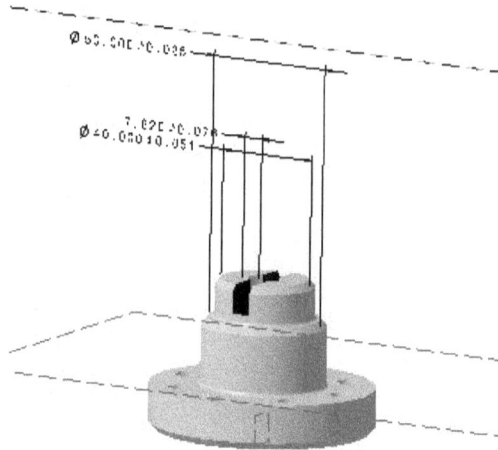

Figure 5–41

Task 4 - Display existing captures.

1. Right-click on **CAP-ALL** and select **Display Capture**, as shown in Figure 5–42, to display all annotations.

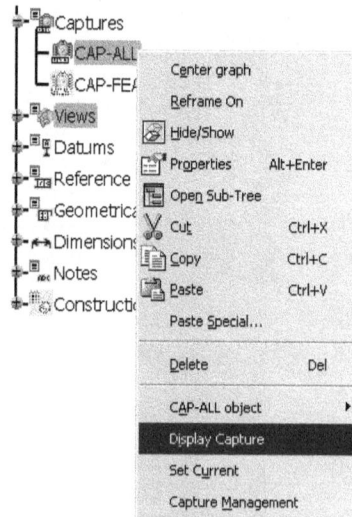

Figure 5–42

The default CAP-ALL capture displays as shown in Figure 5–43.

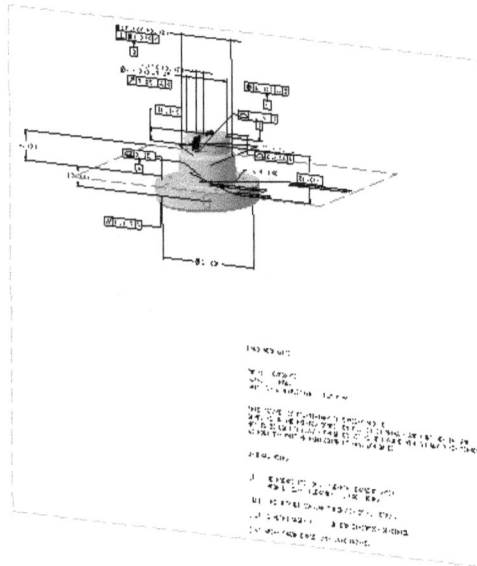

Figure 5–43

2. Right-click on **CAP-FEATURE_001** and select **Display Capture**. The model displays as shown in Figure 5–44.

*A capture uses the current annotation plane. The **CAP-FEATURE_001** capture orients to the **Front.View.1** annotation plane because you left the Viewpoint as Automatic.*

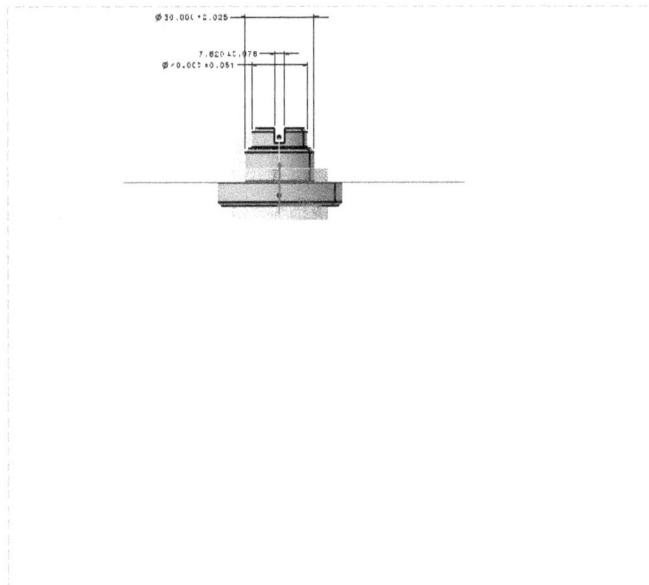

Figure 5–44

3. Right-click on **CAP-ALL** and select **Display Capture**.

Task 5 - Create a new capture.

1. Click [⇥] (Filter). The Filter dialog box opens.

2. Select **By type** and **Position Orientation and Runout** as the *Filter* options, as shown in Figure 5–45.

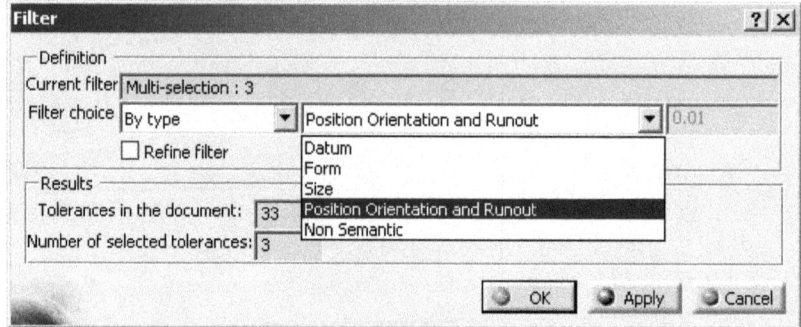

Filter

Definition
Current filter | Multi-selection : 3
Filter choice | By type ▼ | Position Orientation and Runout ▼ | 0.01
☐ Refine filter

Datum
Form
Size
Position Orientation and Runout
Non Semantic

Results
Tolerances in the document: | 33
Number of selected tolerances: | 3

● OK   ● Apply   ● Cancel

Figure 5–45

3. Click **Apply**. Only the geometric tolerances display as shown in Figure 5–46.

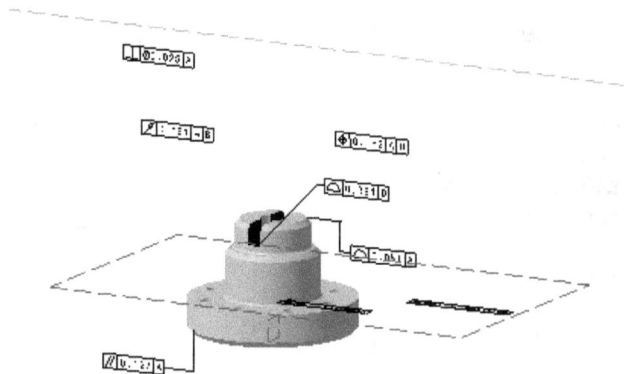

Figure 5–46

4. Select the **Show geometry attachments** option, as shown in Figure 5–47.

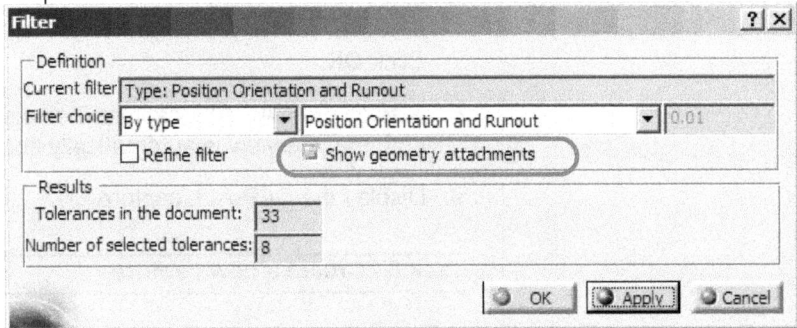

Figure 5–47

5. Click **OK**.

6. Zoom in on the model. The associated dimensions display as shown in Figure 5–48.

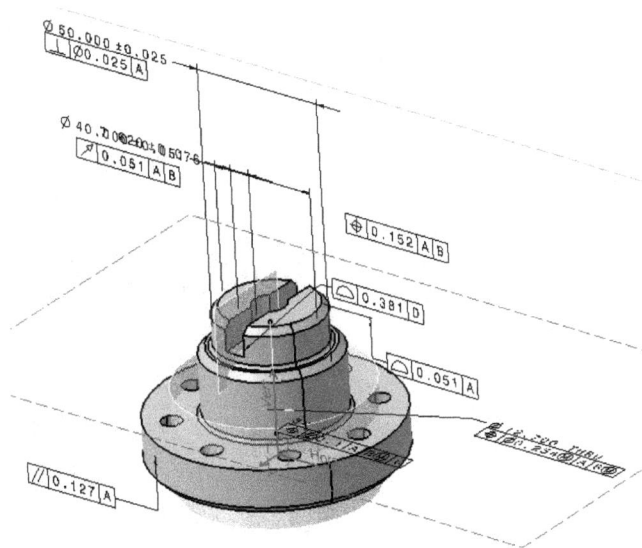

Figure 5–48

1. In the View toolbar, click (Named views).

2. Click **Add** and edit the name to **CAP-GDT**.

3. Click **OK**.

4. Select **Insert>Capture>Capture**.

5. Edit the *Name* to **CAP-GDT** in the Capture Creation dialog box.

6. In the Viewpoint drop-down list, select **CAP-GDT**.

7. Click **OK**.

8. Display the CAP-ALL capture then display CAP-GDT and note that the view is automatically zoomed.

9. Display the CAP-ALL capture.

Task 6 - Create a new capture.

1. Click [icon] (Filter).

2. Select the following using <Ctrl> in the specification tree:

   - **Flatness.1** (Geometrical Tolerances)
   - **Position surfacic profile.1** (Geometrical Tolerances)
   - **Basic dimension.4** (Dimensions)

3. Click **OK** to apply and complete the filter.

4. Click [icon] (Clipping Plane).

5. Click [icon] (Normal View) and select **Front View.1** from the specification tree.

   The model displays, as shown in Figure 5–49.

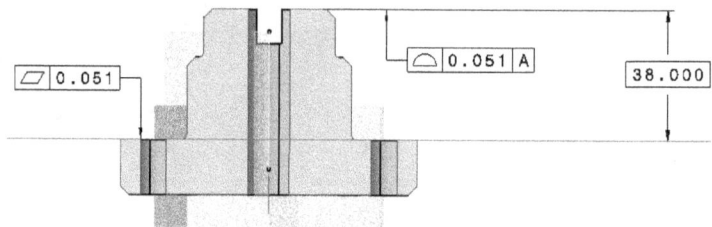

Figure 5–49

6. Click [icon] (Named views).

7. Click **Add**.

8. Enter **CAP-SECTION** as the name and click **OK**.

9. Select **Insert>Capture>Capture**.

10. Edit the *Name* to **CAP-SECTION** in the Capture Creation dialog box.

11. In the Viewpoint drop-down list, select **CAP-SECTION**.

12. Click **OK**.

13. Display the CAP-ALL capture. The model displays as shown in Figure 5–50.

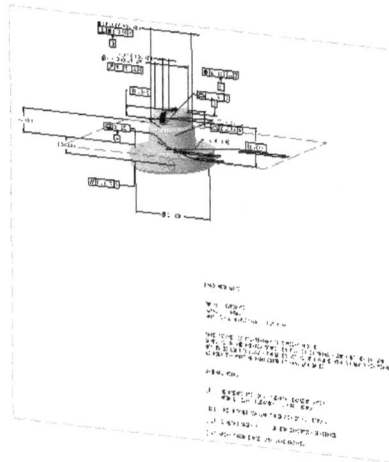

Figure 5–50

14. Display the CAP-SECTION capture. The model displays as shown in Figure 5–51.

The section display is not persistent. To make the section visible in the capture, apply sectioning in the Filter Workbench.

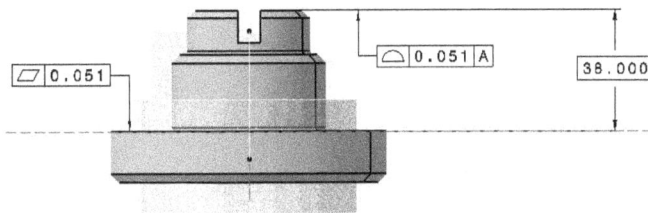

Figure 5–51

15. In the Specification Tree, double-click on **CAP-SECTION** to enter the Capture workbench.

16. In the Filter workbench, click ⬚ (Clipping Plane).

17. Click ⬆ (Exit from capture).

18. Display the CAP-ALL capture, then display the CAP-SECTION capture again.

19. The capture now displays as expected, as shown in Figure 5–52.

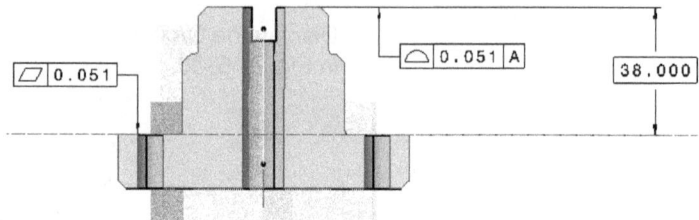

Figure 5–52

20. Display the CAP-ALL capture.

21. Save the model and close the file.

Practice 5b	# Capture

Practice Objectives

- Change the annotation standard.
- Create captures while keeping the Hide/Show status.
- Modify clipping planes.

In this practice, you will create captures that retain the visibility settings of both solid bodies and geometrical sets. You will then modify the appearance of clipped sections in a body by changing its material properties. The model used in this practice is shown in Figure 5–53.

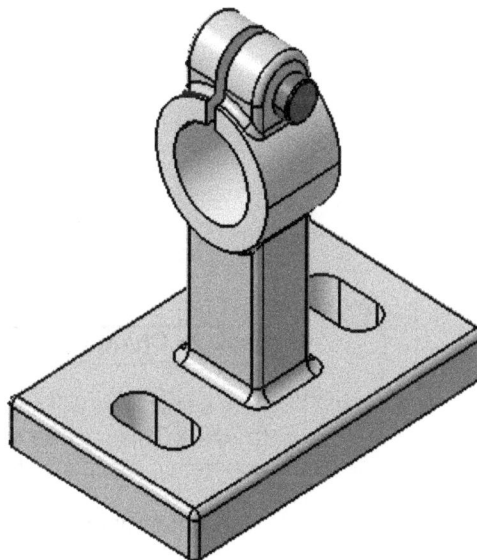

Figure 5–53

Task 1 - Open a part containing multiple bodies.

1. Open **FlangeLock_Capture.CATPart**. The part displays, as shown in Figure 5–54. Note that the part includes geometrical sets, two solid bodies, and an annotation.

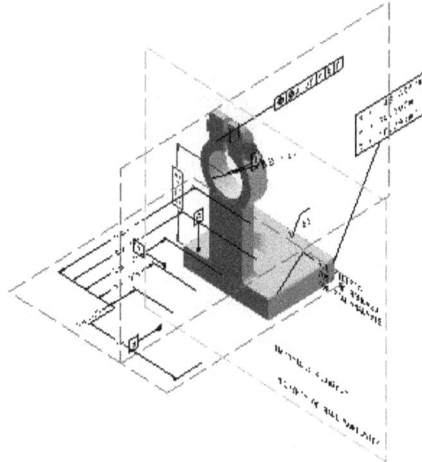

Figure 5–54

Task 2 - Change the annotation standard.

In this task, you will change the annotation standard from ASME to ANSI. This is done to demonstrate the ability to change the annotation standard at any time during the tolerancing process.

1. Right-click on **Annotation Set.1** and select **Properties**.

2. Select the *Standard* tab. Select **ANSI** in the drop-down list, as shown in Figure 5–55.

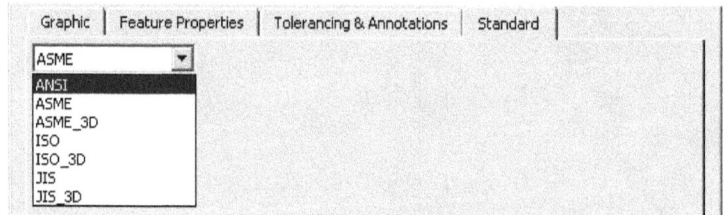

Figure 5–55

3. Click **OK** to change the annotation standard and close the Properties dialog box.

4. Right click **Annotation Set.1** and select **Local Update**.

Task 3 - Create a default capture.

In this task, you will create a default capture that displays all geometry and annotations. This capture is used to return the model to its original display.

1. Select **Tools>Options>Mechanical Design>Functional Tolerancing & Annotation**.

2. Select the *View/Annotation Plane* tab and ensure that the **Manage the visibility of Part instances, bodies and geometrical sets** option is selected.

3. In the View toolbar, expand [icon] (Isometric) and select [icon] (Named views).

4. Click **Add** and edit the *Name* to **DefaultCap**.

5. Click **OK**.

6. Select **Insert>Capture>Capture**.

7. Edit the *Name* to **DefaultCap** in the Capture Creation dialog box.

8. In the Viewpoint drop-down list, select **DefaultCap**.

9. Click **OK**.

Task 4 - Create a capture with hidden components.

1. Hide the following elements:

   - **LockingPin body**
   - **Geometrical Set.1**

2. Create a second capture and name it **FlangeOnlyCap**. Set the *View Point* to **iso**, and click **OK**.

3. The **Geometrical Set.1** and **LockingPin** elements remain hidden, as shown in Figure 5–56.

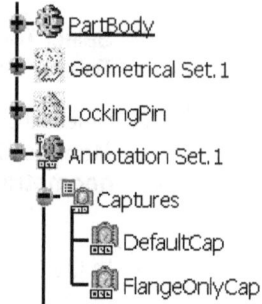

Figure 5–56

4. Display the **DefaultCap** capture by right-clicking on it in the specification tree and selecting **Display Capture**. The model displays with the **LockingPin body** and **Geometrical Set.1** visible.

5. Use the same method to display **FlangeOnlyCap**. The model displays with the **LockingPin body** and **Geometrical Set.1** hidden, as shown in Figure 5–57.

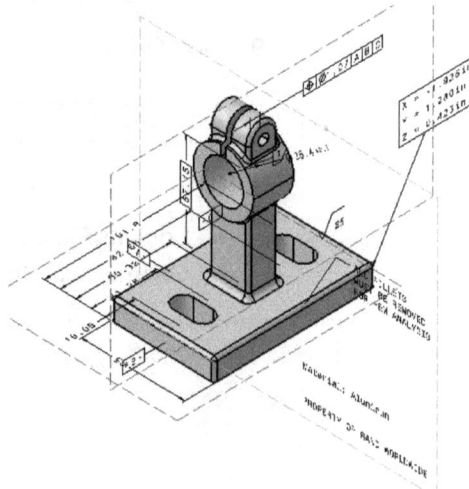

Figure 5–57

Task 5 - Modify and view the clipping plane visualization.

1. Select **Tools>Options>Mechanical Design>Functional Tolerancing & Annotation** and select the *Display* tab.

2. In the *Hatching, coloring or dotting for clipping plane* area, ensure that the **Display** option is enabled, as shown in Figure 5–58.

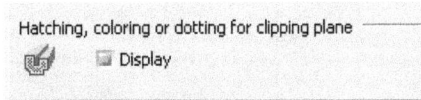

Hatching, coloring or dotting for clipping plane

☐ Display

Figure 5–58

3. Click **OK** to close the Options dialog box.

4. Click (Shading with Material).

Design Considerations

To display a hatched, colored, or dotted clipping plane, the following conditions must be met:

• A material must be applied to the part or product.

5. Expand the PartBody branch in the specification tree, right-click on Aluminum, and select **Properties**, as displayed in Figure 5–59.

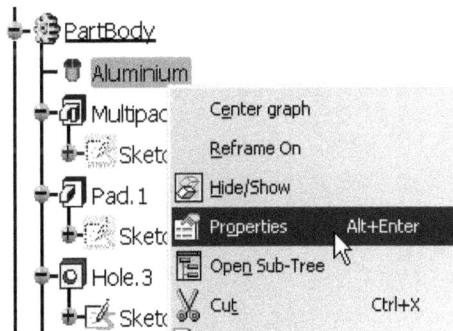

Figure 5–59

6. Select the *Drawing* tab.

7. In the *Number of hatchings* field, enter **2**.

8. Enter **60 deg** in the *Angle* field of the *Hatching11* tab and **-60 deg** in the *Hatching22* tab.

9. Ensure that the color is set to green and the line type is set to **1** in both tabs, as shown in Figure 5–60.

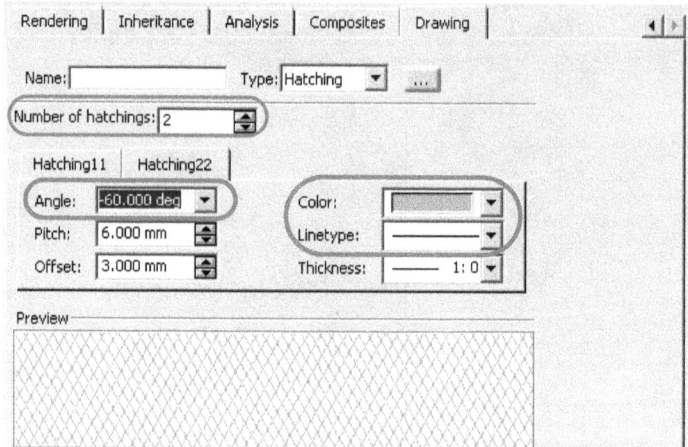

Figure 5–60

10. Click **OK** to close the Properties dialog box.

11. Activate (Clipping Plane) and switch off Annotation Set.1. The model displays, as shown in Figure 5–61.

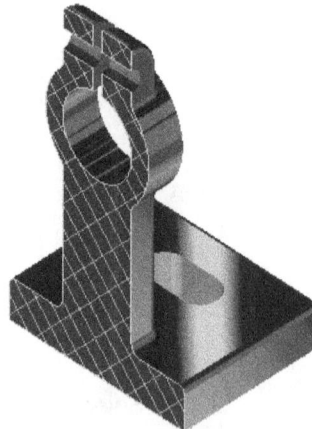

Figure 5–61

12. Display the DefaultCap capture.

13. Save the model and close the file.

Geometry Connection Management

Practice Objectives

- Add a Datum Reference Frame.
- Edit a geometrical tolerance.
- Edit a datum.

In this practice, you will modify the references of existing annotations to become familiar with the Geometry Connection Management tool, and the **Replace Datum Reference Frame** options. You will use the model shown in Figure 5–62.

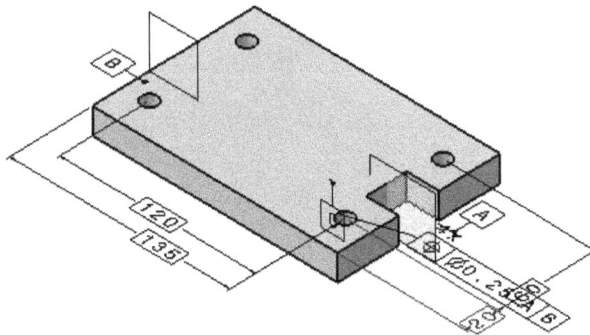

Figure 5–62

Task 1 - Open a part file and investigate annotations.

1. Open **LockingPlate.CATPart**. The model displays, as shown in Figure 5–63.

You need to deactivate

(Clipping Plane) to see the model.

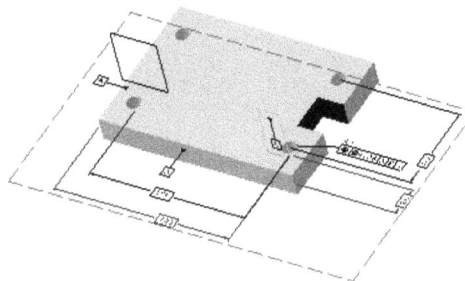

Figure 5–63

2. Click (Normal View), and select **Top View** in the specification tree, as shown in Figure 5–64.

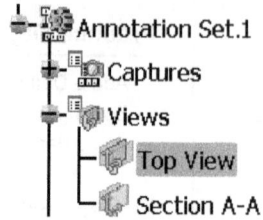

Figure 5–64

The model displays, as shown in Figure 5–65. Note the location and reference surface of datum A.

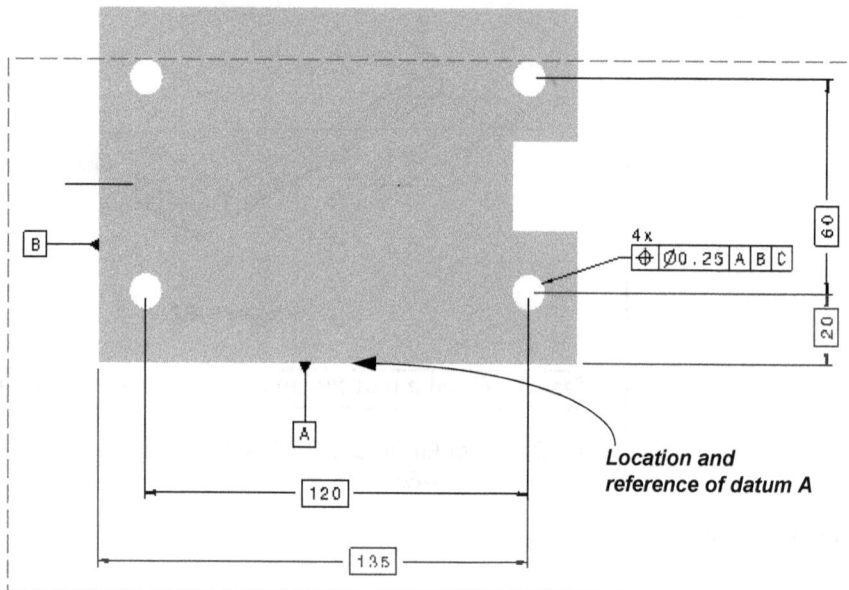

4 x
⊕ | Ø0.25 | A | B | C

Location and reference of datum A

Figure 5–65

3. The positional tolerance (**Position.1**) references the (**A|B|C**) Datum Reference Frame, as shown in Figure 5–66.

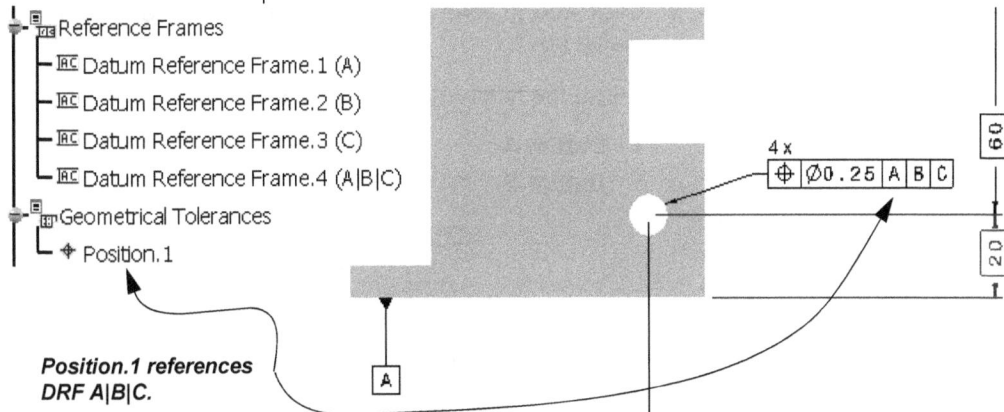

Figure 5–66

Design Considerations

The overall goal of this practice is to change the positional geometrical tolerance that now references datums A|B|C, and have it reference a new datum reference frame A|B. The second goal is to change the reference of datum A.

Task 2 - Create a datum reference frame.

In this task, you will create a new datum reference frame that references datums A and B.

1. Click (Tolerancing Advisor). The Semantic Tolerancing Advisor dialog box opens listing the current datum reference frames, as shown in Figure 5–67.

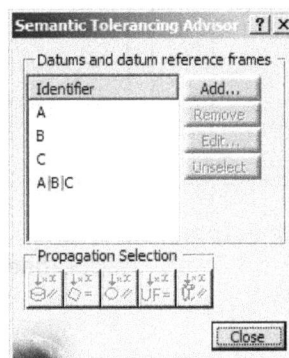

Figure 5–67

2. Click **Add** to open the Datum and datum reference frames dialog box.

3. Select the following datums, as shown in Figure 5–68:

   • **Datum A**
   • **Datum B**

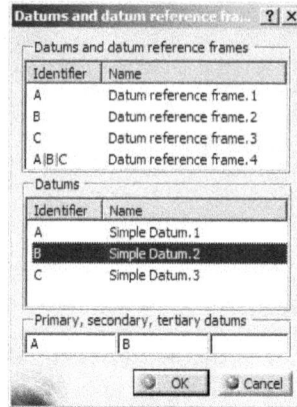

Figure 5–68

4. Click **OK** to complete the Datum Reference Frame. The Semantic Tolerancing Advisor dialog box opens, as shown in Figure 5–69. Note the addition of the A|B Datum Reference Frame.

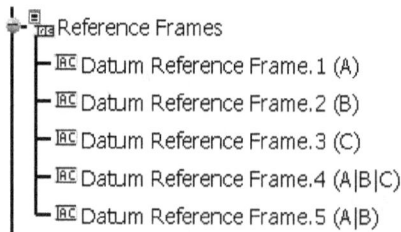
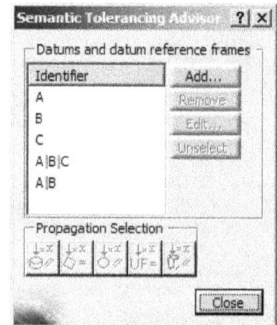

Figure 5–69

5. Click **Close**.

Task 3 - Change the datum reference frame.

In this task, you will change the datum reference frame reference for a geometrical tolerance.

1. Right-click on the **Position.1** tolerance in the specification tree and select **Replace Datum Reference Frame**, as shown in Figure 5–70.

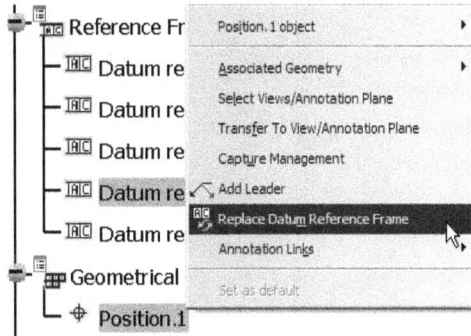

Figure 5–70

2. Select **Datum Reference Plane.5 (A|B)** in the specification tree, as shown in Figure 5–71.

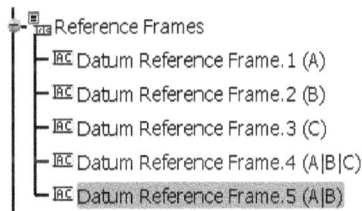

Figure 5–71

The **Positional.1** tolerance now references only datum A|B rather then A|B|C, as shown in Figure 5–72.

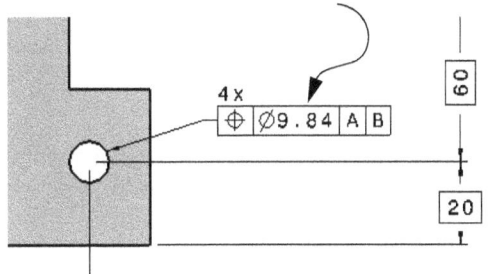

Figure 5–72

Task 4 - Create construction geometry.

In this task, you will create construction geometry that is used to relocate a datum.

1. Preselect the two surfaces shown in Figure 5–73.

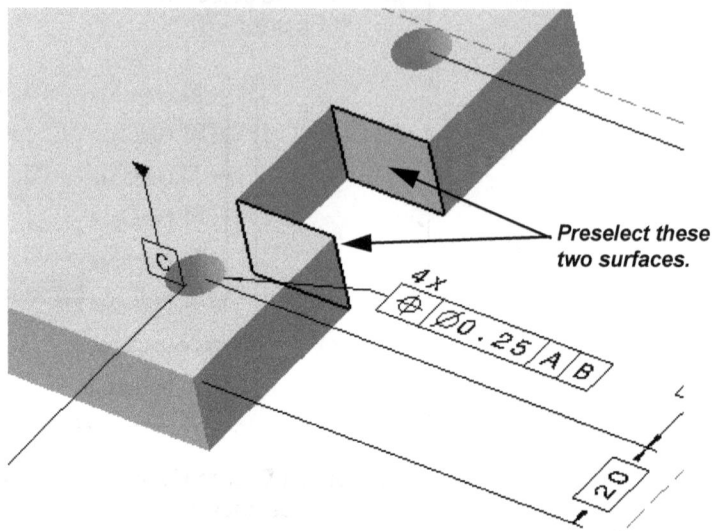

Figure 5–73

2. Click ![icon] (Constructed Geometry Creation). Make the following change, as shown in Figure 5–74:

    • Select **Plane**.

Figure 5–74

3. Click **OK** to complete the geometry, that displays as shown in Figure 5–75.

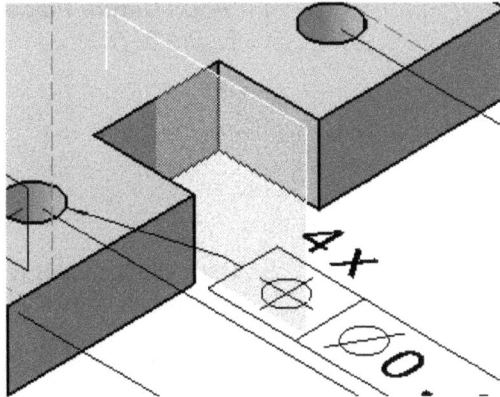

Figure 5–75

Task 5 - Relocate Datum A.

1. Select **Simple Datum.1 (A)** in the specification tree, as shown in Figure 5–76.

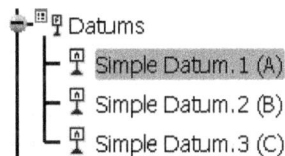

Figure 5–76

2. In the Geometry for 3D Annotations toolbar, click

    (Geometry Connection Management). The Connection Management dialog box opens.

3. Right-click on **Geometric Component.5** and select **Connect**, as shown in Figure 5–77.

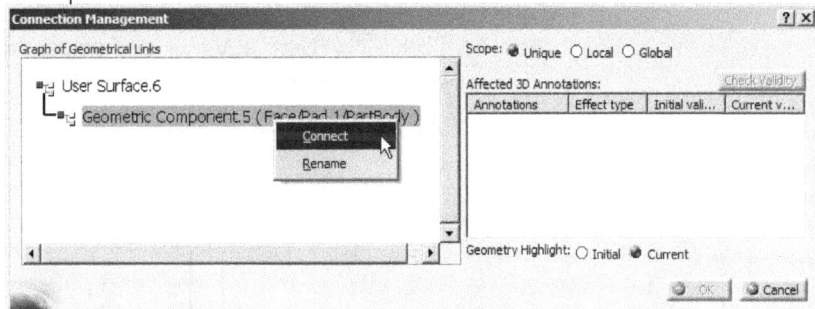

Figure 5–77

---

4. Select **Center Plane.1** in the specification tree, as shown in Figure 5–78.

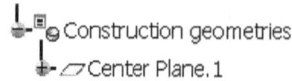

Figure 5–78

5. Click **Check Validity**. The Connection Management dialog box updates, as shown in Figure 5–79.

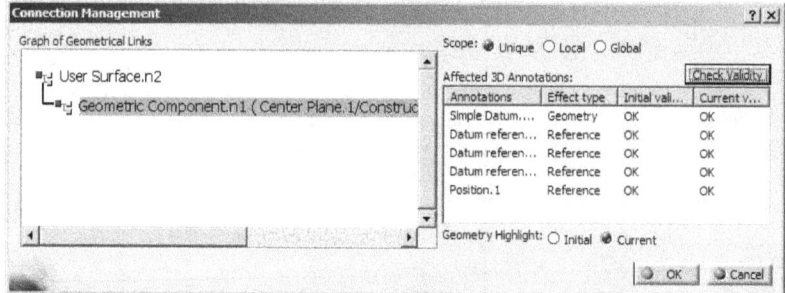

Figure 5–79

Design Considerations

Performing a validity check is important when reconnecting datums to ensure that annotation positions are still valid. You use **Check Validity** in this practice to ensure that the new datum connection is valid for all current annotations. The Current column shows that all annotations are valid when referencing the new geometry.

6. Click **OK** to complete the modification.

Task 6 - View the change to Datum A.

1. Click (Normal View), and select the **Top View** in the specification tree, as shown in Figure 5–80.

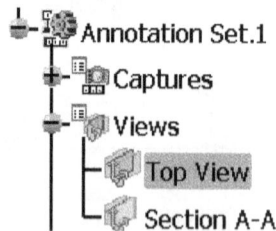

Figure 5–80

2. Modify the attachment of Datum A to switch it to a
   perpendicular leader. The view displays, as shown in
   Figure 5–81. Datum A now references the construction
   geometry that you have created.

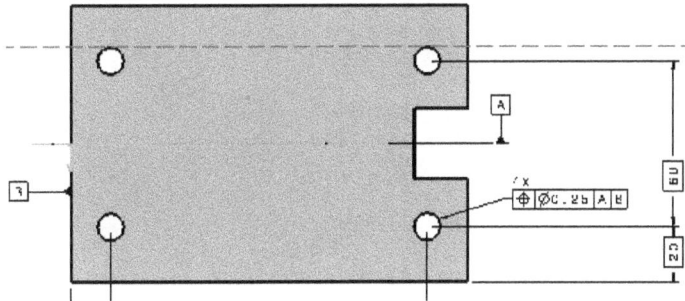

Figure 5–81

3. Save the model and close the file.

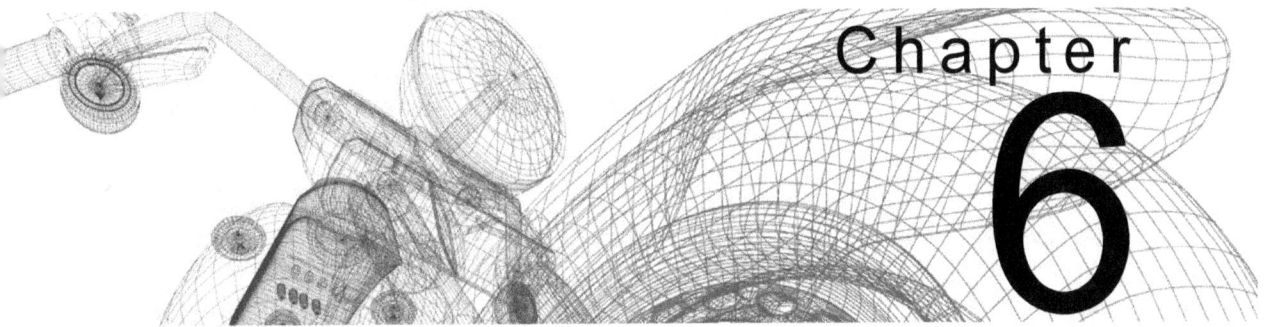

Additional Annotation Tools

This chapter introduces additional tools that are required to develop specialized annotations on your model. Restricted areas are used to divide the face of a model so that two different annotation or tolerance conditions can be defined. The FT&A workbench has the ability to display thread representations and annotations for threaded bosses and holes that have been created in the Part Design workbench.

Learning Objectives in this Chapter

- Understand how restricted areas are used when a portion of a surface needs to be toleranced differently from the rest of the surface.
- Learn how to use the Thread Representation Creation tool to view the graphical representations of threads.

6.1 Restricted Areas

Restricted areas are used when a portion of a surface needs to be toleranced differently from the rest of the surface, as shown in Figure 6–1.

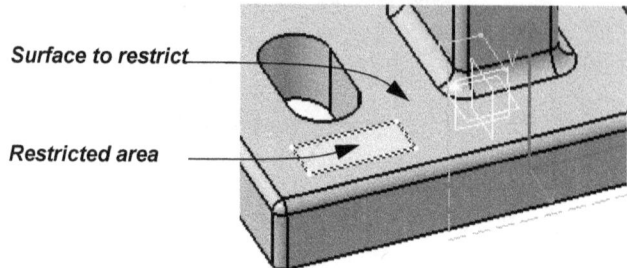

Surface to restrict

Restricted area

Figure 6–1

How To: Create a Restricted Area

1. Click (Restricted Area) to open the dialog box, as shown in Figure 6–2.

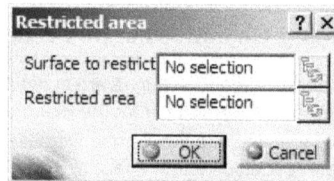

Figure 6–2

2. Select the surface to restrict reference in the model, as shown in Figure 6–1. The surface to restrict is the larger surface that contains the smaller surface. The selected reference displays in the Surface to restrict field.
3. Select the restricted area in the model, as shown in Figure 6–1. The selected reference displays in the restricted area field. The restricted area is a smaller portion of the larger surface, which can be created using the Generative Shape Design workbench.
4. Click **OK** to complete the feature.

Display Properties

The default display properties of a restricted area can be controlled by selecting **Tools>Options>Mechanical Design> Functional Tolerancing & Annotation** and selecting the *Display* tab.

In the *Restricted Area* tab, you can control the color, transparency, and edge properties for the restricted area, as shown in Figure 6–3.

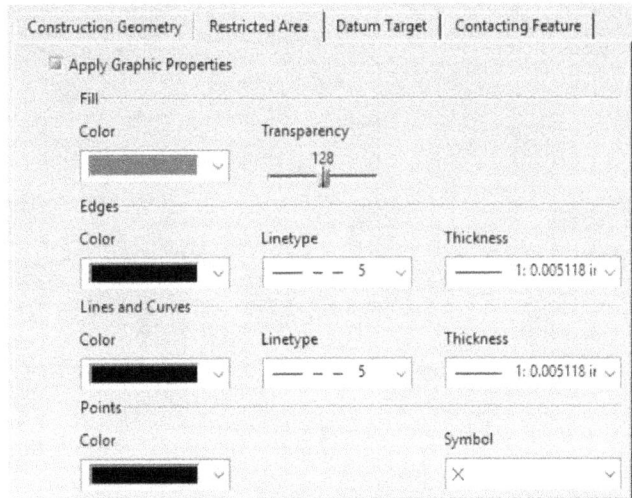

Figure 6–3

When the **Apply Graphic Properties** option is enabled, the referenced geometry in any restricted areas shows the display properties defined in the Options dialog box.

6.2 Threads

When threads are created in the Part Design workbench, their graphical representations cannot be seen in the model. To view the threads, you need to use the Thread Representation Creation tool. An example displays, as shown in Figure 6–4.

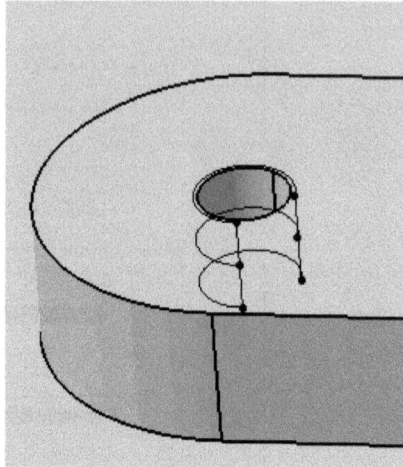

Figure 6–4

How To: Create Thread Representations

1. Click 🗗▾ (Thread Representation Creation). The Thread Representation Creation dialog box opens, as shown in Figure 6–5.

Figure 6–5

2. Select the threaded feature individually or select the **All Threads** option to automatically select all threaded features. A preview of each thread displays in the model, as shown in Figure 6–6.

Threads need to be defined before a thread representation can be created.

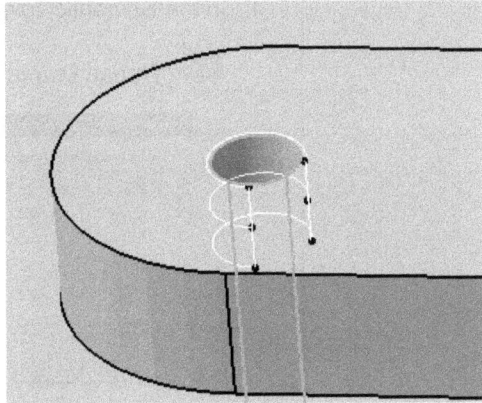

Figure 6–6

3. Click **OK** to complete the feature.

Annotating Thread Representations

How To: Annotate Thread Representations

1. Activate the annotation plane to define the orientation of the thread annotation.
2. Select the middle arc of the thread on which you want to annotate, as shown in Figure 6–7.

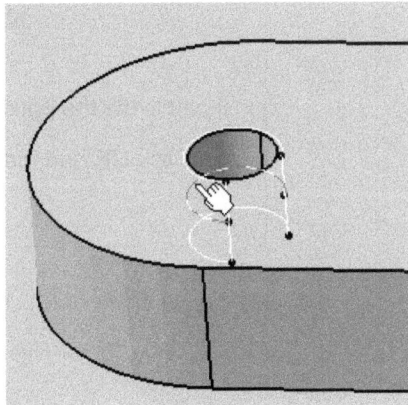

Figure 6–7

3. Click 🎓 (Tolerance Advisor).

4. In the Semantic Tolerancing Advisor dialog box, click

   ▦ (Thread Diameter), as shown in Figure 6–8.

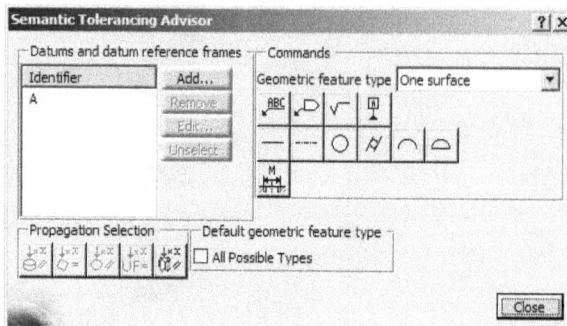

Figure 6–8

The Limit of Size Definition dialog box opens as shown in Figure 6–9.

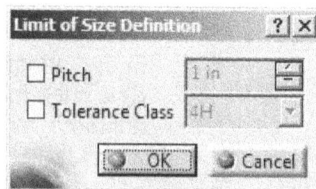

Figure 6–9

5. Activate the option(s) you want to display in the annotation.

6. Click **OK** and then **Close** to complete the feature.

Practice 6a

Annotation Tools

Practice Objectives

- Create a restricted area.
- Annotate a restricted area.
- Display threads and thread annotations.

In this practice, you will develop additional annotations for SimplePad.CATPart. These annotations include a parallelism tolerance that varies across the top face of the part. As well, you will display thread representations and annotations. The completed model displays, as shown in Figure 6–10.

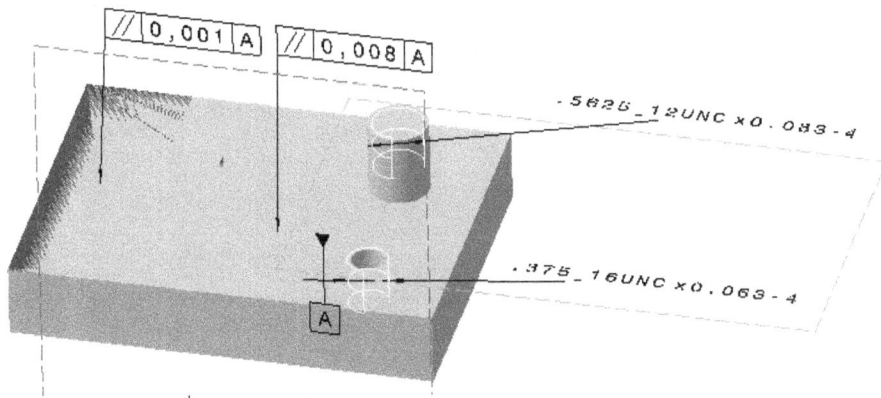

Figure 6–10

Task 1 - Open a part file.

1. Open **SimplePad.CATPart**. The model displays, as shown in Figure 6–11.

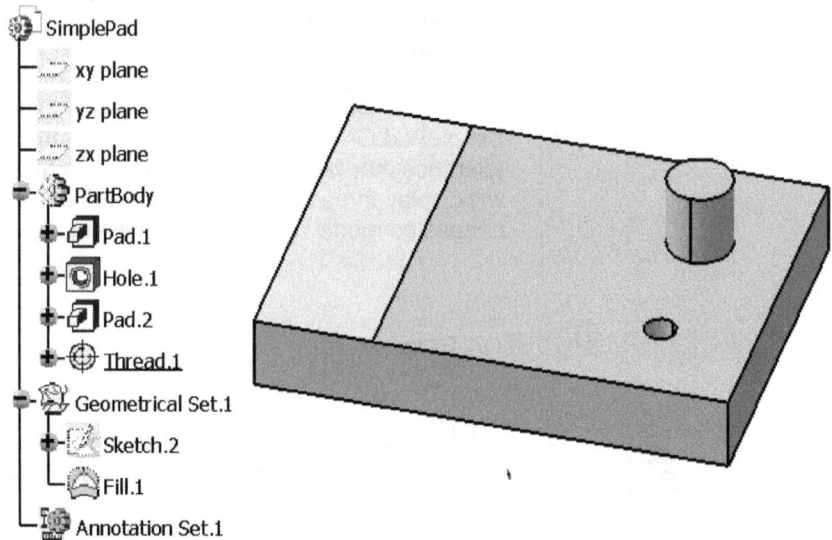

Figure 6–11

2. Investigate the features in the model. The following features are of specific interest during this practice:

   - **Hole.1** - The feature symbol indicates that the hole has been defined as threaded.
   - **Thread.1** - This thread has been added to **Pad.2**.
   - **Fill.1** - This surface has been added to the model to define a restricted area on the top face of the model.

Task 2 - Set options.

1. Select **Tools>Options**.

2. Select **General>Parameters and Measure** and select the *Units* tab. Ensure the Length units are set to **Inch (in)**.

3. Select **Mechanical Design>Functional Tolerancing & Annotation** and select the *Tolerances* tab. Ensure that *Precision* is set to **0.001**.

4. Leave the dialog box open for the next task.

Task 3 - Set the partial surface display properties.

1. If required, select **Mechanical Design>Functional Tolerancing & Annotation**.

2. Select the *Display* tab.

3. Make the following selections in the *Restricted Area* field:

   - Select **Apply Graphic Properties**.
   - *Fill Color:* **Blue**
   - *Edge Color:* **Black**

4. Click **OK**.

Task 4 - Create a restricted area.

In this task, you will define a restricted area on the top face of the part. You will define the restricted area to enable a variation in a parallelism tolerance between the left and right sides of the part, as shown in Figure 6–12.

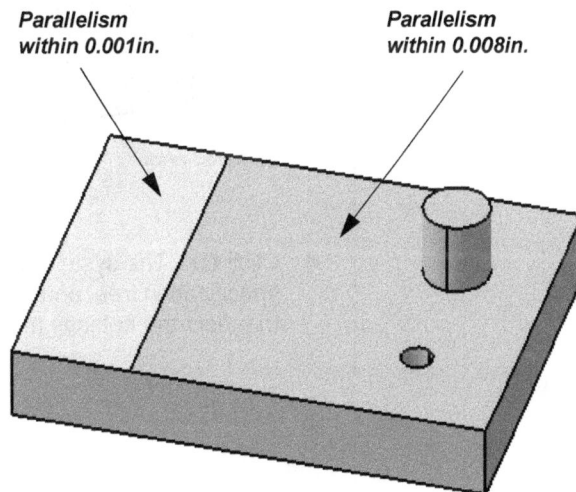

Parallelism within 0.001in.

Parallelism within 0.008in.

Figure 6–12

1. Switch on **Annotation Set.1**.

2. In the Geometry for 3D Annotations toolbar, click

   (Restricted Area). The Restricted Area dialog box opens, as shown in Figure 6–13.

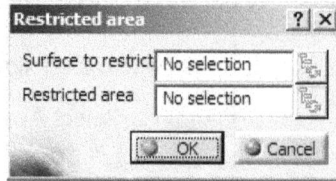

Figure 6–13

3. Select the *Surface to restrict* and *Restricted area* surfaces shown in Figure 6–14.

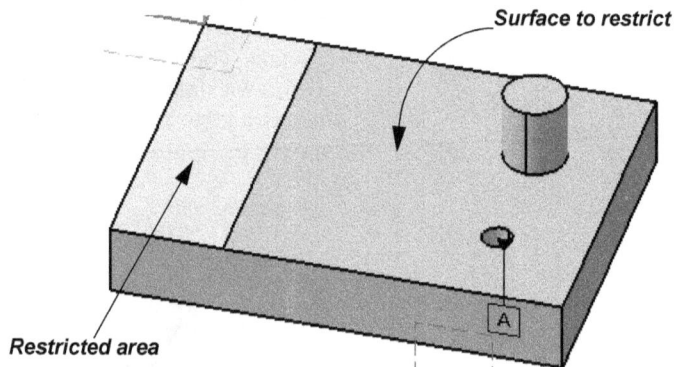

Figure 6–14

4. Click **OK**. The system adds **Restricted Area.1** to the specification tree, and modifies the display properties of **Fill.1** to reflect the settings made in the previous task.

Task 5 - Add a parallelism tolerance to the top face.

1. Activate the Side annotation view.

2. Activate the Tolerance Advisor and make the following selections:

   - Select DRF **A** in the *Datums and datum reference frames* area.
   - Select the top face of the part. The dialog box displays as shown in Figure 6–15.

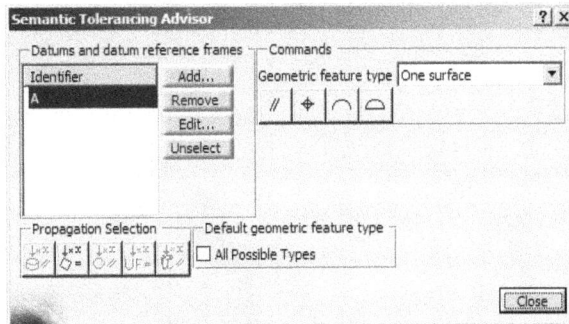

Figure 6–15

3. Click ⬜ (Parallelism Specification) to create a parallelism tolerance with a **0.008in** tolerance value, as shown in Figure 6–16.

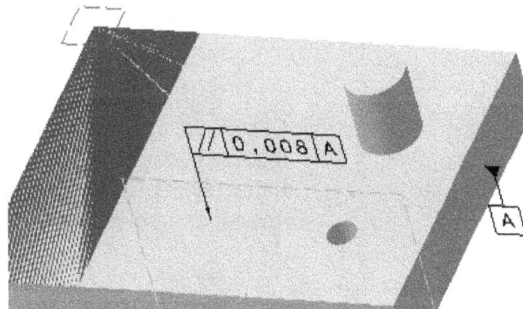

Figure 6–16

4. Complete the tolerance creation.

Task 6 - Create a parallelism tolerance on the restricted area.

1. Activate the Tolerance Advisor and make the following selections:

   • Select DRF **A** in the *Datums and datum reference frames* area.
   • Select **Restricted Area.1** under the **Restricted Areas** branch of the specification tree.

2. Create a parallelism tolerance with a **0.001in** tolerance value, as shown in Figure 6–17.

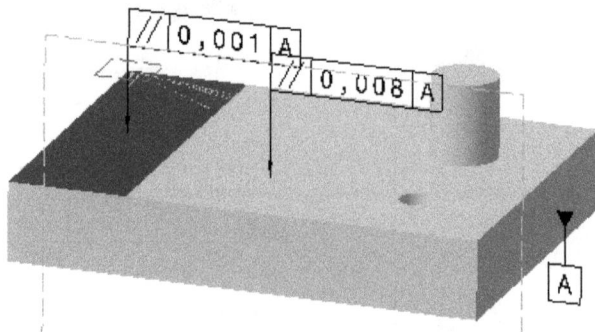

Figure 6–17

3. Apply a filter, using **Filter choice = None** to hide the two geometrical tolerances and the semantic datum.

Task 7 - Display the thread representations.

1. Click (Thread Representation Creation) in the flyout in the Geometry for 3D Annotations toolbar, as shown in Figure 6–18. The Thread Representation Creation dialog box opens, as shown in Figure 6–18.

Figure 6–18

2. Select **All threads** and click **OK**. The model displays, as shown in Figure 6–19.

Thread representations

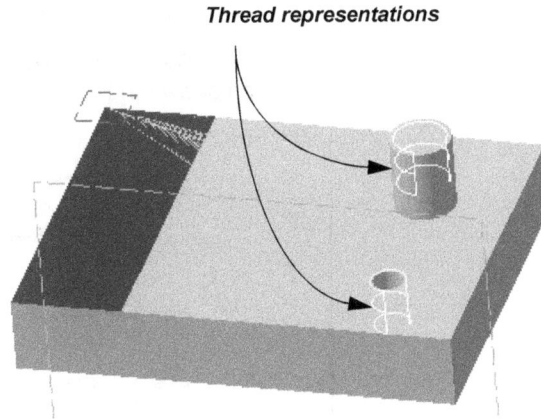

Figure 6–19

Design Considerations

Two thread representation branches have been added under the Construction geometries branch in the specification tree. The thread representation consists of three separate features named Upper Thread Plane, Lower Thread Plane, and Thread Cylinder, as shown in Figure 6–20.

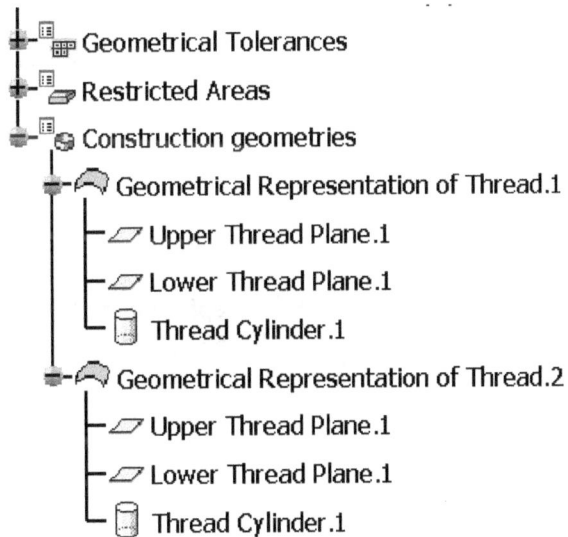

Figure 6–20

Task 8 - Display the thread annotations.

1. Activate the Front view.

2. Preselect the middle curve on the thread for the hole feature, as shown in Figure 6–21.

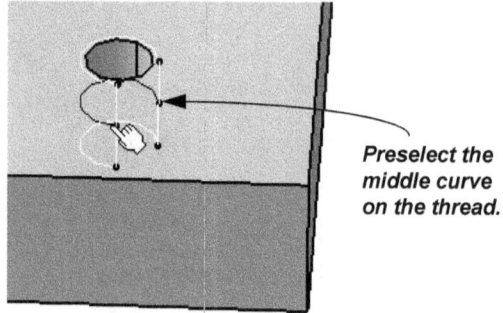

Preselect the
middle curve
on the thread.

Figure 6–21

3. Activate the Tolerance Advisor.

4. Click (Thread Diameter). The Limit of Size Definition dialog box opens, as shown in Figure 6–22.

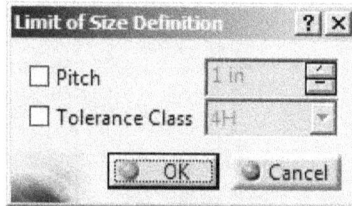

Figure 6–22

5. Accept the default values, and select **Pitch** and **Tolerance Class**.

6. Complete the operation. The model displays, as shown in Figure 6–23.

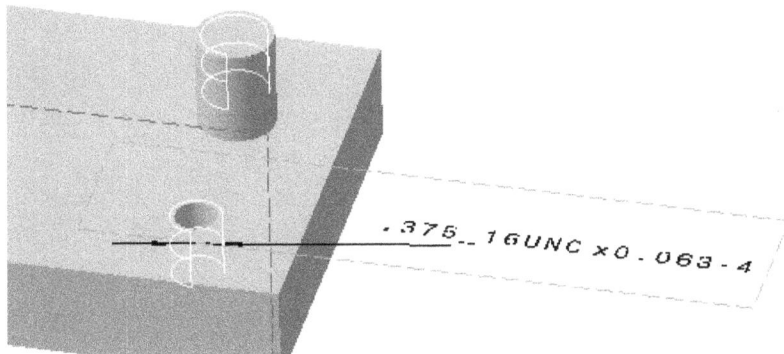

Figure 6–23

7. Repeat this process to display the threaded annotation for the threaded boss. The model displays, as shown in Figure 6–24.

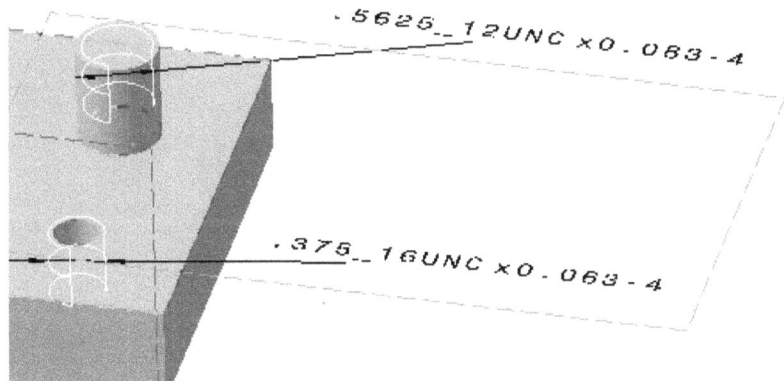

Figure 6–24

8. Save the model and close the window.

Product FT&A

Products are annotated in a different workbench than part models. This chapter introduces the Product Functional Tolerancing & Annotation workbench, and describes its similarities and differences from the part level FT&A workbench.

Learning Objectives in this Chapter

- Understand that the Product Functional Tolerancing & Annotation workbench enables you to create annotations between different parts in an assembly.
- Recognize the various contexts for working with Product FT&A.

7.1 Overview

The Product Functional Tolerancing & Annotation workbench enables you to create annotations between different parts in an assembly. This ability increases the control over the design as specifications become more precise, when dealing with not only the shape and quality of part features, but also the ways in which those features impact the overall assembly.

All tools available in the Functional Tolerancing & Annotations workbench are available in the Product Functional Tolerancing & Annotations workbench. To access the workbench, select **Start> Mechanical Design>Product Functional Tolerancing & Annotations**, as shown in Figure 7–1.

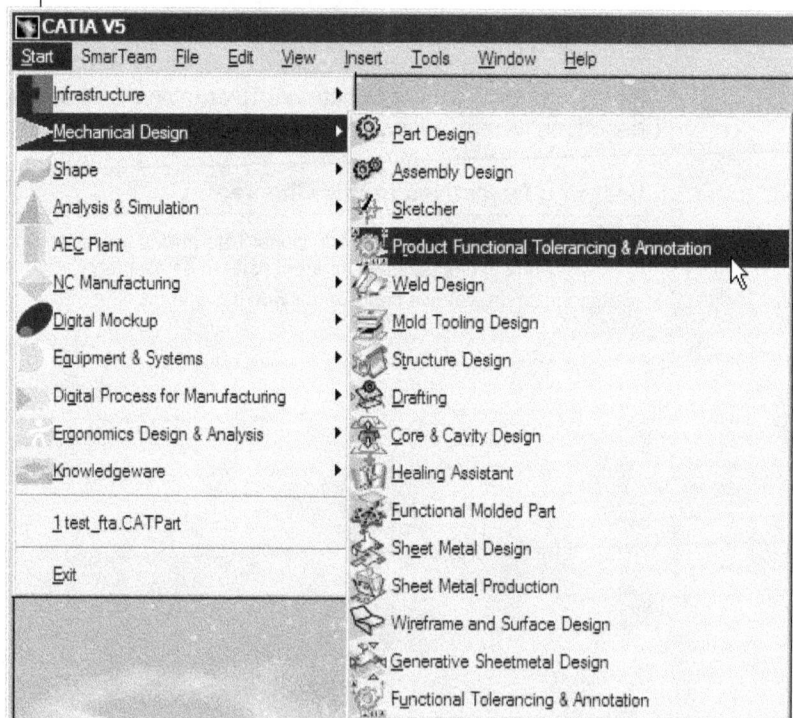

Figure 7–1

7.2 Working Context

Part annotations should be used to their full extent (i.e., to document every aspect of a part to ensure that all standards are met). Product annotations should be used only when the annotation references or refers to more than one assembly component. Keep the design specifications in the individual part to help maintain control of annotation display.

Use product level annotations to define how a product must be assembled. Dimensions in the product level are not intended to drive manufacturing, but to provide valuable information on the maximum allowable deviation when combining deviations from individual parts in an assembly. Annotations can also be used to note assembly instructions, and to point out features, tolerances, and properties common to multiple components in the assembly.

Annotations created in the Product FT&A workbench displays below the constraints in the specification tree, as shown in Figure 7–2.

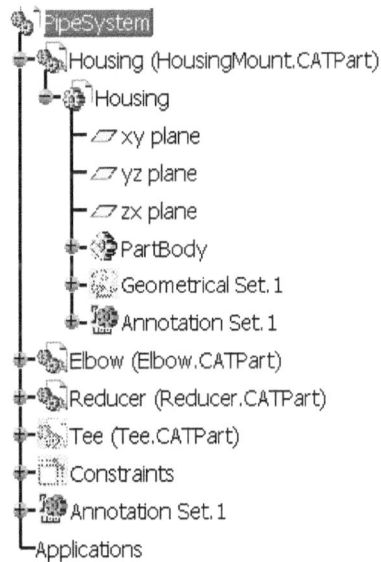

Figure 7–2

Individual annotations from the part annotation sets can be hidden without activating the part using the **Annotation Set Switch On/Switch Off** option.

You can control the display of multiple part-level annotation sets in a single operation by clicking ![icon] (List Annotation Set Switch On/Switch Off) in the Visualization toolbar. The Annotation Set Switch On/Switch Off dialog box opens, as shown in Figure 7–3.

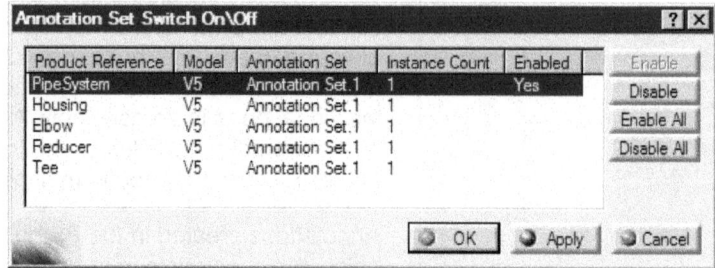

Product Reference	Model	Annotation Set	Instance Count	Enabled
PipeSystem	V5	Annotation Set.1	1	Yes
Housing	V5	Annotation Set.1	1	
Elbow	V5	Annotation Set.1	1	
Reducer	V5	Annotation Set.1	1	
Tee	V5	Annotation Set.1	1	

Figure 7–3

To control the display of an annotation set, select it in the list and use the buttons on the right side of the dialog box.

When displaying a part-level capture, all other components of the assembly are hidden. Hiding the dimensions in an Annotation Set cannot be undone; therefore, toggle off the entire annotation set or select the annotations individually.

© 2018, ASCENT - Center for Technical Knowledge®

7.3 Product FT&A

This section describes the primary differences between working in the Part and Product FT&A workbenches, which include the following:

- Annotation Planes

- Captures

- Cameras

Annotation Planes

Default reference planes do not exist and new reference planes cannot be developed at the product level. Therefore, annotation planes for the Product FT&A workbench typically reference part-level geometry.

Construction geometry can be created in the assembly annotation set. This geometry can be used to define annotation planes.

Carefully consider which references to select for annotation planes. If the part changes and the geometry is modified or deleted, or the assembly constraints are modified, it can affect the annotations. Annotations should be the last step in designing an assembly. If the assembly is still in its design phase, assign annotations to annotation planes that do not change. These annotations can be transferred to more appropriate annotation planes at the end of the design cycle.

Captures

When you create a capture at the product level, it can contain annotations that have been created in either the product or a component (such as a part or subassembly) that has been added to the assembly.

In contrast, when you create a capture at the part level, it displays within the context of an assembly. The system does not display any product-level annotations or annotations that were created in any other parts.

Cameras

When a camera is added using [icon] (Named views) in the Product Functional Tolerancing & Annotation workbench, it is listed in the specification tree, as shown in Figure 7–4.

```
⊕-Applications
  ⊕-Camera
     └─🎥 Default
```

Figure 7–4

You can double-click on the camera in the specification tree to orient and position the model. This should not be done when creating a capture because it forces an exit from the Tolerancing Capture workbench.

You can delete a camera from this branch by right-clicking and selecting **Delete**. You can also modify the position and orientation defined by a camera by dragging the manipulators that appear on the model.

Practice 7a

Product Level FT&A

Practice Objectives

- Create product level datums.
- Create product level geometric tolerances.

In this practice, you will develop a series of annotations for the PipeSystem.CATProduct model shown in Figure 7–5 using the Product FT&A workbench.

You will dimension and tolerance the flanges on the Elbow, Reducer, and Tee components with respect to the A datum reference frame, which is located at the base of the Housing component. Since all of these annotations reference more than one component, they are stored in the product annotation set. Annotations that only reference geometry from a single part should always be stored in the part annotation set.

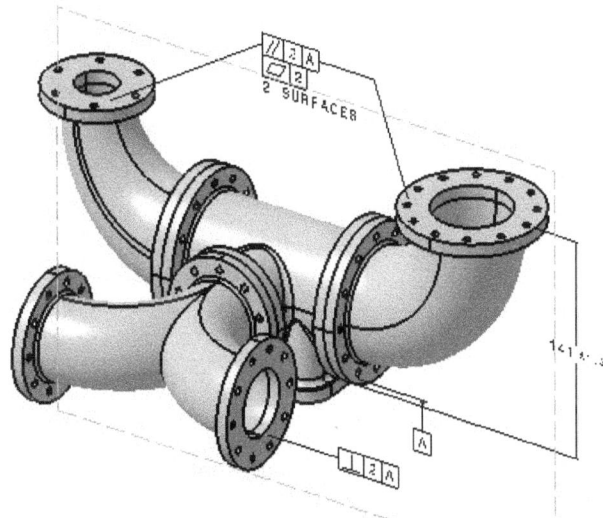

Figure 7–5

Task 1 - Open a product file.

1. Open **PipeSystem.CATProduct** from the PipeSystem folder. The assembly displays as shown in Figure 7–6.

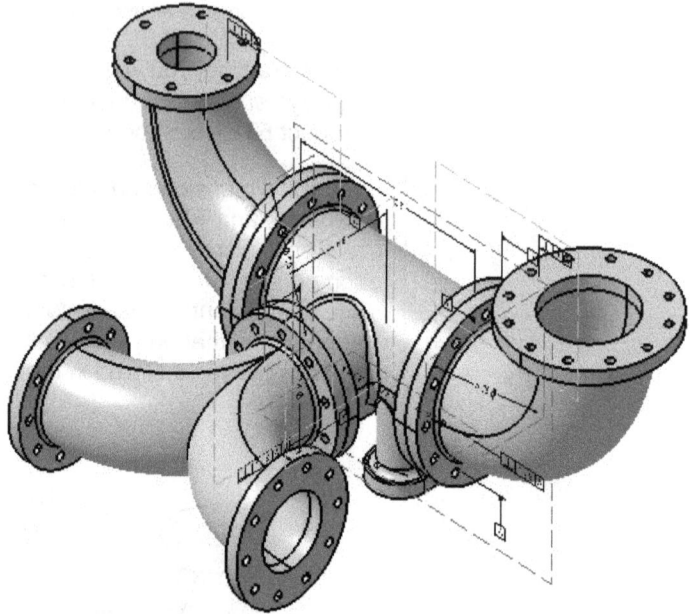

Figure 7–6

2. If you are not in the Product Functional Tolerancing & Annotation workbench, select **Start>Mechanical Design> Product Functional Tolerancing & Annotation**.

Task 2 - Set options.

Review the existing annotations. Note that they are in metric. You will continue to create the annotations and tolerances in metric.

1. Select **Tools>Options**.

2. Select **General>Parameters and Measure** and select the *Units* tab. Set the *Length* to **Millimeter (mm)**.

3. Select **Mechanical Design>Functional Tolerancing & Annotation** and select the *Tolerances* tab.

4. Ensure that the *Geometrical Tolerance Precision* is set to **1**.

5. Click **OK**.

Task 3 - Manage the display of annotations and components.

In this task, you will manage the display of an annotation set that exists at the part level. You will also hide a component to simplify the display of the assembly.

1. Expand the Housing branch of the specification tree, as shown in Figure 7–7. Part-level annotation sets have been created in each component of the assembly.

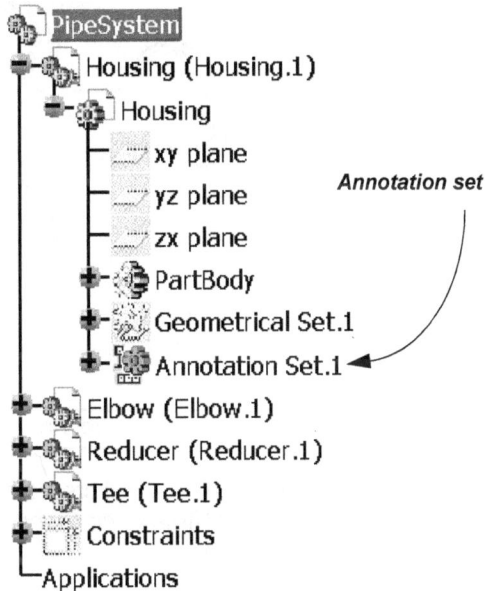

Figure 7–7

2. In the Visualization toolbar, click ⬚ (List Annotation Set Switch On/Switch Off). The Annotation Set Switch On\Off dialog box opens as shown in Figure 7–8.

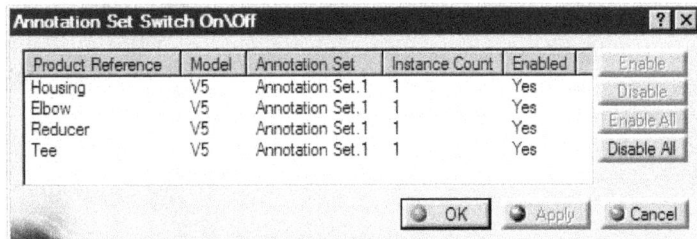

Product Reference	Model	Annotation Set	Instance Count	Enabled	
Housing	V5	Annotation Set.1	1	Yes	Enable
Elbow	V5	Annotation Set.1	1	Yes	Disable
Reducer	V5	Annotation Set.1	1	Yes	Enable All
Tee	V5	Annotation Set.1	1	Yes	Disable All

OK   Apply   Cancel

Figure 7–8

3. To toggle off all of the part-level annotation sets click **Disable All**.

4. Click **OK**. The assembly displays, as shown in Figure 7–9.

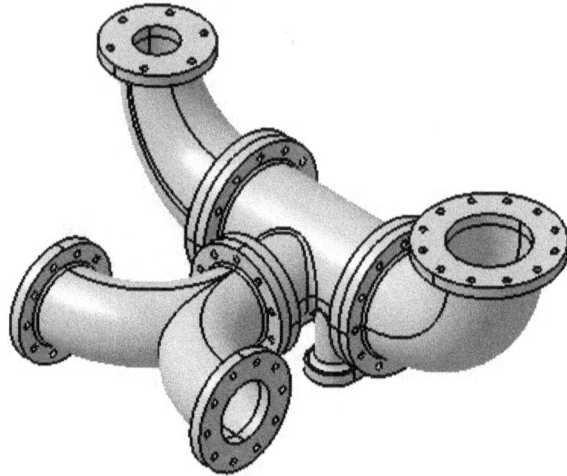

Figure 7–9

5. Hide the Tee component in the specification tree.

Task 4 - Create a view at the product level.

In this task, you will create a view. You must use the Product Functional Tolerencing workbench to create a view and annotations.

1. Select the face, as shown in Figure 7–10.

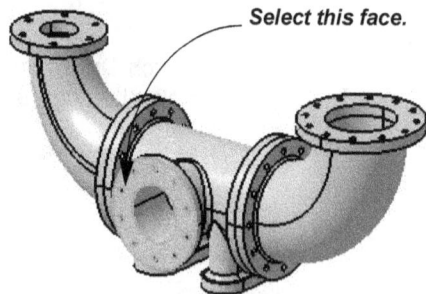

Select this face.

Figure 7–10

2. Create a Projection View view and name it as **TeeFlangeView**. Ensure the view is oriented, as shown in Figure 7–11.

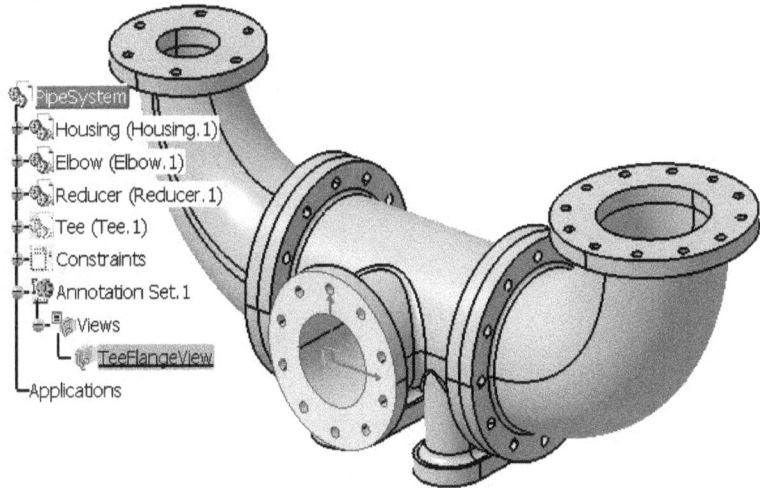

Figure 7–11

Task 5 - Create a product level semantic datum and dimension.

1. Preselect the surface shown in Figure 7–12.

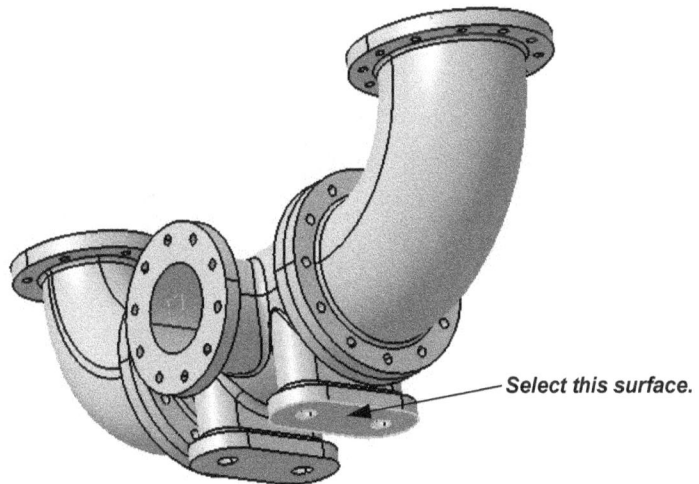

Select this surface.

Figure 7–12

2. Use the tolerancing advisor to create the following:

- **Semantic Datum (A)**
- **Datum Reference Frame** (enable **From this datum feature**)

The completed datum displays, as shown in Figure 7–13 (move the datum to the position shown in the image).

For clarity, annotations have been enlarged to 7.0mm.

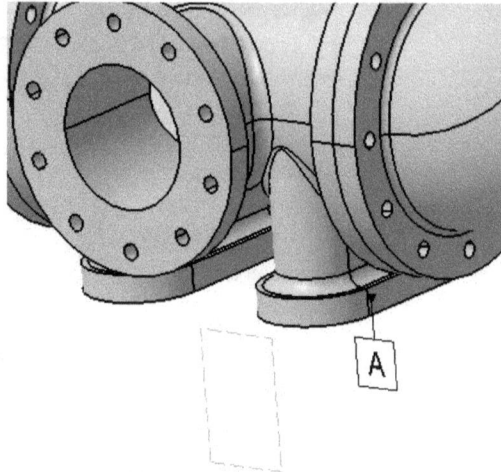

Figure 7–13

Next, you will create a dimension between the surface representing the A datum and the top flange surface.

3. Preselect the two surfaces shown in Figure 7–14.

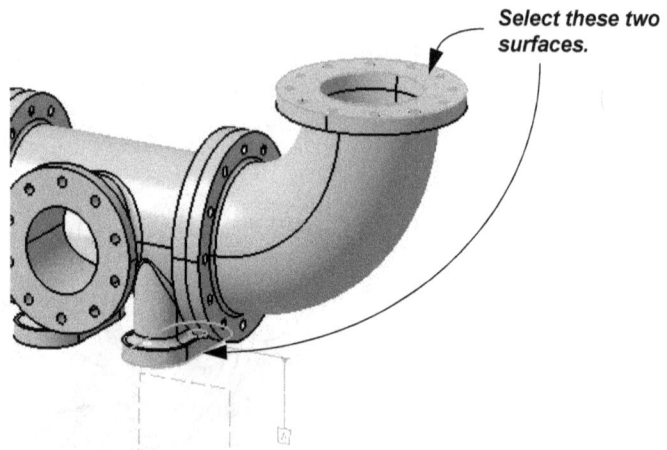

Select these two surfaces.

Figure 7–14

4. Use the tolerance advisor to create a semantic dimension with a symmetrical tolerance of **1.5mm**, as shown in Figure 7–15.

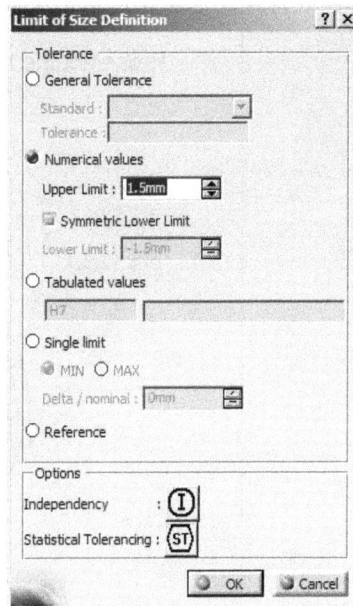

Figure 7–15

5. Use the Numerical Properties toolbar to change the units to **NUM.DIMM**.

6. Move the completed dimension to the location shown in Figure 7–16.

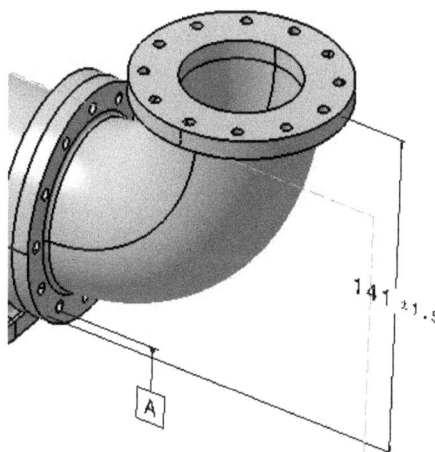

Figure 7–16

Task 6 - Create a product-level semantic tolerance.

In this task, you will create a geometric tolerance that controls the two top flanges relative to datum A.

1. Preselect the two surfaces shown in Figure 7–17.

Select these two surfaces.

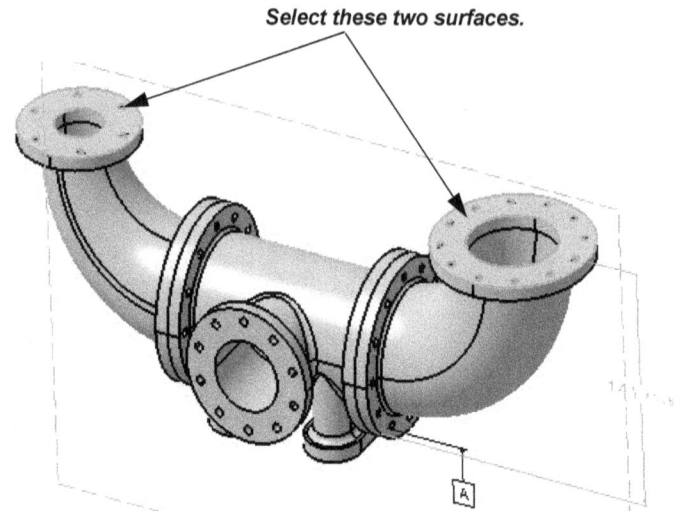

Figure 7–17

2. Use the tolerance advisor to create an **N geometrical features in Collection (NX)** feature type with Flatness Specification, as shown in Figure 7–18.

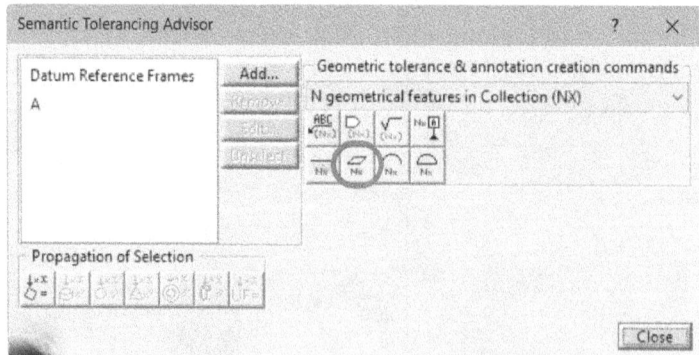

Figure 7–18

3. Enter a tolerance of **2mm**, as shown in Figure 7–19.

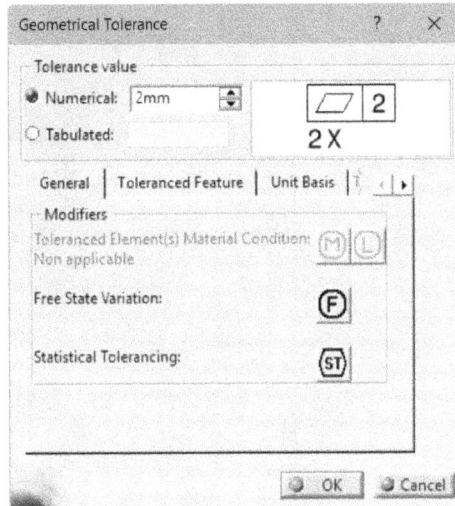

Figure 7–19

4. Click **OK**.

5. Select datum **A** in the *Identifier* section and click **Parallelism Specification**, as shown in Figure 7–20 to create a parallel geometrical tolerance relative to the datum A.

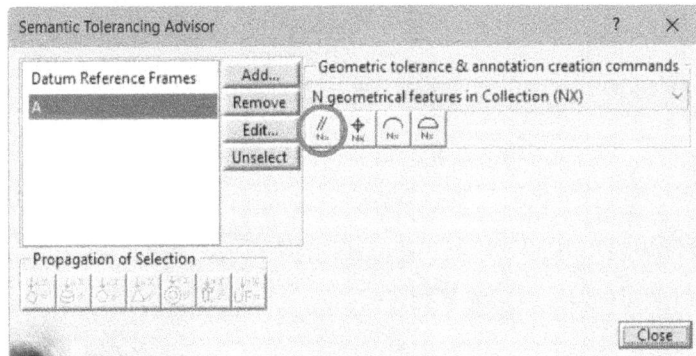

Figure 7–20

6. Enter a tolerance value of **2mm**.

7. Click **OK**.

8. Click **Close**.

9. Move the Geometric Tolerance, as shown in Figure 7–21.

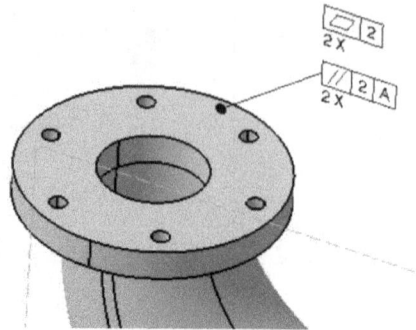

Figure 7–21

Your geometric tolerance might be located on the other surface. The tolerance will be placed closest to the last selected surface.

Note that the geometric tolerance created points to only one of the selected surfaces. In the following steps, you will add another leader to point to the other surface.

10. Right-click on the geometric tolerance and select **Add Leader**.

11. Select somewhere close to the other referenced surface in the view frame area.

Note that you will not be able to select the surface, so simply select a location near it.

12. Right-click on the endpoint of the leader that you just added and select **Add Extremity Link**.

13. Select the applicable flange surface to update the leader placement.

14. Add a Breakpoint to the new leader and place the geometric tolerance, as shown in Figure 7–22.

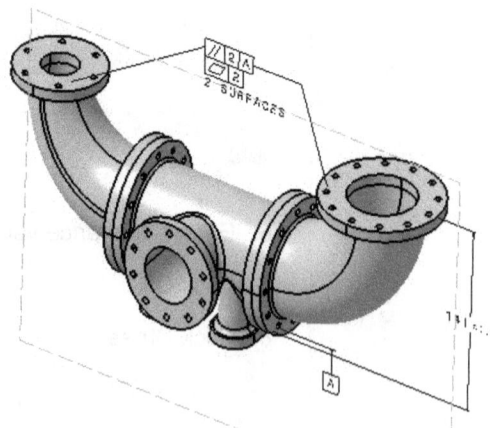

Figure 7–22

15. Show the Tee component.

16. Preselect the surface shown in Figure 7–23.

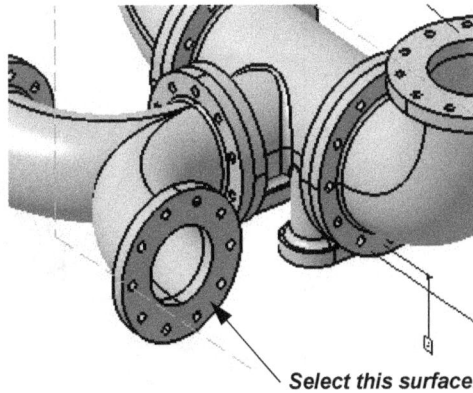

Select this surface.

Figure 7–23

17. Use the Tolerance Advisor to create a geometric tolerance that specifies the selected surface be perpendicular to datum A by **2mm**. The completed tolerance displays, as shown in Figure 7–24.

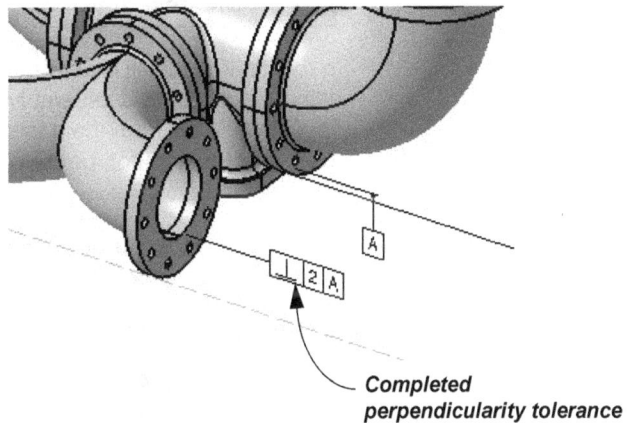

Completed perpendicularity tolerance

Figure 7–24

18. The completed product annotation displays, as shown in Figure 7–25. Save the file.

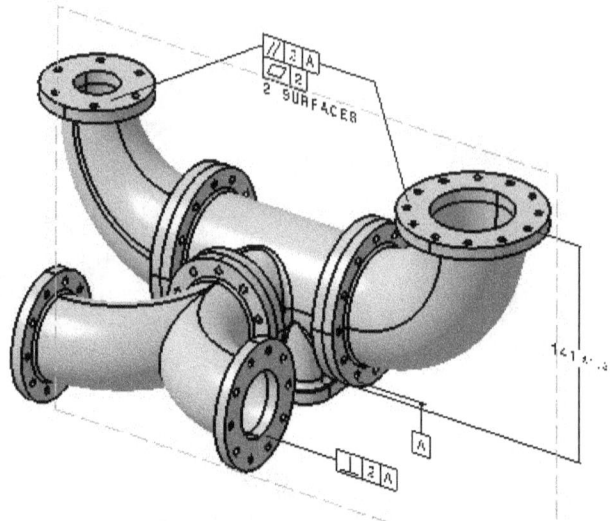

Figure 7–25

Task 7 - Create a drawing.

In this task, you will create a new drawing and add two views using the annotated assembly. The first view uses the TeeFlangeView from the assembly. The second view is created from the Housing component. To do this, you will switch the annotation set for Housing back on.

1. Using the **List Annotation Set Switch On/Switch Off** tool, enable the annotation set for the housing.

2. Create a new empty drawing using the following parameters:

   • *Standard:* **ASME**
   • *Sheet Style:* **D ANSI**

3. Click [⊞] (View from 3D) and select **Window> PipeSystem.CATProduct**.

4. Select **TeeFlangeView** in the product annotation set.

5. Click somewhere on the background. The new view displays, as shown in Figure 7–26.

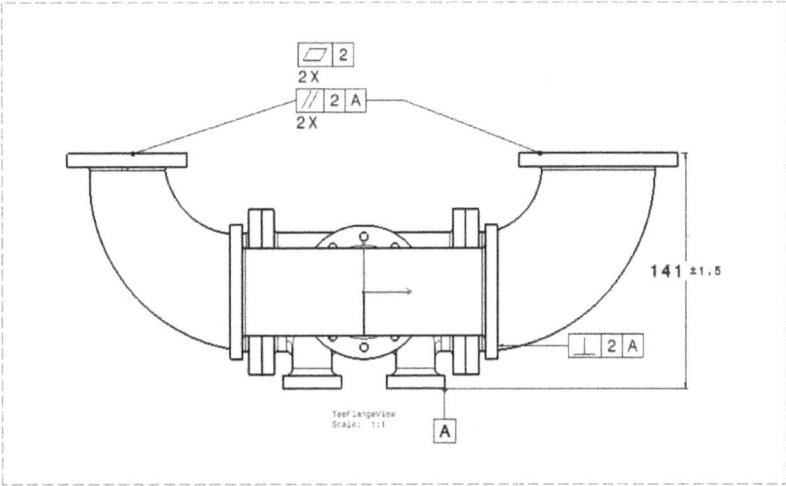

Figure 7–26

6. Create a second view and reference RunFlangeView in the Housing annotation set. The view displays, as shown in Figure 7–27.

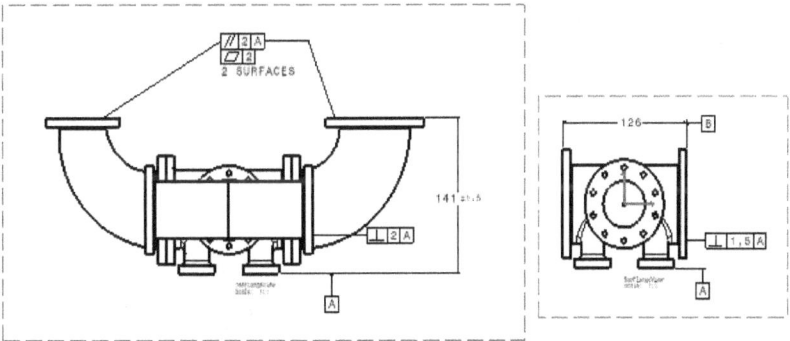

Figure 7–27

7. Add an isometric view of the assembly to the drawing.

8. Right-click on the drawing views in the tree and select **Properties** to toggle off the view frame for all three views. The drawing displays, as shown in Figure 7–28.

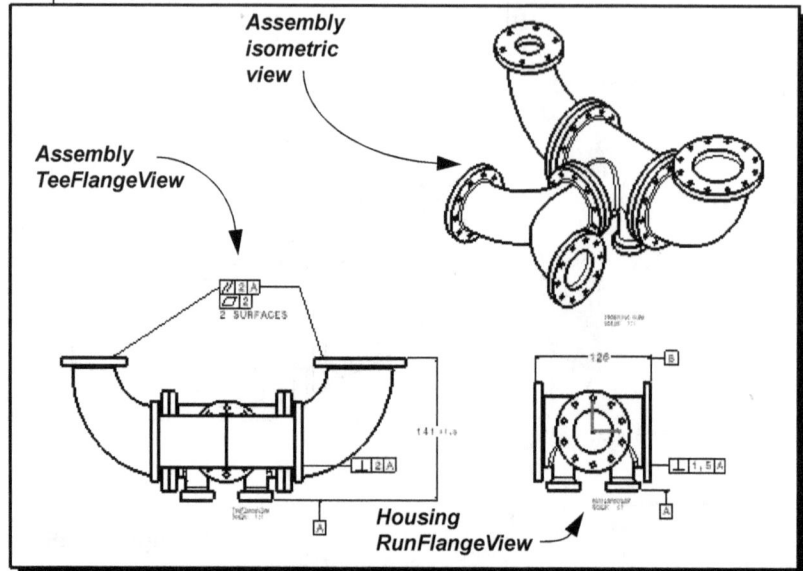

Figure 7–28

9. Save all files and close all windows.

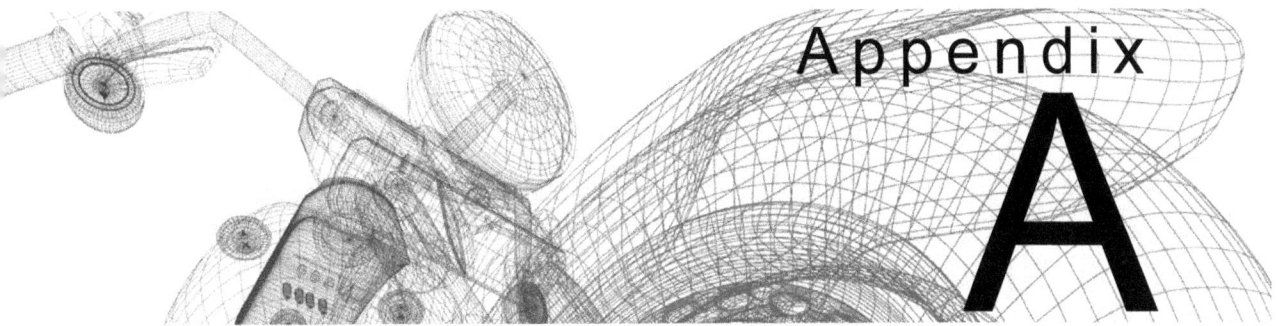

FT&A Projects

These projects are to be completed with minimal instruction. Complete on your own or as a group, as time permits.

Projects in this Chapter

- Flange Part
- Spindle Part
- Coupling Part
- Threaded Ball
- Pressure Plate
- Coaxial Parts Case

Practice A1 | Flange Part

Practice Objective

• Specify runout relative to datum surface and diameter.

In this project, you will add tolerances and annotations to a part and create a drawing view to display them. The completed drawing displays, as shown in Figure A–1.

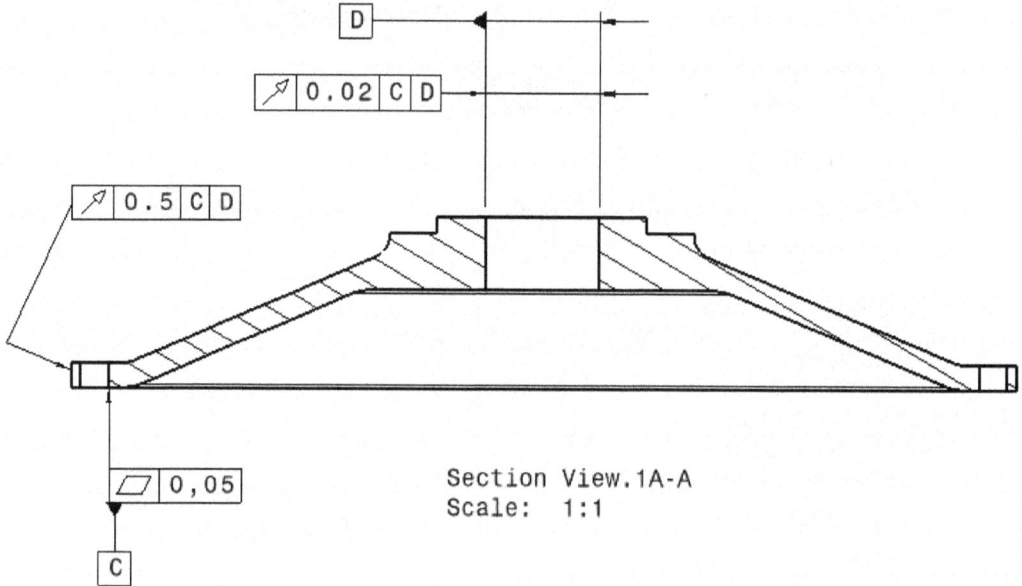

| D |

| ⟋ | 0.02 | C | D |

| ⟋ | 0.5 | C | D |

Section View.1A-A
Scale: 1:1

| ▱ | 0,05 |

| C |

Figure A–1

Task 1 - Open a part file.

1. Open **Flange.CATPart** from the Projects folder. The part displays, as shown in Figure A–2.

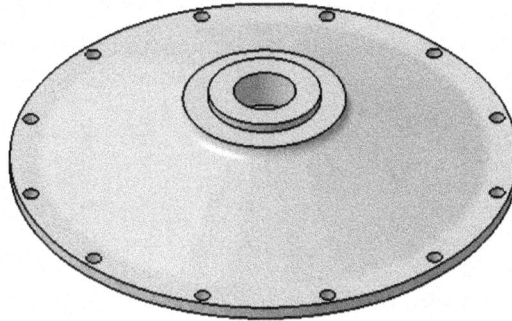

Figure A–2

Task 2 - Create semantic datums and geometrical tolerances.

1. Create semantic datums and geometrical tolerances on a section view plane, as shown in Figure A–3 (you can also reference Figure A–4).

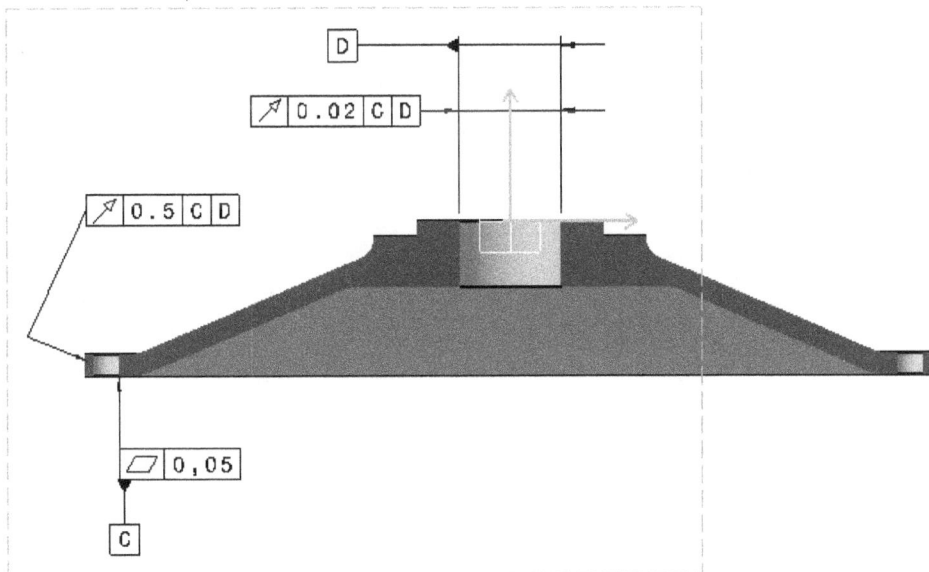

Figure A–3

Task 3 - Create a drawing.

1. Create the following drawing:

   - *Standard:* **ASME**
   - *Format:* **C ANSI**

2. Create the view shown in Figure A–4.

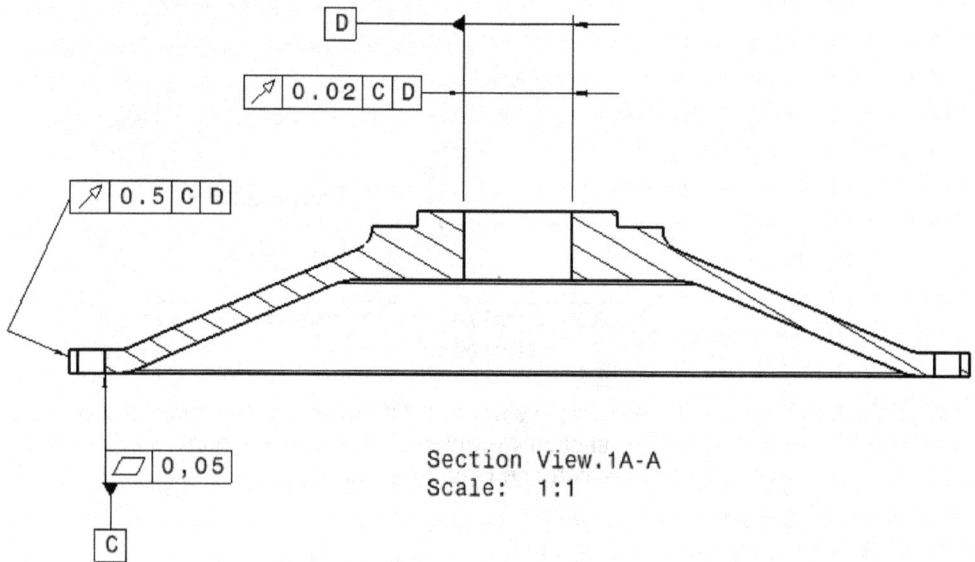

```
Section View.1A-A
Scale:  1:1
```

Figure A–4

3. Save and close all files.

Practice A2 | Spindle Part

Practice Objective

- Specify runout relative to two datum diameters.

In this project, you will add tolerances and annotations to a part and create a drawing view to display them. The completed drawing displays, as shown in Figure A–5.

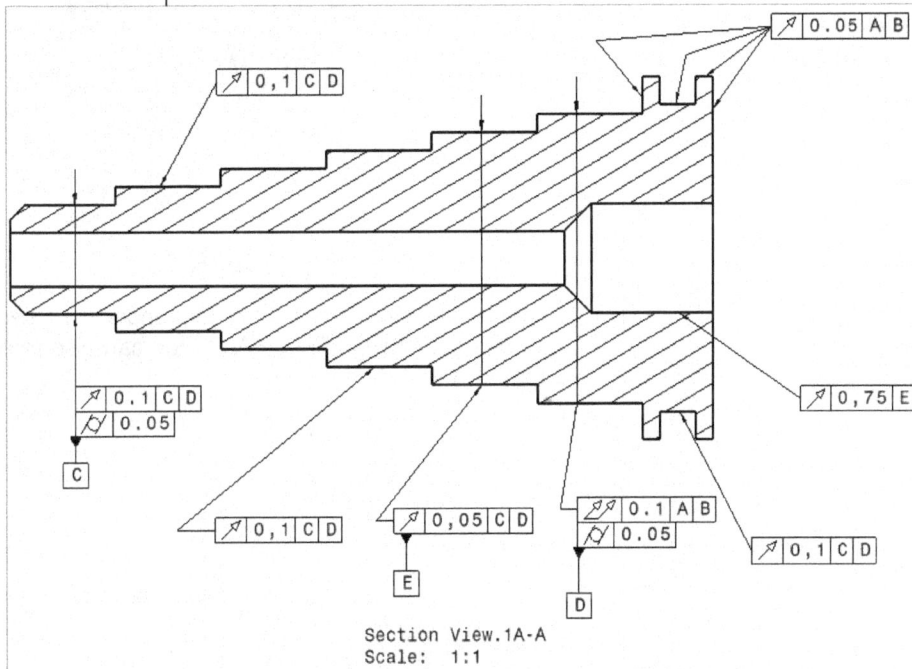

Section View.1A-A
Scale: 1:1

Figure A–5

Task 1 - Open a part file.

1. Open **Spindle.CATPart** from the Projects folder. The part displays, as shown in Figure A–6.

Figure A–6

2. Create semantic datums and tolerances on a section view plane, as shown in Figure A–7 (you can also reference Figure A–8).

Figure A–7

Task 2 - Create a drawing.

1. Create the following drawing:

   - *Standard:* **ASME**
   - *Format:* **C ANSI**

2. Create the view shown in Figure A–8.

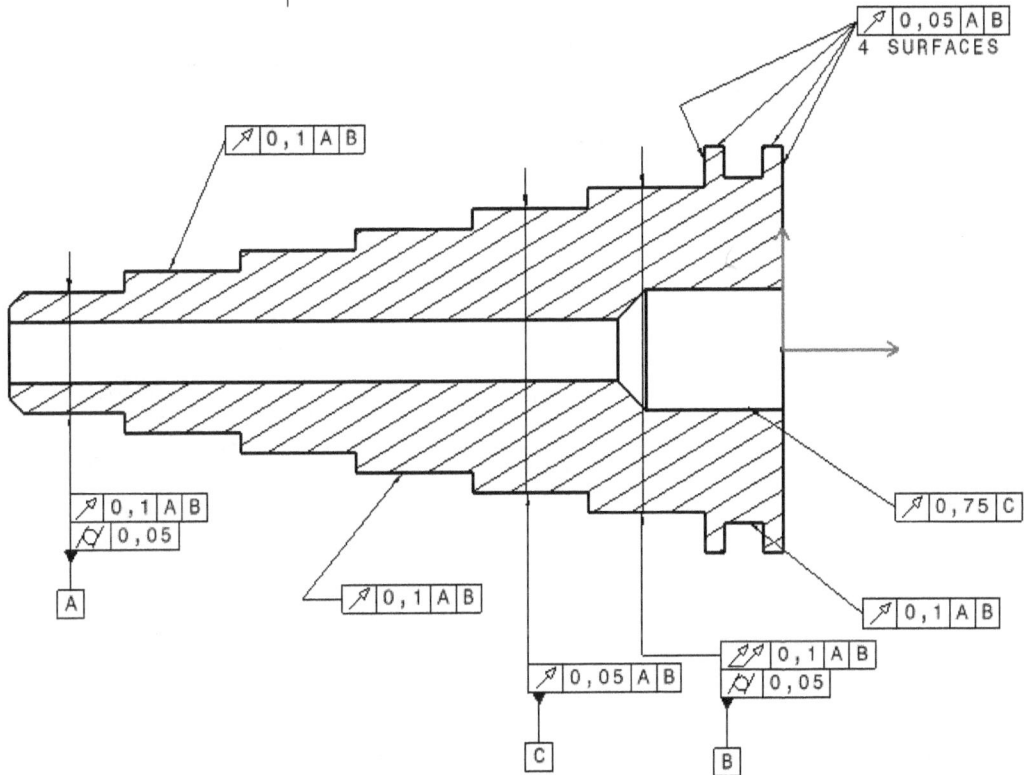

Section View.1A-A
Scale: 1:1

Figure A–8

3. Save and close all files.

Practice A3

Coupling Part

Practice Objective

- Create a radial hole pattern located by composite positional tolerancing.

In this project, you will add tolerances and annotations to a part and create a drawing view to display them.

Task 1 - Open a part file.

1. Open **Coupling.CATPart** from the Projects folder. The part displays, as shown in Figure A–9.

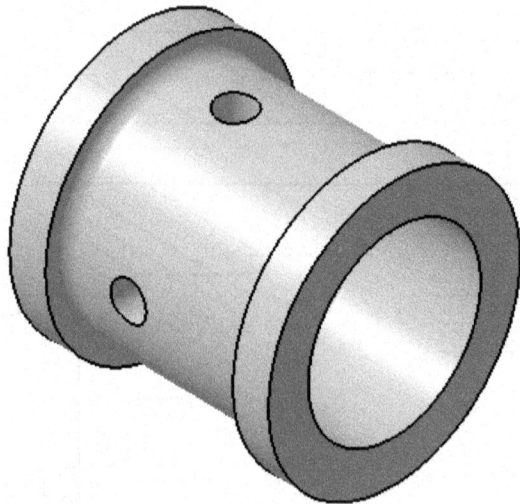

Figure A–9

2. Select **Tools>Options**.

3. Select **General>Parameters and Measure** and select the *Units* tab. Verify that the units are set to **Inch(in)**.

4. Select **Mechanical Design>Functional Tolerancing & Annotation** and select the *Tolerances* tab. Verify that *Precision* is set to **0.001**.

Task 2 - Create semantic datums, dimensions, and tolerances.

1. Create a section view plane and select the YZ plane as a reference.

2. Create the following:

- Semantic datums
- Semantic dimensions
- A basic dimension
- Composite positional tolerance

The required dimensions and annotations are shown in Figure A–10 (you can also reference Figure A–11).

*If a 28mm dimension displays instead of the intended 14mm, right-click on the dimension while placing it and select **Half Dimension**.*

To create this dimension, select the CircPattern.1 from the PartBody in the specification tree.

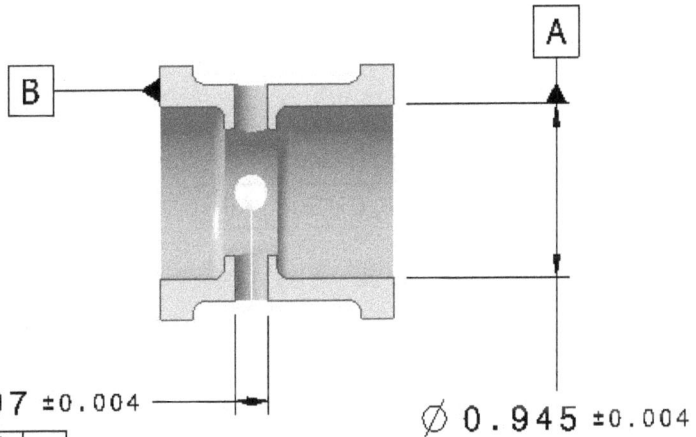

$4 \times \quad \emptyset \, 0.197 \, \pm 0.004$

| $\oplus$ | $\emptyset 0,03$ | A Ⓜ | B |
| $\oplus$ | $\emptyset 0,008$ Ⓜ | A Ⓜ | |

$\emptyset \, 0.945 \, \pm 0.004$

Figure A–10

Task 3 - Create a drawing.

1. Create the following drawing:

   - *Standard:* **ASME**
   - *Format:* **A ANSI**

2. Create the view shown in Figure A–11.

A

B

4 X   ∅ 0.197 ±0.004

| ⊕ | ∅0,03 | A Ⓜ | B |
| ⊕ | ∅0,008Ⓜ | AⓂ | |

∅ 0.945 ±0.004

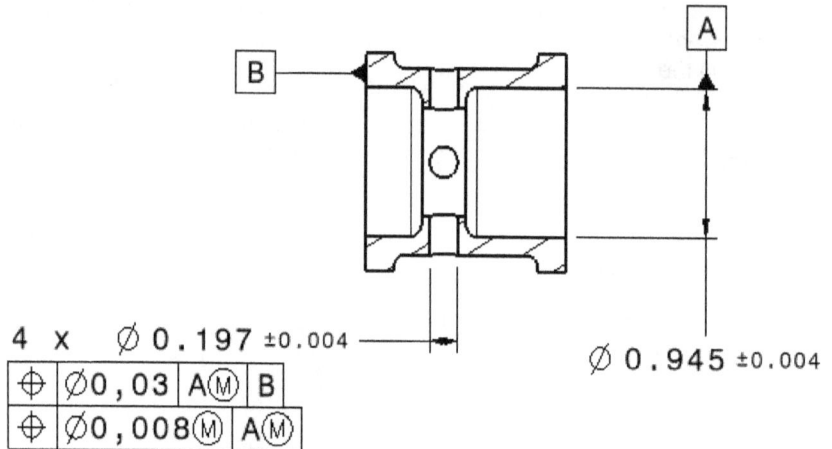

Section View.1A-A
Scale: 1:1

Figure A–11

3. Save and close all files.

Practice A4 | Threaded Ball

Practice Objectives

- Display a thread representation.
- Create a thread annotation.

In this project, you add tolerances and annotations to a part, and create a drawing view to display them.

Task 1 - Open a part file.

1. Open **ThreadedBall.CATPart** from the Projects folder. The part displays, as shown in Figure A–12.

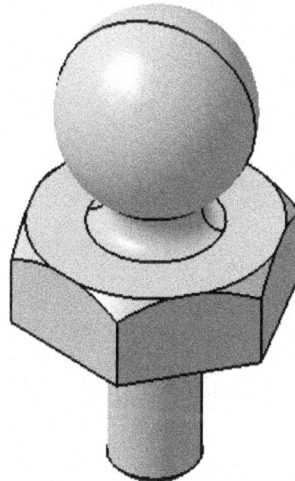

Figure A–12

Task 2 - Create semantic datums, dimensions, and tolerances.

*Note that the units are in metric. Set the global units to **Millimeter (mm)** and use the Numerical Properties toolbar to convert the dimensions to metric.*

1. Create the following:

   - Front view plane
   - Thread representation
   - Thread diameter annotation
   - Semantic datums
   - A semantic dimension
   - A basic dimension
   - A positional tolerance

The required dimensions and annotations are shown in Figure A–13 (you can also reference Figure A–14).

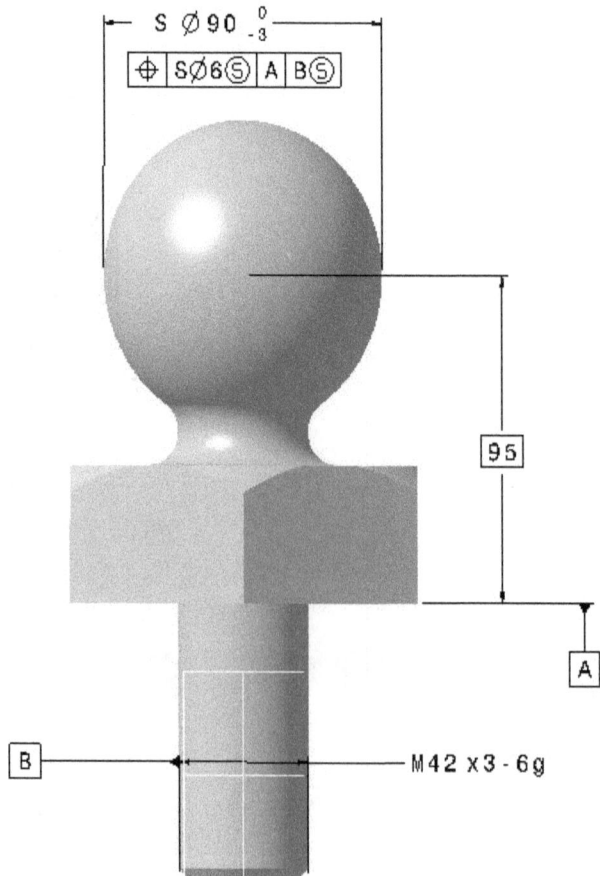

Figure A–13

Task 3 - Create a drawing.

1. Create the following drawing:

    - *Standard:* **ASME**
    - *Format:* **B ANSI**
    - *Portrait:* **Select this option**

2. Create the view shown in Figure A–14. Verify that the thread and axes display.

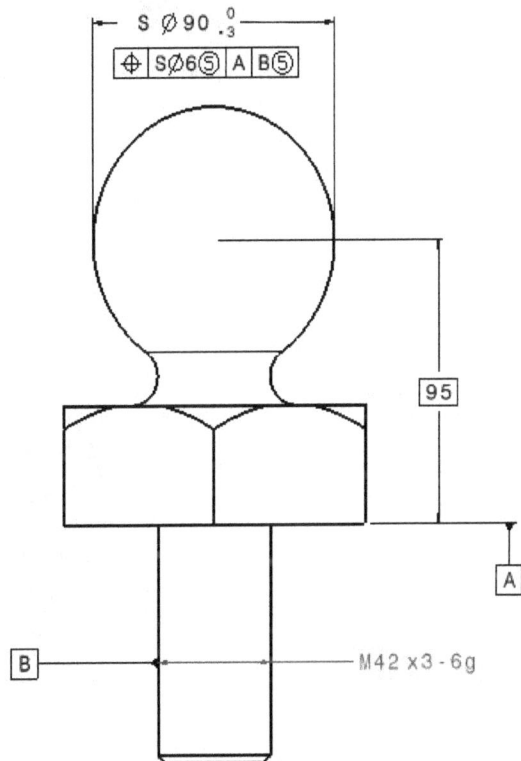

Front View.1
Scale: 1:1

Figure A–14

3. Save and close all files.

Practice A5

Pressure Plate

Practice Objectives

- Annotate a part model.
- Create drawing views of an annotated model.

In this project, you add tolerances and annotations to a part, and create a drawing view to display them.

Task 1 - Open a part file.

1. Open **PressurePlate.CATPart** from the Projects folder. The part displays, as shown in Figure A–15.

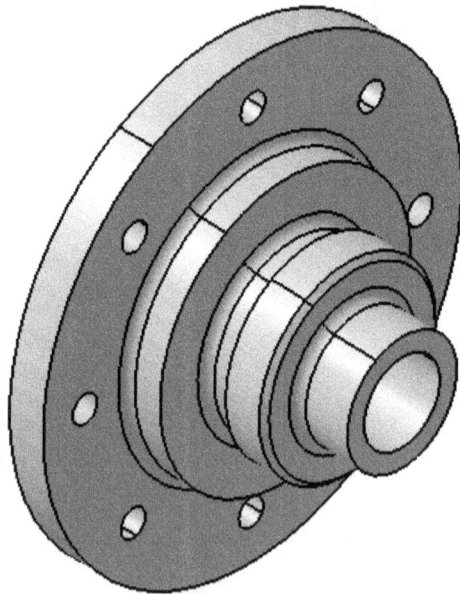

Figure A–15

*Note that the units are in
metric. Set the global
units to **Millimeter (mm)**
and use the Numerical
Properties toolbar to
convert the dimensions
to metric.*

*Use the Generative
Dimensions tool to
create the chamfer
dimension.*

1. Create the following:

    *   Section view plane
    *   Toleranced dimensions
    *   Semantic datums and required datum reference frames
    *   Geometrical tolerances
    *   Thread representation
    *   Thread diameter annotation

The required dimensions and annotations are shown in
Figure A–16 (you can also reference Figure A–18).

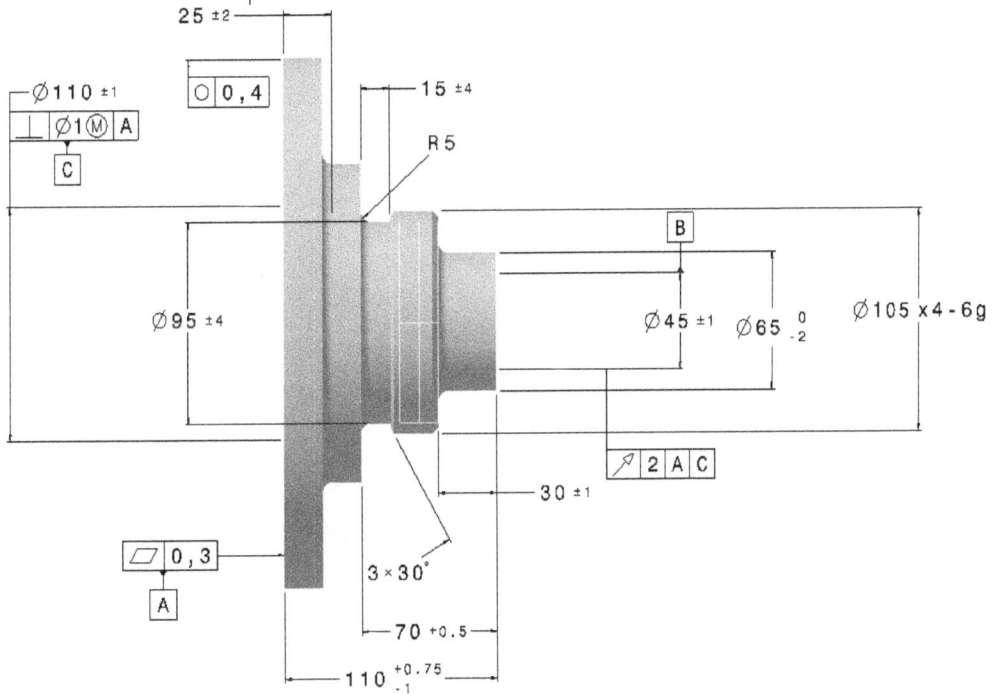

Figure A–16

2. Create the following:

- Front view plane
- Construction geometry
- Semantic dimensions
- Position geometrical tolerance

The required dimensions and annotations are shown in Figure A–17 (you can also reference Figure A–19).

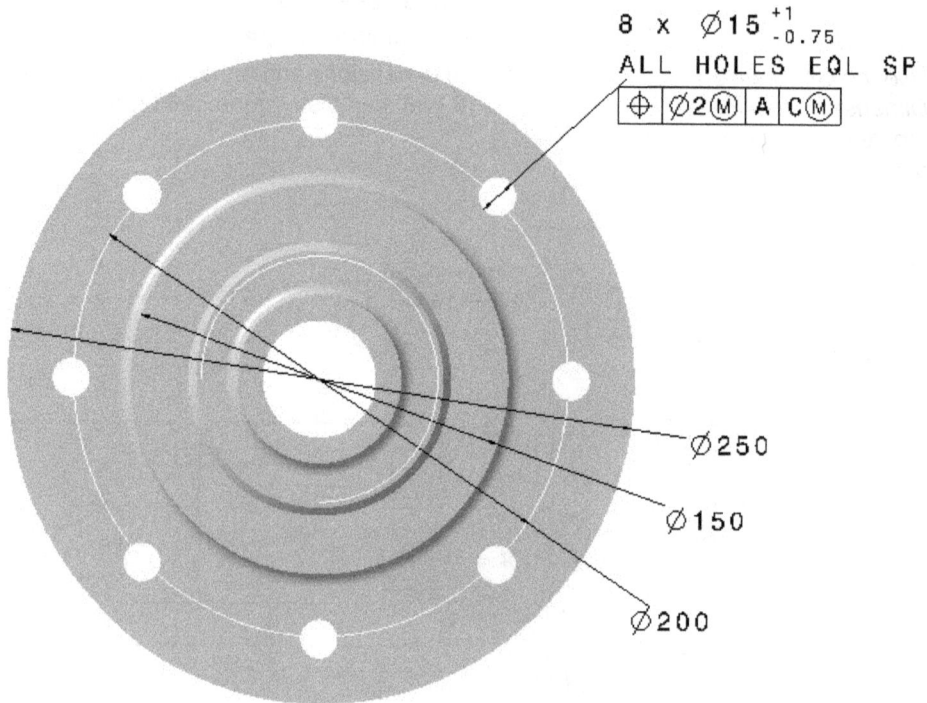

Figure A–17

Task 3 - Create a drawing.

1. Create the following drawing:

    *   *Standard:* **ASME**
    *   *Format:* **E ANSI**
    *   *Landscape:* **Select this option**

2. Create the view shown in Figure A–18 and Figure A–19. Verify that the thread and axes display.

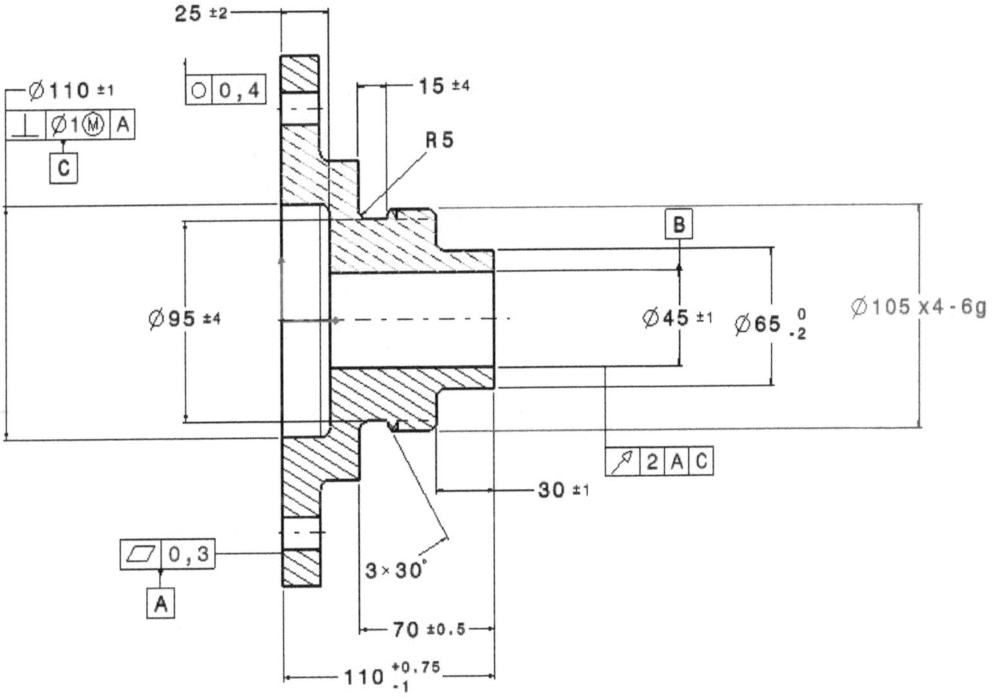

Figure A–18

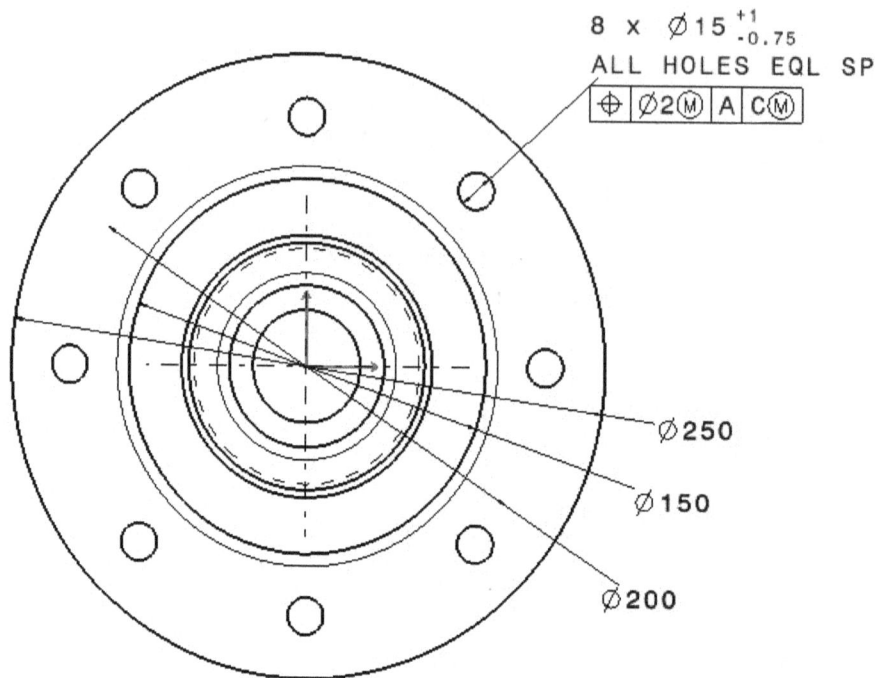

8 x $\varnothing 15^{+1}_{-0.75}$
ALL HOLES EQL SP

| ⊕ | $\varnothing 2$Ⓜ | A | CⓂ |

$\varnothing 250$

$\varnothing 150$

$\varnothing 200$

Figure A–19

3. Save and close all files.

Practice A6 | Coaxial Parts Case

Practice Objective

- Determine tolerance for two coaxial mating parts.

In this project, you will determine the geometric tolerance for each coaxial mating part. You will use a formula to find the available tolerance and divide it unequally between the two parts. At the end of the practice, you will create a drawing of the assembly and create a view from 3D for the parts of the assembly. The completed drawing displays, as shown in Figure A–20.

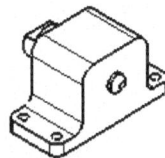

Isometric view
Scale: 1:2

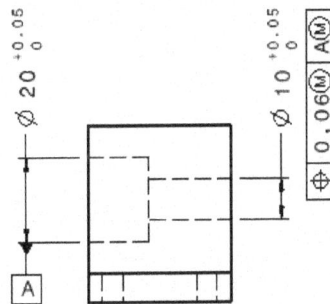

Front View.1
Scale: 1:1

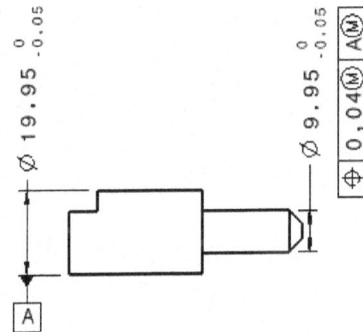

Front View.1
Scale: 1:1

Figure A–20

Task 1 - Open a product file.

1. Open **CoaxialParts.CATProduct** from the Projects folder. The two part assembly displays, as shown in Figure A–21.

Figure A–21

This assembly consists of two parts that share an axis (coaxial) and therefore also share the datum that defines that axis. In this practice, you will create semantic datums and dimensions for each part. You will then apply a floating fastener case formula to determine the geometric tolerance value in the context of this assembly.

2. Close the **CoaxialParts.CATProduct** file.

Task 2 - Set options.

1. Select **Tools>Options**.

2. Select **General>Parameters and Measure** and select the *Units* tab. Verify that the *Length* units are set to **Millimeter (mm)**.

3. Select **Mechanical Design>Functional Tolerancing & Annotation** and select the *Tolerances* tab. Verify that *Precision* is set to **0.001**.

4. Click **OK**.

Task 3 - Open a part file.

In this task, you will open one of the parts that belong to the CoaxialParts assembly and create a semantic datum and dimensions.

1. Open **Seat.CATPart**. The part displays, as shown in Figure A–22.

Figure A–22

2. Create a Front View/Annotation Plane by referencing the YZ plane. Verify that the plane is oriented, as shown in Figure A–23.

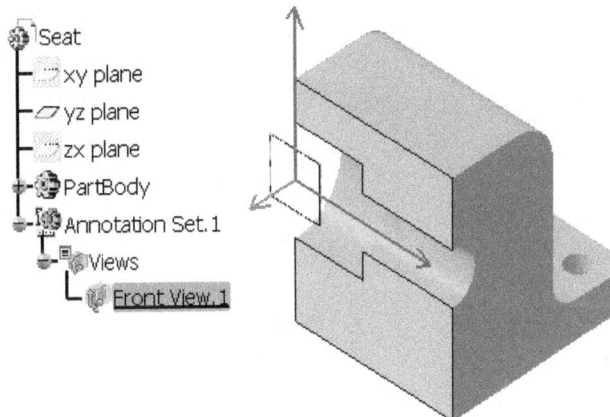

Figure A–23

3. Preselect the larger of the two bores, as shown in Figure A–24.

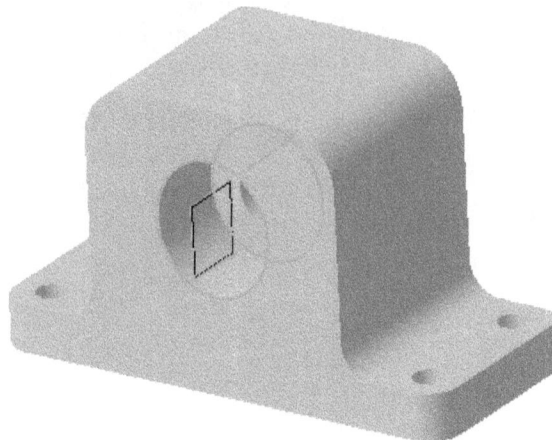

Figure A–24

4. Use the Tolerance Advisor to create semantic datum A with a DRF.

5. Position datum A, as shown in Figure A–25.

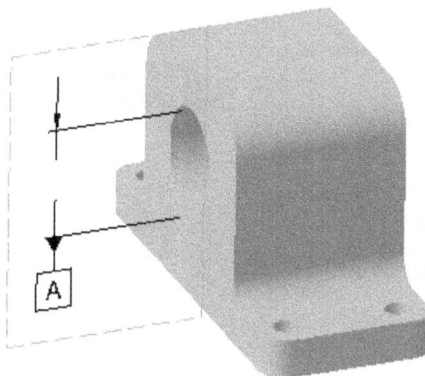

Figure A–25

6. Create a semantic diameter dimension for the same bore. Add the following tolerance.

- *Upper Limit:* **0.05mm**
- *Lower Limit:* **0.0mm**

7. Use the Numerical Properties toolbar to change the units to **NUM.DIMM**.

8. Position the completed diameter dimension, as shown in Figure A–26.

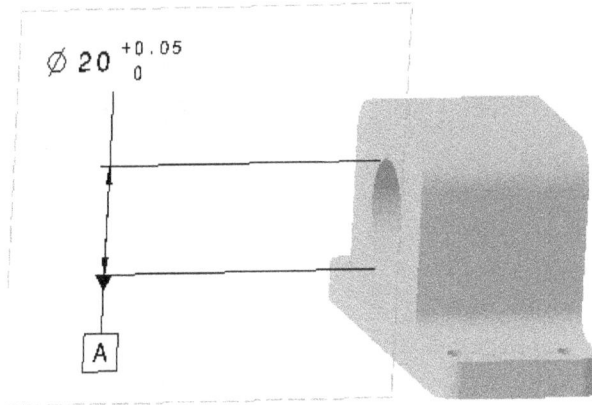

Figure A–26

9. Create a semantic dimension for the smaller bore. Add the following tolerance, as shown in Figure A–27:

   • *Upper Limit:* **0.05mm**
   • *Lower Limit:* **0.00mm**

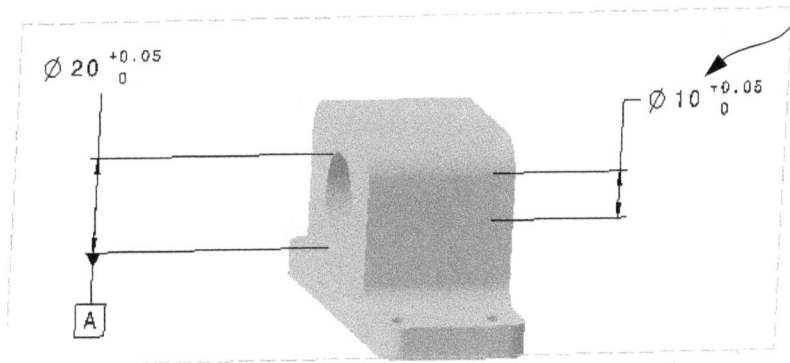

Figure A–27

10. Save the Seat.CATPart file.

Task 4 - Open the mating part.

1. Open **Post.CATPart**. The part displays, as shown in Figure A–28.

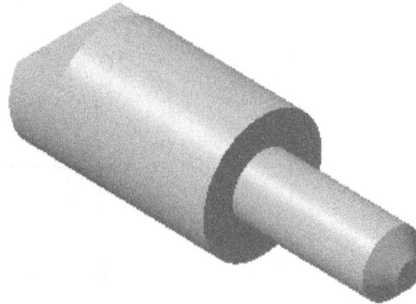

Figure A–28

2. Create a Front View/Annotation Plane by referencing the YZ plane.

3. Create a semantic datum with DRF on the large diameter geometry and position it as shown in Figure A–29.

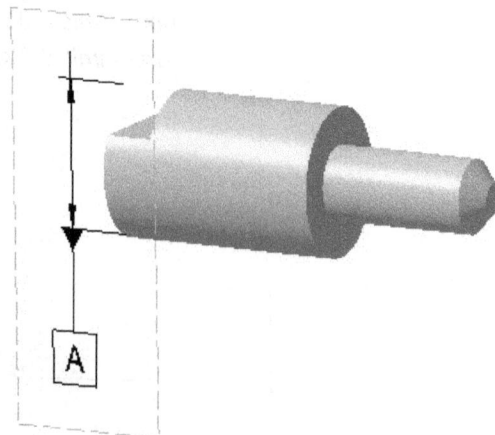

Figure A–29

4. Create the semantic diameter dimension shown in Figure A–30. Add the following tolerance:

- *Upper Limit:* **0.0mm**
- *Lower Limit:* **-0.05mm**

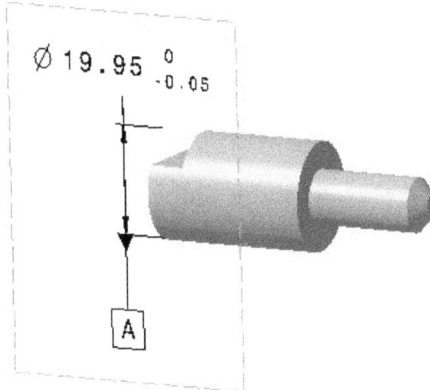

Figure A–30

5. Create the semantic diameter dimension shown in Figure A–31. Add the following tolerance:

- *Upper Limit:* **0.0in**
- *Lower Limit:* **-0.05in**

The completed annotations display, as shown in Figure A–31.

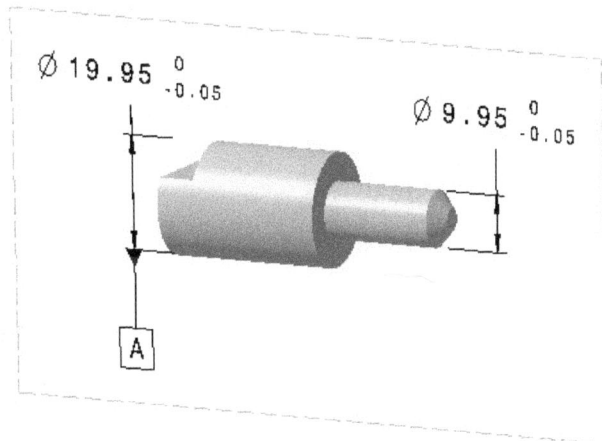

Figure A–31

Task 5 - Determine the tolerance for both parts.

Design Considerations

When two or more parts are assembled (such as bolts and nuts) and all parts have clearance holes, it is termed a *floating fastener case*. Use the following formula to determine the positional tolerance required for a floating fastener case, as shown in Figure A–32 and Figure A–33:

Where:

- F = max. diameter of fastener at MMC

- H = min. diameter of clearance hole at MMC

- T = positional tolerance diameter

$T = H - F$

Therefore:

$T_1 + T_2 = (H_1 + H_2) - (F_1 + F_2)$

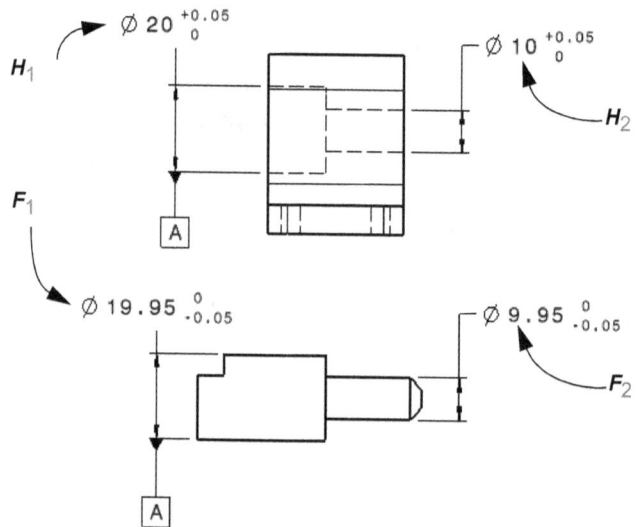

Figure A–32

$T_1 + T_2 = (20 + 10) - (19.95 + 9.95)$

$T_1 + T_2 = 0.1$ total available tolerance

If $T_1 = 0.06$ then $T_2 = 0.04$

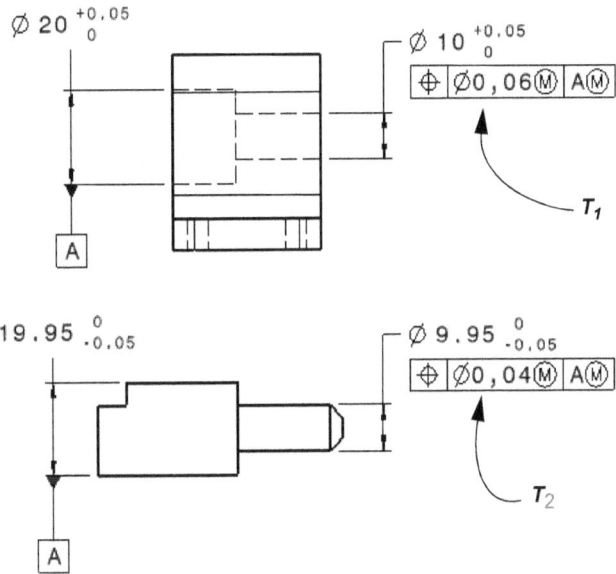

Figure A–33

Task 6 - Create positional tolerances for two mating parts.

1. Activate the Seat.CATPart window.

2. Create the positional tolerance shown in Figure A–34 for the small bore.

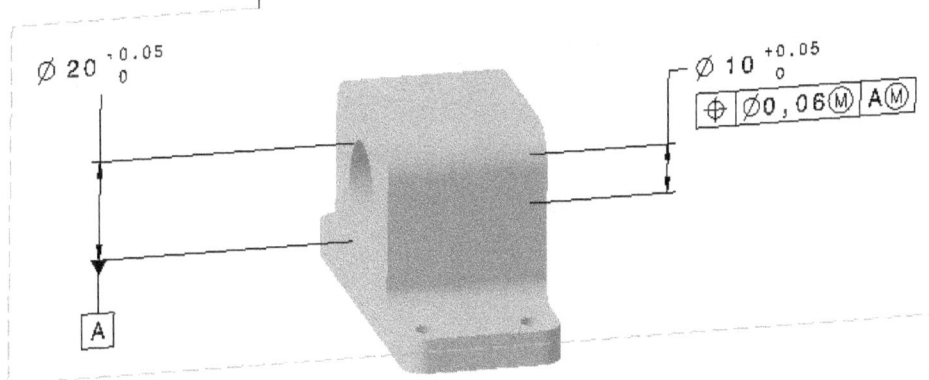

Figure A–34

3. Save the part.

4. Activate the Post.CATPart window.

5. Create the positional tolerance shown in Figure A–35 for the small bore.

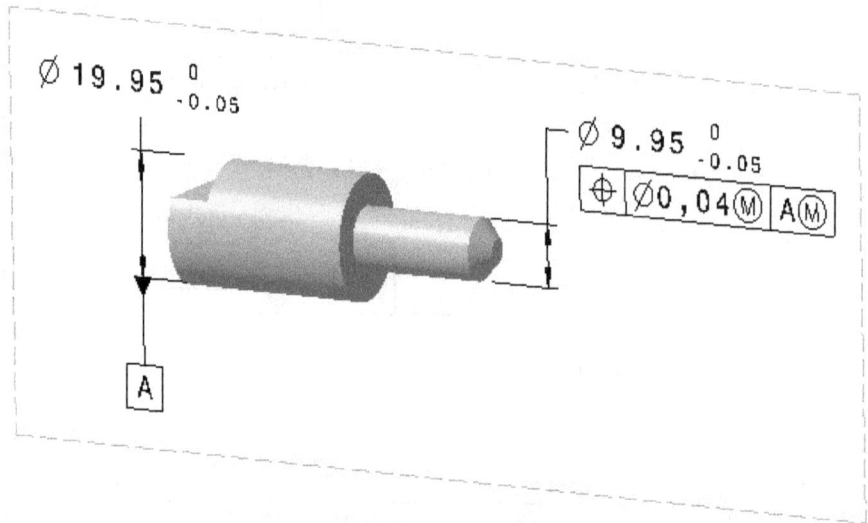

$\varnothing\, 19.95\ {}^{0}_{-0.05}$

$\varnothing\, 9.95\ {}^{0}_{-0.05}$

⊕ | $\varnothing 0,04$ Ⓜ | A Ⓜ

A

Figure A–35

6. Save the part.

Task 7 - Create a drawing.

In this task, you will create a drawing and show a view of the assembly. You will also show the tolerance information for individual parts of the assembly.

1. Create the following drawing:

- *Standard:* **ASME**
- *Format:* **B ANSI**

2. Create the three views shown in Figure A–36.

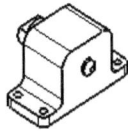

Isometric view
Scale: 1:2

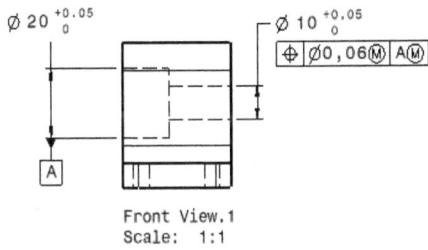

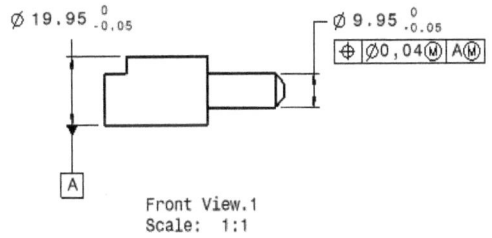

Ø 20 $^{+0.05}_{0}$

Ø 10 $^{+0.05}_{0}$

⊕ | Ø0,06Ⓜ | AⓂ

A

Front View.1
Scale: 1:1

Ø 19.95 $^{0}_{-0.05}$

Ø 9.95 $^{0}_{-0.05}$

⊕ | Ø0,04Ⓜ | AⓂ

A

Front View.1
Scale: 1:1

Figure A–36

3. Save and exit all files.